THE UNIT
COMMANDER

Other Books by Sue Cullins Walls

The Cat Who Couldn't Purr
Who Killed Norma Jean?
The Mystery of the Cabin in the Woods
The Search
Reach the author at suewalls1475@aol.com

A hero is an ordinary individual who finds the
strength to persevere and endure in spite of
overwhelming obstacles.-- Christopher Reeve

THE UNIT
COMMANDER

Mark Fuller's Story

Sue Cullins Walls

THE UNIT COMMANDER
MARK FULLER'S STORY

iUniverse books may be ordered through booksellers or by contacting:

iUniverse
1663 Liberty Drive
Bloomington, IN 47403
www.iuniverse.com
1-800-Authors (1-800-288-4677)

ISBN: 978-1-5320-3402-2 (sc)
ISBN: 978-1-5320-3403-9 (e)

Print information available on the last page.

iUniverse rev. date: 11/20/2017

DEDICATION

This book is dedicated to all of the men and women who risk their lives every day to protect our country and keep it free from terrorists and others who would destroy our freedom. This includes all the military and Federal Agents, as well as all local and state police, Sheriffs Departments and, of course, the Homeland Security Agents.

ACKNOWLEDGMENTS

I wish to thank my husband, Harrison, again, for his patience while I wrote this book. As always, I also thank my sister, Joyce Price, for her encouragement and my brother, John Cullins, for the hard work of proofing my text. I especially want to thank my nephew, Dale Weatherman, Donna's husband, for his invaluable information. I also would like to thank my friends and family who have purchased my books and have said they enjoyed reading them.

DISCLAIMER

THE UNIT COMMANDER

The Federal Security Unit (FSU) is a fictional elite unit of the Federal Security Commission (FSC). The FSC is a fictional department of the Central Intelligence Agency (CIA).

Jim Ryan and Mark Fuller are fictional Unit Commanders of the fictional FSU. In this position, they are in charge of missions to combat foreign and domestic espionage, arrest perpetrators and protect citizens from all terrorist attacks, both foreign and domestic.

Due to the nature and secrecy of their missions, Jim Ryan would usually operate out of an office inside his home. He and Mark would report to their supervisor, who is located in the FSC Headquarters Building. They must give a report to their superior after the completion of each mission.

The FSC Board of Review is a fictional panel of authorities who are authorized to hear cases of charges against any of the officers who are employed by the FSC. Their decisions are final. They have the authority to either dismiss or reinstate a suspended officer.

There is no attempt by the author to depict any real department of the CIA. This book is a work of fiction. Names, characters, places and incidents (except for names of countries and military facilities mentioned) are the product of the author's imagination or are used fictitiously. Any resemblance to actual events, locales, or persons, living or dead, is coincidental.

My apologies to those who are reality purists in their works of fiction. I have taken the liberty to add some incidents that would probably not happen in real life. I have done this to add to the interest of the story. If I have gone a little too far out in left field for you, I apologize again, but, after all, it is fiction.

CHAPTER 1

Doctor Sanders removed the bandages from Mark Fuller's eyes slowly, layer by layer. When all of the gauze was gone and only the pads directly on his eyes remained, Dr. Sanders said, "I want you to shut your eyes now, and open them slowly."

Mark shut his eyes and began to open them slowly, as the doctor had said. The light hurt at first and he blinked. Then he opened them again. There was a smoky haze there, but he could tell that there was light shining through the haze. Then he could see a shadow at the foot of the bed where Cat had positioned herself at Mark's request.

"Can you see anything," Dr. Sanders asked.

"Only shadows," Mark answered. "I know Cat is standing there, but I can't see her."

"Close your eyes again and open them slowly again," the doctor said.

Mark did as Dr. Sanders asked. Still he could see only shadows.

"I can still only see shadows," Mark said, showing his disappointment.

"Maybe it'll clear up in a few days," the doctor said. "If it doesn't, then I'm afraid you'll never be able to see again."

Mark took a deep breath and sighed, "I guess I deserved that. It's my own fault. I should have been more careful when we raided the alleged terrorist house."

"Don't get so discouraged so soon," Dr. Sanders said. "I've seen it take up to two weeks sometimes. We'll just give it time. I've prescribed some drops for you to use four times a day. That may help. It doesn't hurt to try anyway. I'm also giving you a prescription for an antibiotic. You are to take it four times a day. Be sure and take all of them or they won't do you any good. Here is also a prescription for pain medication. You'll need that for a while."

Then he turned to Cat, "Will you be taking him home, Miss?" he asked.

"Yes, probably," Cat answered.

"Then, here are some instructions for you. Please follow them exactly or he could get an infection. That would really be bad."

He gave Cat the instructions and she put them into her purse. "Do you want to go home with me, Mark?" she asked.

"Sure, if my other choice is the nursing home. I'll take your place any day," Mark answered.

"OK, that's settled," the doctor said. "The nurse will be here to discharge you shortly. I'll leave an appointment for you. I want to see you in my office in one week. After the cast comes off in a few weeks, you'll be set up for some therapy. Is there anything you want to know?"

"The only thing I really want to know is if I'll ever be able to see again, but you've already answered that, so I guess there's nothing else I need to know. Do you have any questions, Cat?"

"No, I guess not. I have these instructions and, if I have any problems, I'll just call the doctor's office."

"That's right, Miss," Dr. Sanders said. "If there are no other questions, then I'll see you in a week. Be safe." Then he left and the nurse came in to discharge Mark. Cat went on downstairs to get the car while the nurse pushed Mark down in a wheelchair.

After the nurse loaded Mark into Cat's car, Cat went around and got into the driver's seat. "Do you feel like stopping long enough to have your prescriptions filled or do you want me to take you home and come back for them?" Cat asked Mark, as she started the engine.

"There's not any sense in your making another trip back to

town for my meds. I'll just wait while you have them filled," Mark answered.

When Cat got to the pharmacy, she asked Mark if he wanted to go in with her. Since it was a beautiful Fall-like day, he said he would just wait for her in the car.

Cat hurried into the pharmacy and turned in his prescriptions. When they were ready, the cashier asked for Mark's birthdate. Cat had no idea what Mark's birthdate was. "I'm sorry," she said. "I'm picking these up for a friend. I can't remember his birthdate. He's waiting in the car. He has had an injury to his eyes and doesn't feel like coming in."

"I'm sorry," the cashier said. "I can't let you have these without the proper identification. Can he either come in or give you his ID?"

"He isn't in any shape to come in," Cat said. "I'll get his ID, if that's all you need."

When she arrived back at the car, Mark was asleep. She hated to waken him, but she had no other choice. She shook him gently and called his name. He awoke with a start.

"I'm sorry to have to waken you, Mark, but I need your ID," Cat said.

"Oh, I should have given it to you," Mark said grogily. "I should have known you would need it. Here it is," he said, handing it to Cat, after a search through all of his pockets finally revealed it in his shirt pocket.

Cat took the ID he handed to her and noticed it was his FSC ID. She noticed that it didn't contain his birthdate. "Mark, I need your driver's license, if you have it. This doesn't have your birthdate on it."

"It's October 15, 1985," he said.

Cat gave him a strange look, but just said "Do you have your driver's license? I know it has it on it."

Mark moved around painfully and tried to find his wallet in his back pocket, but he gave up because of the pain. "I can't find it, Cat. I don't know where it is. It must be in some of my things. Just give them that and tell them my birthdate. Maybe that will satisfy them."

3

So Cat made the trip back into the pharmacy armed with Mark's ID and his birthdate. This time, she was successful. When she got back to the car, Mark was asleep again.

She got into the car as quietly as she could, but when she closed the door, Mark jumped. "I'm sorry, Mark, I didn't mean to waken you. Are you all right?" she asked as she handed him the medicine and his ID card.

"Yes, I'm OK. I think the pain shot that the nurse gave me before I left the hospital has finally taken effect," he said. "I hope I can get out of the car when we get to your place."

When Cat pulled up in front of the cabin and stopped, Mark awoke with a start again.

"We're here, Mark," Cat said, and she walked around the car and opened the door for Mark. "Put your arm around my shoulders and use your crutch. Maybe we can make it into the house without falling down. At the door, she braced Mark against the wall while she unlocked and opened the door.

"Do you want to lie down on the sofa in the den?" Cat asked.

"Yes, that would be fine," Mark answered.

Cat helped Mark to the sofa and he fell onto it. "That was a chore," Mark said.

"Was it as hard for you as it was for me?"

"It was hard," Cat chuckled as she answered. "Maybe it'll get easier after we practice for a while. You just lie down and I'll bring your things in. Do you want me to put them in your room upstairs or do you want them down here?" Cat asked, as she headed for the door.

"If you don't mind, I'd like to stay down here for a while. I hate tackling those stairs already."

"Sure, you can stay down here as long as you feel you need to." Then she disappeared and reappeared shortly with his things.

"Mark, I'll put your things right over here, so they'll be handy for you, but they'll be out of the way," Cat said, as she picked a spot that would be easy for Mark to get to, but wouldn't be in his way.

"Are you hungry?" Cat asked after she got Mark settled.

"I could eat something, but don't go to any trouble," he said.

"I've made some vegetable beef soup and cornbread muffins. I like soup and cornbread on cool nights like this. Is that OK with you?"

"That would be fine," Mark answered. Then he lay back on the pillow that Cat had given him and went to sleep again.

Cat went into the kitchen and put the soup on the stove to heat and placed bowls and spoons onto the table.

When it was ready, she helped Mark to the table. She said a short prayer and then filled Mark's and her bowls with the steaming hot soup. "Cat, do you mind directing me to the bowl," Mark said a little embarrassed. "I can't tell for sure where it is and I don't want to make a mess."

"That's OK, Mark, let me help you," Cat said, as she took Mark's hand and directed it to the bowl. "Would you like for me to help you?" she asked when she saw that he was still having a difficult time.

"That would be great," Mark answered. So Cat sat next to Mark and helped him eat. "Would you like some dessert?" she asked. "I have a pecan pie."

"I'm pretty full, but I can't pass up pecan pie," Mark answered. "Just give me a small piece."

Cat cut Mark a small piece of pie and helped him eat it. "That was very good, Cat. I didn't know you could cook," Mark said, as he patted his stomach.

"Thanks," Cat said. "When Molly and Barbara were cooking for us, I had no reason to cook. Now that I'm the only one here, I didn't see any reason for Barbara to cook for only one person. I told her she might as well leave, if she wanted to go somewhere else. She's working at the hunting lodge now. They have groups that come in during hunting season. She enjoys cooking for a lot of people, so she's happier there. She comes and visits me every now and then. Molly retired and stays home and takes care of her grandchildren. She always wanted to do that, so she's very happy, too."

Then Cat went to the stove and dipped up a container of soup and put some cornbread muffins into a plastic bag. "I fix dinner for Carol sometimes, when I have time. It helps her out. She teaches at the high school in town and comes home exhausted. She has a little girl, who will be three years old this month. As a matter of fact, her birthday is October 15, also. Do you remember my sister, Carol?"

"Yes, I remember Carol. Wow, that's a coincidence about our birthdays, isn't it?" Mark said, amazed at the coincidence.

"Let me help you back to the sofa," Cat said. "Then I'll clean up the kitchen."

"Can't I stay here while you do that?" Mark asked. "I would really like to talk to you while you do that."

"Sure, you can stay," Cat answered. "I just thought you might need to rest."

Then there was a knock on the door. When Cat answered it, Carol came rushing into the room. "Gee, it's beginning to get cold out there," she said. "I didn't know it was supposed to turn this cold so soon."

"Why didn't you wear a jacket?" Cat asked.

"I didn't realize it was so cold," Carol said, as she headed toward the kitchen, but she stopped when she saw Mark.

"Who's that?" she mouthed without saying a word.

"Carol, do you remember Mark Fuller?" Cat said, as she urged Carol toward Mark. "He was Jim's Second-in-Command, remember?"

"Oh, yeah, I remember him," Carol said. "What happened to you, Mark?"

"Hi, Carol," Mark said, as he held out his hand in Carol's direction. "I had an accident. Your wonderful sister was kind enough to volunteer to help me get well."

"Yeah, Cat's really kind like that," Carol said frowning. "She's always taking in strays; a stray cat here, a stray dog there. Now, I guess she's taken in a stray person."

"Yes, that's me," Cat said. "I'm a very compassionate person.

Now, Carol, don't you need to get this soup home before it gets cold?"

"I guess I do," Carol said, reluctant to leave. "Help me get out, Cat."

When they reached the door, Carol turned on Cat. "Cat, are you crazy? What are you doing? You can't let Mark stay here. Not just the two of you."

"Hush, Carol," Cat said, as she pushed her out the door. "I know what I'm doing. He didn't have anyone. He needed me and, frankly, I need him."

"You can't be serious, Cat," Carol said. "I thought you said you thought he killed Jim."

"I was mistaken," Cat said. "Now, go on home. I'll be fine."

"I don't like it, Cat," Carol persisted.

"It's OK, Carol," Cat said. "Just go on home."

She shut the door behind Carol and walked back into the kitchen.

"She doesn't like me much does she?" Mark asked.

"She'll get over it," Cat said. "It's my fault. You know I blamed you for Jim's death. I'm sorry that I did that, now, but I was crazy with guilt and grief. If I hadn't insisted on going on that assignment when Jim didn't want me to go, he would still be alive. It was all my fault that he died and I couldn't accept that fact. I had to have someone else to blame and you were the nearest one. I have to apologize to you, Mark. I know I made your life miserable. I hated myself and I couldn't stand it. It hurt too much to realize that I killed the one that I loved most in this world." Cat started to cry and Mark held out his hand in the direction he thought Cat was standing.

"It's OK, Cat," he said when he found her hand and squeezed it. "I was glad that I could help you vent your frustration. It hurt that you believed I had killed Jim when I had tried so hard to save him, but maybe I deserved the accuation. I'm not saying that I didn't do everything I could to save him, because I did. I'm just saying, maybe I should have insisted that he go first and let me cover you. That's all over now, though, and we can't go back and change it. No matter how much we wish we could, we still can't change it."

Cat was sobbing now. It was hard to stop crying. "Maybe we both have something to feel guilty for, Mark, but maybe time will heal us and we can get on with our lives," she said.

"Let's hope so," Mark said, then he was silent for a few minutes while Cat composed herself.

"Are you ready to go back to the den?" Cat asked.

"I am if you are," he answered.

"Here, let me help you get up," Cat said, as she put her arm around Mark's waist and steadied him so he could get up.

As they passed Jim's office, Mark sensed that they were near it. "Do you mind if I just go into Jim's office for a few minutes?" he asked.

"I haven't been in there since Jim's death," Cat answered with tears in her eyes. "I didn't even look to see what it looked like after you took all of the FSC stuff out. I just couldn't make myself go in there. I hated that room. Jim spent too much time in there, time that I wasn't allowed to share. There were too many memories. It hurt too much. Yes, you can go in if you would like."

Cat opened the door and pointed Mark in the direction of Jim's desk. She stood in the doorway and watched as Mark found the desk and caressed the edges of it. He then made his way around to Jim's chair. He caressed the back of the chair then he cautiously sat down.

Cat stood and watched, as long as she could stand it and then walked back to the kitchen. After a while, she returned to the office to find Mark with his head on Jim's desk and he was sobbing just like she had done before. Cat stood and watched Mark for a few minutes without saying anything. She thought it was best to let him grieve. She knew how long it had taken her to come to grips with her loss and she realized now that Mark had lost Jim also. It was funny, she had never even thought that Mark had lost his best friend when Jim died. She knew that Mark and Jim had been feuding just before Jim died, but she also knew that he still cared a great deal for Jim.

"Mark," she finally said softly. "Let's go back to the den." Then she went in and took his hand and led him back to the sofa.

Mark sat there for a long time not saying anything and Cat didn't want to intrude into his thoughts, so she just sat beside him and left him alone with his thoughts.

"Thanks, again, Cat," Mark finally said. "I appreciate what you're doing for me. I don't really have anyone who cares whether I live or die, not like Jim did. Everyone loved Jim, but my team really doesn't even respect me, I think. I would have had a hard time at the barracks. I think Ted's still mad because I made Commander and he thought he should have. The rest of the men go along with Ted. They think he should have been Commander, too. Now, he can be the Commander. I'll never be able to command my team ever again."

"You don't know that, Mark," Cat said. "The doctor said that sometimes it takes a couple of weeks for your eyes to adjust. This is only the first day."

"I know, Cat. I also know how I feel, and I feel that I'll never get well," he said.

"Mark, you never want to give up," Cat said, taking his hand and squeezing it. "I almost gave up, but someone cared for me and came and forced me to go to church. I didn't want to go, but if I hadn't, I would still be that same empty shell that I was three years ago. I appreciate what you did for me, Mark. You helped me to want to live again. I can never repay you for that. I'm going to do all I can to help you the same way. You'll see. It's not as bad as it seems. There is a light at the end of the tunnel."

"Cat, what I did for you, I did because I love you. You don't have to try to repay me. Just to know that what I did helped you is all the repayment I could ask for," Mark said.

Cat leaned over and gave Mark a quick kiss on the lips. He pulled her to him and kissed her back. Then he kissed her again, this time more urgently and passionately. He put all of his pent up love for Cat into his kiss. For a moment he forgot everything except his love for Cat.

"Wait, Mark," Cat said, as she shoved Mark back and stood up. "I didn't intend to start something that I couldn't stop. We have to take it a step at a time. First you have to court me. Then, after a while, when we know that we're really in love, you can ask me to marry you. I may say yes and then we'll get married. After that, we'll make love. We don't skip any steps."

"I'm sorry, Cat. I lost my head. Do you want me to leave?" Mark asked.

"No, Mark, of course not. I just want you to know how we stand. The courting comes first."

"Why would you want a blind, broken-down lover like me, anyway, Cat. I'm sorry that I overstepped my boundary. I'll try not to let it happen again."

"I think I better go on upstairs," Cat said. "Here, lie back and let me put these drops into your eyes."

After she put the drops into Mark's eyes, Cat went into the kitchen for a glass of water.

"Here, take this pill," she said. "It's your antibiotic. Do you need a pain pill?"

"It wouldn't hurt to take one," he answered. "I probably won't sleep without it."

"Here, take it," she said.

After he took the pill, she asked if there was anything else he needed.

"No, Cat. I'm sorry that I took advantage of your sympathy and forced myself on you," Mark said.

"You didn't do anything that I didn't want you to do, Mark. I'll see you in the morning. Good night."

Then she covered him up, turned out the light and ran upstairs to her bedroom.

CHAPTER 2

The next morning, when Cat came downstairs, Mark was still asleep on the sofa. She went into the kitchen and began preparing breakfast. Mark awoke and slowly made his way into the kitchen by following the wonderful aroma of freshly brewed coffee and frying bacon.

"Good morning, Cat," he said. He assumed it was Cat, anyway.

"Good morning, Mark. Did you sleep well?" Cat asked.

"I must have. I don't remember moving all night," Mark answered. "Something smells good. May I have some coffee?"

"Sure," Cat said, as she poured some coffee into a cup and set it in front of Mark. "Do you want anything in it?"

"No, I just drink it black," Mark said, as he felt around for the handle.

"Be careful; it's hot," Cat cautioned.

"Wow! It sure is," Mark said when he took a drink.

"Mark, I have to go to work for a while," Cat said. "I'll leave you some sandwiches for lunch in case I don't make it back in time. Here is your pill for now and they'll be due again at 2:00 p.m. I'll try to get back by 2:00, but if I don't, I'll leave them here on the table for you. Lean back and I'll put the drops into your eyes."

Mark leaned back and Cat put the drops into his eyes and handed him a tissue to wipe the excess off.

"The refrigerator is right behind you, Mark." Cat said. "There's a little slot that you can put your glass into. When you push it, it dispenses ice. I've put your sandwiches and some Cokes on the middle shelf, where it'll be easy for you to reach them. Here are some paper plates. I think you should be able to take care of lunch, don't you?" she asked.

"Yeah, I can handle that. I can see a little. Its foggy, but I can at least see the refrigerator," Mark said. "Thanks."

"OK, here's your breakfast. It's bacon and eggs. I didn't know how you like your eggs, so I just scrambled them. I hope that's all right."

"That's fine, Cat," Mark said, as he felt around for his silverware. Cat picked up his fork and put it into his hand. "Do you need anything else?"

"No, I'm fine. You go ahead and run along. I can take care of myself," Mark said, as he began eating.

Cat leaned over and kissed him on the cheek. "Have a good day, Mark. I'll be back as soon as I can."

"Goodbye, Cat. I'll see you later," he said, as he turned in her direction and watched as she headed toward the door.

Cat was busy most of the day and, when she finally finished and started home, she stopped and picked up some Chinese carry-out for dinner.

When she arrived home, Mark was asleep on the sofa. He awoke with a start when she touched him. "I'm home," she said softly. "Are you all right?"

"Yes, I'm OK," Mark answered. "I had to take a pain pill. It put me to sleep as usual. I feel much better now."

"I'm glad you're feeling better," Cat said. "I brought Chinese carry-out for dinner. I didn't know if you liked it or not, but Sherry Rene loves it. She loves to eat with the chopsticks. You should see her. She gets more on herself and the table than she does in her mouth, but she loves it."

"Sure," Mark said, as he sat up. "I'll eat just about anything that doesn't eat me."

"I'll fix it in a little bit. I'm going to call Carol first," she said, as she picked up the phone.

Shortly, there was a knock at the door and Carol came in, led by a rambunctious three-year-old.

"Aunt Kitty, wook wat I drawed," she said, as she ran over to Cat. Then she stopped when she saw Mark.

"Who zat?" she said pointing to Mark.

"He's a friend of mine. His name is Mr. Mark," Cat said, as she picked up the little girl, kissed her and walked over to Mark.

"Mark, this is my niece," Cat said.

"Hi," Mark grinned and held out his hand toward Cat. "What's your name?" he asked Sherry.

"My name is Sherry Rene," she said. "What happen to you?"

"I had an accident," Mark said.

Sherry wiggled until Cat set her down on the floor beside the sofa.

She walked over to Mark and touched his face. "Does it hurt?" She asked.

"Yes, it does hurt," Mark said.

"I kiss it. Make it betta," Sherry said, as she crawled up into Mark's lap and started kissing his face. Then she kissed his right arm and started to kiss his leg.

"No, no, you've kissed enough," Cat said, as she picked her up.

"I kiss Mista Mok. I make he well," she said. "Does it feel betta?"

"Yes, Sherry, it feels a lot better. Thank you," Mark said, smiling at Sherry.

"Sherry Rene," Sherry said putting emphasis on the Rene.

"I'm sorry," Mark said. "Yes, I feel much better, Sherry Rene." He put emphasis on the Rene just like she had done.

"Wook wat I drawed," she said holding it up to Mark.

"Oh, that's beautiful," Mark said, even though he could barely make out the paper, much less what she had drawn on it.

"Thanks, Mista Mok," she said, as she took it over to Cat and showed it to her.

"See Aunt Kitty. I drawed a picture of you."

"Oh, yes, I agree with Mister Mark. It is beautiful. Come see what I brought you," Cat said, as she led Sherry to the kitchen.

"Oh, China food," she said. "Did you bwing the sticks?"

"Yes, of course, you know I did," Cat said. "Now, let me fix it so your mother can take it home for your dinner."

Sherry hopped up into the chair at the table and stood on her knees watching Cat, as she separated the food. Carol came up behind Cat and whispered into her ear while she was separating the food.

"I can't believe he's still here, Cat. Have you lost your mind?" Carol whispered.

"No, Carol, I know exactly what I'm doing." Cat finished separating the food and put some for Carol into a plastic bag and left some on the table for Mark and herself.

"Here, you need to take this home for dinner before it gets cold," Cat said, shoving it into Carol's hands.

"It's already cold," Carol said frowning. "Are you rushing me off?"

"Yes," Cat said.

"Come on, Sherry. Let's go home before our food gets cold," Carol said sarcastically.

"I gotta kiss Mista Mok first," she said, as she ran over to the sofa. "Bend ova so I kin reach you Mista Mok," she said.

Mark complied and Sherry kissed him several times all over his face. She started to kiss his arm, but Mark said, "That's OK, Sherry Rene. My arm is better now. You don't have to kiss it."

"Come on, Sherry," Carol called from the door. "Let's go."

"Bye, Mista Mok," Sherry said, as she waved and ran to the door.

"Bye, Sherry Rene," Mark said, and waved in the direction of the door hoping he was waving toward Sherry.

After Carol and Sherry were gone, Mark said, "I see why you love her so much. She is a precious little girl, isn't she?"

"Yes, she is," Cat smiled. "She's the most beautiful little girl in the world. Now come on into the kitchen. Let's eat. I'm starving."

She helped Mark to his feet and led him into the kitchen. She set a plate in front of him and started putting food on it. "I'll just put some of everything on your plate. If you don't like it, just leave it."

"Like I said before, I eat just about anything that doesn't eat me. I was raised in an orphanage and you had to learn to eat everything they gave you or you went to bed hungry."

"I didn't know you were an orphan," Cat said surprised.

"Yeah, my folks died when I was very young. My relatives didn't want me. They already had kids of their own and were having trouble feeding what they had. They weren't very close to my folks, anyway. So I just wound up in an orphanage. The people who came to adopt didn't want me either. I don't blame them. I was a skinny kid, who was always getting into trouble. The first family I ever had was Jim and you. I thought of Jim as the brother I never had. I thank you for taking me in and making me a part of your family."

Cat had tears in her eyes. She took Mark's hand and squeezed it. "I never knew," she said.

"Well, I didn't go around broadcasting it," Mark said. "I really hated for people to feel sorry for me; you're the first person I wanted to feel sorry for me. I thought if you felt sorry for me, then maybe you'd fall in love with me. That's why Jim and I argued sometimes. He was jealous of me, I think. He thought I was trying to take you away from him. I guess I was, but I know now that I never had a chance. You would never have left Jim for me."

"You're right, Mark. Jim was the first man I ever loved. I thought we would be together for the rest of our lives. I thought he would be the last man I ever loved. I guess I was wrong." Cat began to cry and Mark took her hand, kissed it and cried with her.

Cat got a glass of water from the kitchen and gave Mark his medicine, then she asked him to lie back, so she could put some drops into his eyes. After she put the drops into his eyes, he pulled her down to his chest and kissed her. When she didn't pull away, he kissed her again passionately. He kissed her again and again. Then he started to unbutton her blouse.

"No, Mark," she said. "I told you. You have to take one step at a time. You have to court me first."

"You're driving me nuts, Cat," Mark said. "What do you mean by courting you, anyway? I thought that was what I was trying to do."

"No, Mark," Cat said. "You have love and sex mixed up. When you get them straightened out, you'll understand what I mean by courting me. I'm tired now. I think I'll go to bed. Is there anything you need before I go upstairs?"

"Yes, but you won't give it to me," he said sarcastically. Then he grinned. "Good night, Cat. Sweet dreams."

"Good night, Mark. See you in the morning."

The next morning, when Cat came downstairs, Mark was already awake and sitting on the side of the sofa.

"Good morning, Mark," she said. "Did you sleep well?"

"No, not really," Mark said. "I had too much to think about. Here," he said, as he handed her a drawing of a beautiful rose.

"I don't have any real flowers to give you, so I drew you a rose. You, my love, are fairer than any rose could ever be. I couldn't see what I was doing, so it may not look much like a rose, though," Mark said.

Cat was surprised. "Thanks. I guess you do understand courting after all. You did a good job, even if you can't see. It's beautiful. It looks just like a rose to me."

"I'm beginning to see a little better," Mark said. "Maybe I'll be able to see again. Who knows?"

"Maybe," Cat said, as she headed for the kitchen. "Do you want a cup of coffee?"

"That would be nice," Mark said, as he hobbled after her into the kitchen. "When is it that I go see that doctor again?" He wanted to know.

"Next Tuesday," Cat answered. "Don't worry. I won't let you forget.

"It'll just take a few minutes to brew the coffee. Why don't you sit down while I fix it?" she said, as she put coffee grounds into the coffee maker and poured fresh water into the carafe.

Mark walked up behind Cat and put his good arm around her waist. "Cat, you can tell me to leave if I'm getting out of hand. It's just that it's so hard to be so close to you and not touch you or kiss you or make love to you. Do you want me to leave?"

"No, of course not, Mark. I just want you to take it slow. I'm still in love with my dead husband. It's going to take time. Do you understand?"

"Sure, Cat, I understand. I apologize for rushing you. Just slap my face if I do it again, OK?"

"OK," Cat answered. "Now, you go sit at the table and I'll bring your coffee."

They ate breakfast in silence and Cat told Mark to go back to the den while she cleaned up the kitchen.

About 10:00 a.m., there was a knock on the door. When she opened it, Ted Ames and Jason Hall were standing there.

"Hello, Cat," Ted said. "I heard that Mark Fuller was here. Is he?"

"Yes, he's here," Cat answered. "Come on in. He'll be glad to see you."

"Mark, it's Ted Ames and Jason Hall," Cat said, as she led them over to the sofa.

"Ted, Jason," Mark said, as he tried to stand. "It's good to see you. Well, to almost see you anyway. I still don't see very well. Come on in."

"Sit down and visit with Mark," Cat said. "I have things I have to do in the kitchen."

"Well, how are you, Mark?" Ted asked.

"Better than I was," he answered. "Cat's a very good nurse."

"I can see that," Ted said.

"How's everything going?" Mark wanted to know.

"Well, some of the guys are still in the hospital, but some have been released. They weren't as bad as you were. Some of them are already wanting to go back to work. When do you think you'll be able to come back to work?"

"I don't know, Ted," Mark said a little sadly. "Maybe never."

"What do you mean by maybe never?" Ted asked.

"I don't know if I'll ever be able to see right again. The doctor said that if I couldn't see by the end of two weeks, chances are good that I won't," Mark answered.

"That's too bad, Mark," Ted said. "What will you do, then?"

"I don't know," Mark answered. "I haven't thought that far ahead yet. What about the unit? How's it doing?"

"It isn't doing at all right now, Mark," Ted answered. "You know, with you out and most of the men injured, we haven't been able to take on an assignment.

"I tried to visit you when you first went into the ICU, but they wouldn't let me.

"They told me if I wasn't a member of your immediate family and my name wasn't on your visitor list I wouldn't be able to see you."

"I'm glad to know that you tried to visit me," Mark said. "I thought maybe you didn't care how I was doing."

"Yeah, I care, Mark," Ted said. "All of the guys care. They ask about you all the time. This is the first time I was able to find out anything, though. I finally got someone at the hospital to tell me where you were. I was really surprised when I found out you were here, especially after the way Cat acted after Jim died. You got something going with Cat?"

"No, I don't have anything going with Cat," Mark said angrily. "She just felt sorry for me and offered to help. I'm not able to do anything, anyway."

"No, I guess not with that heavy cast on your leg," Ted said, tapping Mark's leg. "I just thought it was strange that she let you come here, since she blamed you for Jim's death."

"Well, she asked me to come here," Mark said. "I guess maybe she got over it."

"I guess she did," Ted said.

"Jason, you've been awfully quiet. How're you getting along?" Mark asked.

"I was lucky. I only got a few superficial cuts. I'm doing OK. We miss you down at the unit, though, Mark. I'll be glad when you can get back."

"Don't count on it, Jason," Mark said. "If I do come back, it'll be a long time."

"Would you gentlemen like a Coke or something to drink?" Cat asked, as she came out of the kitchen.

"Not for us, Cat," Ted answered. "We have to be going. We'll come visit again, Mark. Now that we know where you are. You will be here won't you?"

"If Cat doesn't kick me out, I'll be here," he answered.

"That remains to be seen," Cat smiled. "Ted, I have to be gone some tomorrow. Why don't you come back and stay with Mark while I'm gone?"

"We might be able to do that," Ted answered. "What time?"

"It'll be about this same time," Cat answered. "I won't leave until you get here."

"OK, we'll see you tomorrow, then. We've got to go now. Bye, Mark; I'll see you tomorrow," Ted said.

"Bye, Ted, Jason. I'll look forward to seeing you again," Mark said.

Cat showed them to the door, then she came back and gave Mark his medicine. "Now, I'll put your drops into your eyes if you promise there won't be a repeat of last night."

"I can't promise that, Cat," Mark smiled. "I can't help myself when you're so close to me."

"Then I might have to tie your hands down." she said, and they both laughed at that.

"I'll be good, Cat. Just put the drops in. They seem to be helping. I hate to miss them."

After she had finished putting the drops into his eyes, she asked Mark if he would like for her to read to him.

"Yes, I would," he said. "It gets pretty boring just lying here. That is, unless I'm asleep, and I need to quit sleeping so much during the day so I'll sleep at night."

Cat started reading and soon Mark was sound asleep. "I guess he still needs to sleep," she thought, so she quietly got up and started preparing something for dinner. She knew Carol's family all liked spaghetti and it was quick to fix, so she started boiling water and making homemade spaghetti sauce.

Soon, there was a knock on the door and Skip came in carrying Sherry and a handfull of mylar balloons. "Hi, Aunt Kitty," she said, as she wriggled out of Skip's arms. "I bout Mista Mok sum booms," she said. "Hi, Mista Mok. I bout you sum booms," she said, as she ran over to Mark and jumped up into his lap.

"Wook wat it sezs," she said pointing to one of the balloons.

"It says Get Well Soon," Mark said, as he held them up close to his eyes so he could see them. "Thanks, Sherry Rene. They're beautiful. It was so nice of you."

"I got card, too," she said. "Hea."

"Thank you, Sherry Rene. I'll have to have Aunt Cat read it to me," he said.

"Not Aunt Cat. Aunt Kitty," Sherry corrected him.

"Aunt Kitty will you read it to me?" he asked.

"I'll be glad to read it to you," Cat said, as she took the card and opened it.

"Roses are red, violets are blue. I hope good health will soon come to you. I'm sorry you're sick. Hope you are better soon. Love, Sherry Rene Taylor."

"That's so sweet, Sherry," Cat said.

"Sherry Rene," Sherry said, emphasizing Rene. "You always leave out Rene."

"I'm sorry, Sherry Rene," Cat corrected herself. "It's a beautiful card."

"Do you wik it Mista Mok?" she asked.

"Yes, I do, Sherry Rene," Mark answered. "I love it."

"I wuv you, Mista Mok. I kiss you hut. make it betta," Sherry said, as she started kissing Mark's face again.

"That's enough, Sherry," Skip said, as he picked Sherry up off Mark's lap. "Mr. Mark might not like all those kisses. You need to save some for me and Mama."

"I gots kisses left fo you and Mama," she said. "I gots some mo fo Mista Mok and Aunt Kitty, too."

"Well, come on. We need to get on home. Mama's waiting for us."

"Give me some of those kisses before you go, Sherry Rene," Cat said, as she hugged and kissed Sherry.

"You gets lots a kisses, Aunt Kitty," she said, as she kissed Cat. "Bye Aunt Kitty. See you lata. Bye Mista Mok, see you lata."

"Bye, Sherry Rene. See you later, alligator," Mark said.

"See you lata, awagata," Sherry said, as she waved goodbye from Skip's arms.

"Bye, Sherry Rene," Mark said, as he waved in the direction of the door. He hoped that he was waving where she was.

"Thank you, Mark," Cat said with tears in her eyes.

"For what?" Mark asked.

"For being so nice to Sherry. I know she can be a little irritating at times, but you didn't let it bother you. Thanks, again."

"I loved it, Cat," he said. "She's a wonderful little girl. I feel like it's a privilege to be kissed and hugged by her. You don't know what that means to me."

"Mark, you cease to amaze me," Cat said, as she bent over and kissed him lightly on the lips. "I don't think I have ever been so surprised by anyone."

Mark grabbed Cat's arm, as she raised up and pulled her back down and kissed her again. "Once is not enough," he said, but she pulled away before he could kiss her again.

"Let's not get that started again," she said. "I might not be able to resist it tonight."

"I wouldn't want you to resist," Mark said, as he reached for her again, but she slipped out of his reach.

"Not yet, Mark. You know my rules. One step at a time. Are you ready for dinner?" she asked, as she headed for the kitchen.

"Sure. Is it ready?" he asked.

"I'll put it on the table. You can come on in," she answered.

"Why don't you come help me get up?" he said pretending to have difficulty getting up.

"I think you can do it by yourself," she said, as she continued doing what she was doing.

"You can't blame a guy for trying," he said, as he got his crutches and helped himself up and into the kitchen.

"Mmmm, that smells good," he said, as Cat filled their plates with spaghetti.

"Will you bless our meal for us?" she asked. Mark said a short prayer and they ate their meal in silence.

After the meal, Cat gave Mark his medicine again and had him lean back and she put the drops into his eyes. She thought it was better to do it while he was in a sitting position instead of waiting until he was lying down again.

"I need some more paper," Mark said. "Do you have any more?"

"Sure, let me get you some," Cat said, as she got Mark some paper and another pencil. He sat at the table and busily drew on the paper. Cat wondered what he was doing and tried to look over his shoulder, but when she did, he covered it up.

"You can't see it until I finish," he said. "You know it would be a lot better if I could see what I'm doing, don't you?" he asked.

"I'm sure it would be," Cat said.

Mark was still drawing when she finished cleaning up the kitchen. "Mark, I need to go upstairs and get ready for bed. Do you want to stay in here or do you want me to help you get back to the den?"

"You go on and do what you have to do," he said. "I'll get back to the den when I'm ready."

"OK, then, I'll say good night," she said.

"Good night, Cat. I'll see you in the morning."

As Cat soaked in the hot sudsy water of the tub, she thought about Mark. He probably would like to have a bath, but how was she going to handle it? She thought about asking Skip to help him, but she thought Mark might be uncomfortable with Skip.

Then she thought about asking Ted, but she quickly dismissed that idea. She was pretty sure Mark wouldn't want Ted or Jason either one to help him bathe. It looked like it would be left up to her. She was already becoming embarrassed just thinking about it. She thought she would put it off as long as she could. It would have to be soon, though. She knew he must be very uncomfortable. He needed a shave, too. At least she felt that he might be able to handle that if she could find a way for him to use the sink and mirror without having to stand on his leg.

The water in her bath was beginning to cool off, so she got out, dried off and put on her gown and robe. Then she remembered that Mark needed his last dose of medicine and his eye drops. "I'm not going down there like this, though," she thought. "I guess he'll just miss this last dose."

When she got into bed, she couldn't sleep because she felt guilty for not giving Mark his last dose of medicine. She got out of bed, put on an old, unsexy robe and made her way back downstairs. Mark had already turned out the lights and was lying on the sofa. It looked like he was already asleep. She hated waking him up, but, since she went to all the trouble to get up and go downstairs, she was going to see that he had his medicine.

She touched his arm and softly called his name. He jumped and immediately opened his eyes. "Cat, is that you?" he asked.

"Yes, Mark, I forgot to give you your medicine," she said.

"That's OK, I took it, Cat. I figured you probably forgot, so I went ahead and took it. I put my drops in my eyes, too. It ran all over my face, but I think I got enough in my eyes to do some good. What is that robe you have on? Are you trying to be unattractive? If you are, you're not succeeding. You're still the most beautiful woman I have ever seen."

"If I had thought that you might have already taken your medicine, I wouldn't have bothered to come down here," Cat said. "I'm glad you were able to get your medicine yourself. Now I know that you can do it, you will be doing it yourself from now on."

"I'm sorry I let you know," he said. "I like having you give it to me."

"Good night, again, Mark. This time I'm really going to bed. I'll see you in the morning."

"Good night, Cat. I love you," he said.

She turned and gave him a dirty look and went on upstairs. She got into bed, but was unable to sleep. She thought about Mark; he was changing. When she first brought him home, he was so apologetic and shy. He seemed as if he didn't feel worthy of her attention. Now, it seemed like he was demanding her attention. She kind of liked this new Mark in spite of her misgivings. When he kissed her, she felt a tingle run up her spine. He was the only man, besides Jim, who had excited her so with his kiss. Matt had never brought so much excitement to her when he kissed her. What had she done when she brought Mark into her home? She laughed when she thought how she had given him her rules. He had so quickly tossed them away and done what he wanted, anyway. How would she hold him off when he was better? She had better get her bluff in on him now before he was better or she might regret it later. Maybe Carol was right. Maybe she was crazy.

CHAPTER 3

The next morning, Cat hurriedly prepared breakfast for Mark and got ready to go do her volunteer work at the local children's hospital.

About 10:00 a.m., true to his word, Ted and Jason arrived to keep Mark company while Cat was gone.

"There are sandwiches and drinks in the refrigerator. You can push this little lever and get ice for your drinks. I fixed enough sandwiches for all of you. Will you see that Mark eats lunch?" Cat asked.

"You go on and do what you need to do, Cat. We'll take care of Mark," Ted said.

"I'll leave him in your hands, then," she said. "Thanks for coming."

"We were glad we could help. After all, he is our Unit Commander," Ted said. "You run along now. We'll take good care of Mark."

Cat was a little reluctant to leave because Ted's last remark seemed a little sarcastic, but she just had enough time to drive to the hospital before she was due there. She hurriedly gave Mark a light kiss and said, "You behave while I'm gone, now." Then she hurried out the door.

She could hear Ted laughing and teasing Mark as she closed the door. "I hope he doesn't ride Mark too much," she thought. "I would hate for him to be in a bad mood when I return." Then she put Mark out of her mind as she made her way through the traffic to the hospital.

The day went by fast and soon it was time for Cat to go home. She stopped and picked up something for dinner. She had decided it was easier to just stop and get something instead of trying to prepare something, just in case Ted and Jason stayed for dinner.

While Cat was gone, Mark, Ted and Jason had done a lot of reminiscing. Most of it was about adventures they had shared when Jim was alive. They had done some laughing and some crying, and had finally run out of things to talk about.

"Do you think Cat has a deck of cards?" Ted asked.

"I don't know," Mark answered. "Look in the coffee table drawer. If she has one it will probably be there." Sure enough, there was an almost new deck of cards still in the box lying in the drawer.

"Do you think she would mind if we used them?" Ted asked.

"I don't know, but if she gets mad, I'll tell her it was my idea and she can get mad at me," Mark said.

They played a game of poker and Mark had to hold the cards close to his eyes to see what he had. Ted and Jason teased him good-naturedly. Mark took their teasing in stride and laughed with them. Somehow, Cat's name was brought into the conversation, and Ted's teasing became more than light banter.

"Well, Mark, I guess you finally got what you wanted, didn't you?" Ted asked, a little sarcastically. "You wanted his job and his wife. Now it looks like you're getting both."

"What do you mean, Ted?" Mark asked.

"Well, I know that you tried to take Cat away from Jim when he was alive. Remember, I was there that time when Jim was so angry with you," Ted said.

"Look, Ted. What Jim and I had a disagreement about was between him and me.

It had nothing to do with you or the unit. It was none of your business. I was loyal to Jim while he was alive and I don't like your insinuations," Mark said angrily.

Jason could see that Mark and Ted were both becoming angry, so he tried to change the subject.

"Look, Ted, that has nothing to do with us. Let's just get back to the game," Jason said.

Both men gave each other an angry look, but cooled off.

"Ted, I think it's your turn," Jason said, trying to change the subject. He hadn't been a part of Jim's unit when all of Jim's and Mark's arguments occurred, so he didn't know what had started it. He only came after Mark had angrily left for a while. He knew it was none of his business and he really didn't want to get involved. He gathered that it had something to do with Cat, but he didn't want to know what it was. He just hoped he could get Mark and Ted back on friendly terms again. Then he remembered a funny incident that had happened after Mark had become Commander and said something about it. Soon the men were laughing and teasing again. The day had been ruined for Mark, though. He hated to remember how he and Jim had fought shortly before Jim had died. He would have given almost anything to take it back, but there was no way he could.

When Cat came in a few minutes later, they were back to their easy camaraderie. They were laughing loudly when Cat entered, but Mark still felt the sting of Ted's words.

Maybe there was some truth to what Ted had said.

"You guys must have been having a good time," she said, as she walked into the den.

"We found your deck of cards and were playing poker," Mark said. "I hope it was all right for us to use them."

"Sure, I never use them. When I bought them, I thought I would play Solitare with them, but it's more fun to play it on the computer, so I never use them. How did everything go, today?" she asked.

"It went well," Mark said, and Ted and Jason agreed with him.

"I brought some barbecue, baked beans and potato salad for dinner. Would you two like to eat with us?" she asked.

Ted started to say no, but he saw a disappointed look in Cat's eyes, so he said, "Sure. How about it, Jason?"

"You know I would rather have that than what they'll have at the barracks," Jason said.

"You guys continue your game and I'll let you know when it's ready," Cat said. "I'm going to fix something for my sister, Carol's family first. You remember Carol don't you, Ted?"

"Yes, I remember her as many times as Jim had me baby-sit you three women," Ted said.

"I wouldn't put it that way," Cat said, a little peeved at being called a baby. "You protected us from danger."

"Yeah, well, I remember her," Ted said.

They went back to their poker game and Cat went into the kithen to fix a package for Carol. When it was ready, Cat called Carol. Shortly, there was a knock on the door and Sherry Rene ran in followed by Carol.

"Mista Mok, see what I drawed for you," she started, but stopped when she saw Ted and Jason. "Who zat?" she asked Cat.

"They're two of Mr. Mark's friends," Cat answered. "Come over here and I'll introduce you to them."

Sherry became bashful and grabbed Cat's leg and got behind her.

"Are you being bashful, Sherry Rene?" Cat asked. "I've never seen you be bashful before."

Sherry didn't say anything, but when she was close enough to the sofa where Mark was sitting, she let go of Cat's hand and climbed up into Mark's lap.

"You like dem, Mista Mok?" she asked.

"Yes, Sherry Rene," Mark said. "They're friends of mine."

She gave them a long look and then she turned back toward Mark. "I give you kiss," she said, as she kissed him several times on the face. "I drawed you a pic-ture," she said, holding it up to him.

"Sherry Rene, you're being rude to my guests," Mark said. "You need to say hi to them."

She gave them a mean look and said, "No." Then she ran and hid behind Cat again.

"What's wrong with you, Sherry Rene?" Cat asked. "I've never seen you act like this before."

"He don wik Mista Mok," she said pointing to Ted.

"Now you're being silly, Sherry," Cat said. "He's Mr. Mark's friend. He's been here keeping him company while I was gone. Now you apologize to Mr. Ted."

"No," she said and ran over to Carol.

"She's just tired and cranky," Carol said. "She didn't get her nap today. I'm sorry, Ted. I apologize for my child. Really she isn't this rude. Cat, I need to get my stuff and get her on home."

"Sure. I have it all ready for you. I'll just go get it," Cat said, as she hurried into the kitchen. She couldn't imagine why Sherry had been so rude. She had never seen her rude to anyone.

Cat hurried back with the package she had fixed for Carol and Sherry was still behind Carol, hanging onto her leg.

"Come on Sherry. Let's go home," Carol said. "I'm sorry that she was rude, Mark. I apologize, again, Ted. She isn't usually this rude. I don't know what's wrong with her."

"Bye, Mista Mok," Sherry waved. "I see you lata, awagata."

"Bye, Sherry Rene, I'll see you later, alligator," he said, as he waved in her direction.

When they were gone, Cat apologized to Ted again. "I'm really sorry, Ted. Really, she's never acted like that before. I have no idea why she did it. The only thing I can think of is that she was jealous that you were Mark's friend. Sometimes you just can't tell what a child is thinking."

"That's OK, Cat," Ted said, as he stood. "You can't help what your niece does.

I've changed my mind, though. I think we'll be going. Thanks for the invitation, anyway. I'll see you later, Mark. Come on, Jason. Let's go."

After they were gone, Cat apologized again to Mark. "I'm so sorry, Mark. I've never seen her like that. She's always so loving. You know, like she was the first time she saw you."

"That's OK, Cat. I think I know why she acted like she did."

"Why?" Cat asked. "Why do you think she did that?"

"I can't tell you, Cat, but I think she had a good reason."

"What reason?" Cat asked. "She's never seen Ted before. Why would she take such a dislike to him the first time she saw him?"

"Forget it, Cat," Mark said. "He probably won't come back. I think he accomplished what he came here for."

"What do you mean by that?" Cat asked. "What happened while I was gone?"

"Forget it, Cat. Let's go eat. I'm starving." Then he put his arm around Cat's shoulders and said, "Help me get to the kitchen, my love, and feed me."

Cat wondered what had happened, but she knew that Mark would probably never tell her. It was so strange. Something happened just before she had gotten home and Sherry had sensed it. How she knew it had something to do with Ted, she guessed she would never know. "I guess it'll remain a mystery," Cat thought. "Why did Sherry take such a dislike for Ted the minute she saw him?" Ted had always been nice to her. He had been her protector for several years and he had never even said an unkind word to her, even though she had given him a hard time sometimes. "Well, I might as well forget it," Cat thought. "Like Mark said, I probably will never know why Sherry had acted like that."

CHAPTER 4

After dinner, Cat told Mark to go back to the den while she cleaned up the kitchen. "I'd rather just stay here and watch you, if you don't mind, Cat," he said.

"It's OK with me, but it isn't very exciting to watch me wash dishes and put them away," she said.

"You have your idea of excitement and I have mine," he said, as he gave her a quick wink.

Cat gave a little laugh and said, "Suit yourself." Then she went back to doing what she was doing.

"When you get through there, I have something for you," Mark said.

Cat could hardly wait to see what Mark had, so she hurriedly finished the dishes and dried her hands.

When she walked over to the table, Mark handed her a paper. "This is my first installment of Step Number One," he said.

Mark had written something in an uneven handwriting. You could tell it was probably written by someone who wasn't seeing well by the way the words slanted. There was a picture and a group of words next to it and then another picture and more words. It started out:

**"O thou fairest among women, I have
compared thee, O my love,
To a company of horses in Pharaoh's chariots."***

Then there was a picture of a horse hitched to an elaborate chariot.

**"Thy cheeks are comely with rows of jewels,
Thy neck with chains of gold."***

Beside these words was a picture of the head of a woman with a chain of gold around her neck.

**"Behold, thou art fair, my love; behold thou art fair,
Thou hast doves' eyes."***

Then there was a picture of a dove beside these words.

"As a lily among thorns, so is my love among the daughters."*

Here, he drew a picture of a lily.

**"Let me see thy countenance, let me hear thy voice,
For sweet is thy voice, and thy countenance is comely.
Thy teeth are like a flock of sheep."***

Here, he had drawn a little lamb.

**"Thy lips are like a thread of scarlet, and thy speech is comely:
Thy temples are like a piece of a pomegranate."***

Here, he had drawn a pomegranate.

"Thy two breasts are like two young roes."*

Here, he had drawn two small deer.

"Thou art all fair, my love; there is no spot in thee."*

---

* The Holy Bible, KJV

When Cat finished reading, she had tears in her eyes. "When did you do this, Mark?" she asked.

"Last night," he answered. "Do you like it?"

"I love it, Mark." Then she leaned over and kissed him. He pulled her to his chest and kissed her again. "I love you, Cat," he said, as he kissed her again and again. She didn't stop him. She let him kiss her neck and her lips. She could feel his desire for her, but a little voice told her she had to stop him. She didn't want to stop him, but finally she got strength enough to say, "Mark, stop."

He stopped kissing her and let her go, but he was breathing rapidly. He looked at her with disappointment. Neither of them said anything for a few minutes. Then Cat pulled out a chair and sat down.

"You did that last night?" she asked breathlessly.

"Yes," Mark said, as his breathing became steady again.

"How?" she started. "How did you see?"

"I can see better than I did," he answered.

"Did you write that from memory or did you use a Bible? Did you think I wouldn't recognize the Song of Solomon in the Bible*?"

"Yes, I figured you would recognize it. I have to confess. I found a Bible in the bookcase in the den," he said.

She took a deep breath and said, "Mark, I think you made it through the First Step."

"I'm glad, because I don't know how much longer I can wait," he said. Please don't make me wait much longer. It seems like I've waited for you my whole life. I fell completely in love with you the first time I laid eyes on you. You always belonged to someone else, though. How long before you'll belong to me?"

Cat took another deep breath and said, "I'm sorry, Mark. I can't marry you right now. It's too close. I just can't. Maybe after the first of the year. We can start a new year with a new marriage. Can you wait that long?"

"I don't know how I can wait that long, Cat, but I understand.

I didn't even think about how close it would be to November 21. You're right. We need to start a new year with a new marriage. I'll just have to wait."

"Mark, you're so wonderful, I do love you. I love you more than I ever thought I could ever love anyone else. Thank you for understanding. I love your gift. I can see that you put a lot of thought and work into it. I'll treasure it forever. Let's go into the den, now. It's more comfortable there."

"Whatever you say, Cat. I'm happy just being with you."

Cat helped Mark into the den and sat down next to him on the sofa. He put his arm around her and they sat for a long time not saying a word. Each of them were deep into their own thoughts.

"How can I have been so lucky as to have the love of two such wonderful men?" Cat wondered. "God has been so good to me." Then she drifted off to sleep and was awakened later when Mark gently shook her and said, "Cat, I think you need to go upstairs before I do something that I'll regret."

Then she sleepily arose and headed for the stairs. "Can you get your medicine?" she asked.

"Sure, you go on up to bed," he answered.

Cat continued on up the stairs and into her bedroom. She knew her sleep would be punctuated with dreams; dreams of a new love who had surprisingly entered into her life, but who was so much a part of it now.

The next day was Saturday and Cat was still faced with the problem of giving Mark a bath. After breakfast, Cat cautiously broached the subject. "Mark, how would you like a nice hot bath?"

"I would love one, but how can I get one with this heavy thing on my leg?"

"Well, you won't be able to get into the tub, but maybe working together, we can come up with something," Cat said.

She got one of the kitchen chairs and put it in the downstairs bathroom. She helped Mark into the bathroom and seated him on the chair.

"The first thing we'll do is tackle your hair," she said. She wrapped a bath towel around his shoulders. Then she wet a washcloth and wet his hair just enough to make a slight lather when she put a dab of shampoo on it. She gave him a washcloth to cover his eyes and had him lean back and hold his head over the sink. Then she slowly squeezed water from another washcloth over his hair until all of the soap suds were gone. Then she took another bath towel and blotted as much water as she could, out of it.

"When we get through," she said. "I'll take my blow dryer and style and dry your hair."

"Thanks, Cat. It sure feels better already," Mark said.

Next, Cat ran some hot water into the sink and got a clean washcloth. She lathered the washcloth and washed his face. Then she washed his left arm and took his right arm out of the sling and washed it as well as she could.

Now, she was getting into an area that she knew was going to embarrass her. She washed and rinsed his back and then she dried it with a bath towel. Now, it was time to wash his chest. She hesitated for a few minutes.

"What's wrong, Cat?" he asked. "Are you afraid to wash my chest?"

"Yes, I guess I am," she answered. "I haven't touched a man's chest since Jim died."

"Here, give me the washcloth. I'll do it," Mark said.

"I'm sorry, Mark. I thought I could do it, but I can't," she said.

"That's OK, Cat," he said. "If you can get my leg and my feet, I'll do the rest of me."

"Thanks, Mark. That's a deal."

So Cat washed, rinsed and dried his left leg and both of his feet, since the cast wasn't on his right foot, and Mark did the rest. After he was washed and dried, Cat took her blow dryer and styled his hair while she dried it.

"Now, let's tackle those whiskers," Cat said, as she got out a razor and shaving cream.

"Wait a minute, Cat," Mark said. "If you'll hold a hand mirror up for me, I can do that. I don't like the idea of your trying to shave me as nervous as you are about touching me."

"OK, I'll do it that way, then," she said.

After he was shaved, Cat found some after shave lotion that had been Jim's. She splashed it liberally on his face and sprayed some cologne on his chest. "Here's some deodrant. You can rub it under your arms," she said, as she handed it to him.

"There," she said, as she stood back and admired her work. "You look a lot better, anyway."

"I feel 100 percent better," he said.

"Do you have any clean pants and shirts?" she asked.

"I don't know what I have," he said. "I didn't pack my bag. I was kind of out of it when they took me to the hospital. I don't even know who packed it."

"Wait here. I have some of Jim's clothes that I couldn't bear to part with," Cat said. "He was taller and more muscular than you, but maybe they won't swallow you. I'll be back in a few minutes."

Cat picked out the smallest shirt and pants she could find. They still looked like they might be a little big on Mark, but maybe they wouldn't look too bad. She hurried downstairs and helped Mark put them on.

Just as she thought, the pants were about two inches too long and the shirt just hung on Mark. She knew that Jim had been taller and bigger than Mark, but she didn't realize he had been that much larger.

"I can hem up the pants, but I'm sorry, I can't do anything about the shirt. You'll just have to grow into it," she said laughing.

"Well, at least I'm clean," he said, as he laughed, too. Then he hurriedly dressed.

"I think we had better get out of here," Mark said. "I don't think Carol would be too happy to find us in the bathroom together. I really don't think she likes me."

They walked out of the bathroom just in time, for only a short time later, there was a knock and Sherry ran in followed by Carol.

"Aunt Kitty, whea aw you?" she asked.

"Right here, Sherry Rene," Cat said, as she hurried away from the bathroom.

"Is dat mean man hea?" Sherry asked.

"What mean man?" Cat asked.

"You know wut mean man," Sherry said. "Dat one dat wus mean to Mista Mok."

"No, Sherry Rene," Cat said, as she picked her up and gave her a hug. "He isn't here now."

Then she saw Mark, who had made it to the sofa. She ran over to him and hopped upon his lap. "Mista Mok," she said, holding up a picture. "See wut I drawed fo you?"

"Oh, Sherry Rene," he said, as he gave her a hug. "That's beautiful. I love it. Thank you."

"You welcum, Mista Mok," she said.

"While they're occupied, come into the kitchen," Carol said as she led the way into the kitchen. "I want to show you what I have for the party."

"Mark looks and smells cleaner," Carol said, as she sat down at the table. "You didn't give him a bath, did you?" she asked.

"How else was he going to get one?" Cat asked, a little peeved at Carol's insinuation.

"Cat, I think you're treading on dangerous ground with Mark. Can't you see how crazy he is about you? I don't think it would take much of an encouragement to, well you know what. You haven't have you?" Carol asked.

"Have I what?" Cat asked, even though she knew what Carol was hinting at.

"You haven't gone to bed with him have you?"

"Carol, I thought you knew me better than that!" Cat said angrily. "You know I would never do that before marriage!"

"No, I don't know that, Cat," Carol said. "I've seen how he looks at you. It reminds me of a hungry wolf looking at a little lost lamb. I know his kind."

"Well, Carol," Cat said. "I'm not a little lost lamb and I know how to handle Mark. Now, come on, show me what you came here to show me."

"You may think you know how to handle Mark, but you just wait until he's well. You'll find out that it's going to take a lot to hold him back."

"Let's just change the subject," Cat said. "Let me see what you have here."

While Cat and Carol were looking at cakes and party favors, Mark was entertaining Sherry in the den.

"I bot my book. I gonna weed to you, Misa Mok," Sherry said, as she sat on Mark's lap and opened her book.

"Dis is a pig. He go oink, oink," she said and turned the page. "Dis is a cow. He go moooo. Dis is a dog. He go woof, woof."

She continued to read each page and did the sound for each animal, then she looked up at Mark and caressed his face with her tiny hand. "Oh, it smooove, Mista Mok. I like it bedda."

"Your Aunt Kitty helped me shave," he said, as he ran his hand over his smooth face. "I like it better, too."

"Oooo, you smell nice, too," she said

"I had a bath, too," he said.

"You feel bedda?" she asked.

"Yes, I feel lots better," Mark answered.

"I wuv you Mista Mok," she said, as she hugged him and kissed his face. "I don wik dat man to be mean to you."

"It's OK, Sherry Rene," Mark said, as he hugged her back. "He won't be mean to me anymore. I love you, too. Some day I want a little girl just like you," he said.

"You gonna git a widdle gul wik me?" she asked.

"Yes, some day I will," Mark answered.

"Git hua now, so I kin pway wit hua," Sherry said.

"I can't get her right now," Mark answered. "I have to wait until I'm well. Then I need your Aunt Kitty to help me."

"Aunt Kitty kin hep you git a widdle gul?" she asked.

"Maybe. If you ask her real nice, maybe she'll help me get a little girl for you to play with," Mark said with a twinkle in his eye. "Why don't you go ask her if she'll help me get a little girl for you to play with?" He was really feeling mischievous and was anxious to see what Cat would say.

"Aunt Kitty, Aunt Kitty," Sherry called, as she ran into the kitchen.

"What is it Sherry Rene?" Cat asked.

"Mista Mok said he was gonna git a widdle gul wik me, but you havta hep him. He said will you hep him git a widdle gul for me to pway wit?"

"He did, did he?" Cat said, as she looked at Mark in the den. He was trying to stifle a laugh, but he wasn't having much luck at it.

"Yes, Aunt Kitty," Sherry continued. "You need to hep Mista Mok git a widdle gul, so I kin pway wit her."

"We'll just have to think about that," Cat said, as she walked into the den and placed her hands on her hips. "You should be ashamed of yourself, Mark Fuller. Corrupting an innocent child like that."

"I couldn't help it," he said. "It was too good to pass up. Well, when will you help me get a little girl for Sherry Rene to play with?"

"Yeah, Aunt Kitty, when?" Sherry said, as she danced up and down beside Cat.

"Some day, Sherry Rene, but not right now," Cat said, as she gave Mark a dirty look and headed back to the kitchen.

"We'll keep on until she gives in, Sherry Rene. We'll get our little girl soon. Maybe sooner than she thinks," Mark said, as Sherry hopped back up onto his lap and he hugged her again. "Thanks for your help, Sherry Rene. I needed it."

"I told you to watch out for him, Cat." Carol said accusingly, as Cat walked back in and sat back down at the table.

"He's sneaky. Now he's even corrupting my child and getting her to do his dirty work. You better listen to me, Cat. He'll have you in bed before you know it."

"Let's change the subject, OK?" Cat said. "Now show me what you've got here."

"OK," Carol started again. "I was thinking, do we need two individual cakes or just one and decorate each end differently?"

"I think it would be better to have two individual cakes," Cat said.

"OK," Carol said. "I thought Sherry's could be in the Strawberry Shortcake motif or something like that. Then we could take Mark's badge and make a copy of it and make a big one in the center of his. He does have a badge, doesn't he?"

"He has one somewhere," Cat answered. "He probably doesn't know where it is, though. Someone else packed his things when he went into the hospital and he hasn't been back to the barracks since he's been out of the hospital."

"I also thought we could put little guns all around the edge. He does carry a gun, doesn't he?" Carol asked.

"Yes, he carries a gun when he's working, but he hasn't been working since the accident," Cat answered.

"Do you think you can get a picture of his badge and gun for me?" Carol asked.

"I don't know, Carol," Cat answered. "He probably doesn't even know where they are. I hate to ask him right now."

"I know, Cat, but I wanted to order the cakes on Monday. You know, the 15th will be here before you know it and I have to get everything ready in advance."

So Cat went into the den to find Sherry still sitting on Mark's lap and still reading from her book.

"Mark," she said. "I need to ask you something."

"Go right ahead, my love," he said.

"Do you have your badge?" she asked.

"Not on me." he answered. "It may be in my bag. Why do you want to know?"

"I wanted to get a picture of it," she answered. "I knew you didn't have it on you.

May I look in your bag?"

"Of course you may," he answered. "You didn't have to ask."

"I just wanted to ask first," she said, a little miffed at his sharp answer.

She looked through everything in his bag, but his badge wasn't there. She thought it might be in his wallet, but his wallet wasn't there either. The only things in his bag were clothes. He couldn't find his wallet when they stopped at the pharmacy, and he didn't know what had happened to it.

"It isn't there," she told him.

"Why do you want a picture of my badge, anyway," he asked.

"Carol is ordering a cake for your birthday and she wanted to put a picture of your badge on the cake.

"I don't need a cake, anyway, so forget about my badge," he said angrily.

Cat left the room almost in tears. Mark had never talked to her like that and she couldn't understand why he did now.

Sherry was surprised and turned around and looked at Mark.

"Why you mad at Aunt Kitty?" she asked. "You talk mean to Aunt Kitty. Why?"

"I'm sorry, Sherry Rene," he said. "I shouldn't have talked to Aunt Kitty like that. I'll have to apologize to her."

"I think I had better get my child and go home," Carol said. "I think she's getting on Mark's nerves. Oh, are you and Mark going to church in the morning?"

"I don't know. It depends on how he's feeling in the morning," Cat said, still on the verge of tears.

"Skip and I are going to go in time for Sherry to go to Sunday School. She loves Sunday School and I'm glad she does," Carol said, as she gathered up her birthday information, but leaving a brochure for Cat to look at. "I'll call you in the morning before we leave to see if you're going. We'll meet you there if you go. I better go now before Mark blows a gasket."

"Come on, Sherry," Carol said, as she picked her up from Mark's lap. "We have to go. Mama has a lot to do before bedtime."

"Bye Mista Mok," Sherry said, as she waved to Mark. "I still wuv you, even if you hut Aunt Kitty. Don't do dat again, OK?"

"OK, Sherry Rene," Mark said. "I won't do it again."

When Carol and Sherry were gone, Mark hobbled into the kitchen and found Cat sitting at the table silently crying. He came up behind her and put his hand on her shoulder. "I'm sorry, Cat," he said close to her ear. "That was a mean thing to do. I didn't mean to make you cry. Will you forgive me?"

"Since you apologized, I guess I can," Cat said through sniffles. "I just thought you might have your badge with you."

"Well, I don't," he said still a little angrily. "I have no idea where it is. Maybe all my stuff is at the barracks, unless Ted has already thrown it out."

Then he turned and hobbled out of the kitchen and back into the den. Cat decided not to follow him. There was something about his badge that was eating at him and he was still angry at the thought of it. It was best that she stay out of his way until he got it settled.

Carol had left her a copy of the supplies that she had thought that they would need for the party, so Cat picked it up and studied it. Having Mark in her house, and feeling the way she did about him, was beginning to cause her all kinds of problems. Maybe she shouldn't have brought him here. If she hadn't brought him here, though, where would he be by now? "Oh, well, maybe he'll get over it soon and get back to the wonderful, caring person he had been before," she thought. "I sure hope so."

CHAPTER 5

The next morning, Cat arose early in case Mark felt like going to church. She looked in Jim's closet and found a nice suit that had been tight on Jim. She took it out and brushed it with the clothes brush and hung it on the door to air out. She hoped that it would look OK on Mark.

When she went downstairs, Mark was already sitting at the table. "Good morning, Mark," she said. "How are you feeling?"

"Hi, Cat. I'm feeling ashamed," he said. "I apologize for the way I talked to you yesterday. I'm sorry that I hurt your feelings. Please forgive me."

"I forgive you, Mark," Cat said. "If Sherry made you nervous, I'll try to make her leave you alone when she comes back over."

"No, Cat," he said. "That had nothing to do with Sherry. I love Sherry and feel so privileged that she likes me and wants to be with me. Don't make her stop. I just had a bad day. Sometimes the pain gets to me and I have to vent. The closest one to me gets the full effect of it. Just try to overlook me sometimes, if you can. Can you make me some coffee? I tried, but it's hard to do with only one hand."

"Sure," Cat said. "I was just going to make it, anyway."

After Cat had put coffee in the receptacle and poured the water into the coffee maker, she turned it on and walked over to the table and sat down to wait for it to brew.

"Do you feel like going to church this morning?" she asked.

"Not really, but I would like to go if you don't mind helping a cripple get around. You'll have to help me get into and out of the car," he answered.

"Carol wanted to know if we were going," Cat continued. "She and Skip are taking Sherry to Sunday School. She wanted me to let her know if we were going."

"I'll know more after I have my coffee," Mark said. "Tell her we're going, though. I'll go, even if I don't feel like it."

So Cat called Carol and told her that they would be there in time for church. Then Cat fixed a quick breakfast.

After breakfast, she brought Jim's suit down and showed it to Mark. "Would you like to wear this suit? It was really too small for Jim, so he didn't wear it much."

"I'll try it on," Mark said. "It can't look any worse than what I had on yesterday."

"Do you need some help?" Cat asked.

"I'm sure I will," Mark answered. So Cat helped him get into the suit. Her heart skipped a beat when she saw him with the complete suit on. It fit really well. He looked very handsome in it. He almost looked like Jim standing there in front of her. Cat held her breath and ran her fingers over the front of the jacket. It felt like Jim was alive again. She seemed to go into a trance as she looked at Mark standing there in Jim's suit. As she stared at him, Mark became Jim. She could hardly breathe. "Oh, Jim," she said and struggled to keep her heart from beating so fast she could hardly breathe.

"Cat," Mark said, as he put his hand on her shoulder. "Are you OK?"

When he said that, it brought Cat out of her trance and she shook her head. She looked at Mark and shook her head again in confusion.

"Are you OK, Cat," Mark asked again.

Cat didn't say anything. She just caressed Mark's chest. Then she sat down on the sofa and tried to come back to reality. She was still dazed and didn't answer Mark for several minutes.

"Cat, are you OK?" Mark asked even louder this time and he shook her shoulder a little.

"I'm sorry, Mark," she said. "I thought I saw Jim. I have to go upstairs, now. I have to get ready," she said, still in a daze. She arose and slowly walked up the stairs.

When she returned about 30 minutes later, she was ready to go to church.

Mark had taken the suit jacket and tie off. If it made Cat act in such a strange manner, he didn't want to wear it. The pants fit, so he thought he would wear them, but there was no way he was going to put that jacket on again.

Cat came into the den and looked at Mark. Then she looked at the jacket where Mark had thrown it across the back of the sofa. She didn't say anything for a few minutes. Then she walked over and picked up the jacket. She stroked it lovingly for a few minutes and said, "You don't want to wear the jacket?"

"No, Cat, I don't want to wear the jacket," he said through clenched teeth. He hoped that she didn't insist that he wear it.

"I'll take it back upstairs, then," she said, as she turned and went back upstairs.

Mark watched her go till she reached the top of the stairs and then he turned and sat down on the sofa to wait until she was ready to come back down. Somehow he figured she was lying on her bed with the jacket held tightly to her face and she was crying her heart out. How could he ever compete with Jim Ryan? "Even in death, he's a better man than I am," Mark thought sadly. "How do you compete with a dead hero?"

After about 30 minutes, Cat came down the stairs. "I was right," he thought, as he saw her red eyes. "She's been up there crying."

"Are you ready to go?" she asked, as if nothing had happened.

"Yes, I'm ready," Mark answered with a lump in his throat.

Cat picked up Mark's crutches and handed them to him. "You'd better take these. You'll need them," she said, as she led the way to the door. She held the door open for Mark to go through, then she shut and locked it.

She opened the car door and helped Mark get into the car. Then she fastened his seat belt. She walked around to the driver's side and got into the car. Before she started the engine, she turned to Mark and said, "I'm sorry, Mark. I shouldn't have done that, but I can't help it. I didn't know seeing you in his suit would affect me like that. When you're able, we'll get your clothes. I'll never ask you to wear anything of Jim's again."

Then she started the car and didn't say anything else until they reached the church.

She stopped the car and helped Mark get out of the car and into the church. Then she steered Mark over to the pew where Carol, Skip and Sherry were sitting. When Sherry saw them, she ran over to them and yelled, "Aunt Kitty, Mista Mok. Come sit with us."

When they sat down, Sherry climbed into Mark's lap, and whenever anyone came by to shake hands with Cat and Mark she said, "Dis is Aunt Kitty and Mitsa Mok. He gonna git a widdle gul to pway wit me and Aunt Kitty gonna help him."

Cat tried to hold her hand over Sherry's mouth to keep her quiet, but she pulled her hand off and said it again. "Hush, Sherry. That's supposed to be a secret," Cat whispered in her ear, as she tried holding her hand over her mouth again.

"It's a secret?" she asked.

"Yes, Sherry, it's supposed to be a secret and you're blabbing it all over the place."

Everyone got a good laugh at that and told Cat they understood and to not be embarrassed. They thought they knew what she meant.

Soon, the pastor went to the pulpit and preached his prepared sermon. Carol tried to get Sherry to go over to her, but she insisted on sitting in Mark's lap. "Leave her alone," Mark whispered, so Carol let her stay there until the end of the service. After the service, everyone came over and told Cat and Mark they were glad that they had come and invited them to come back again.

"What happened to you?" they all wanted to know.

"I was in an accident," Mark answered. He didn't say what kind of an accident, but he hoped that they would figure it was an automobile accident and not ask anymore questions, which, as it turned out, they did think it was an automobile accident and didn't ask anything else.

"Would you ladies like to go to a restaurant and eat before going home?" Skip asked.

"Yes, of course," Carol answered. "Who wants to cook on Sunday?" she asked.

So they left Cat's car at the church and they piled into Skip's car and went to the popular restaurant downtown.

There was a big crowd there and they had trouble finding a table, but they finally found one. Since the restaurant was set up buffet style, they had a word of prayer before filling their plates.

"Would you like me to fix your plate for you, Mark?" Cat asked.

"Yes, I would," Mark answered. "Don't put very much on it, though. I'm not very hungry."

So Cat put some fried chicken and some vegetables that she knew Mark liked on his plate and brought it and his drink to the table for him.

Carol had taken Sherry over with her, so she could show her what she wanted. Skip went with them to help Carol with Sherry. Then Cat went to the buffet to fill her plate. That left Mark at the table alone. Jason and his family were in the restaurant and when he saw Mark alone at the table, he went over to talk to him.

"How are you doing, Commander?" Jason asked.

"I'm getting better every day," Mark answered. "Please don't call me Commander, though, Jason. I would prefer that you just call me Mark. I don't know if I'll ever be your Commander again."

"You may not be, but I still think of you as my Commander," Jason answered.

"I would still prefer that you just call me Mark," he said.

When Jason started to go back to his table, Mark took hold of his arm. "Jason, will you do something for me?"

"Sure, Mark, anything," Jason answered.

"I need you to go to the barracks and get all of my stuff for me. I want all of my personal stuff as well as my gear. Will you get it and bring it to me at Mrs. Ryan's cabin?"

"Sure, Mark. I'll be happy to do it. Do you want everything, then?"

"Yes, Jason. I want everything."

"I'll do that first thing in the morning, Mark," he said. "I see your family coming back now. I'll go so you can enjoy your meal with them."

"Thanks, Jason. I appreciate your doing that for me," Mark said, as Jason walked away.

"Was that Jason?" Cat asked when she walked up to the table.

"Yes, it was," Mark answered.

"He should have joined us," Cat replied.

"He has his family here," Mark said. "He's eating with them."

As Cat sat down, Carol, Skip and Sherry returned and sat down.

They had just begun eating when another of Mark's team members saw him and came over to speak to him.

"Bob, this is my, I mean, this is Cat Ryan and her sister and brother-in-law, Carol and Skip Taylor and their daughter, Sherry Rene. Everyone, this is Bob Adams, one of my team members."

"Hello, everyone," Bob said and they said hello to him.

"Cat Ryan, are you Jim Ryan's widow?" Bob asked.

"Yes, I am," Cat said hesitantly. She didn't want to go into that here in the restaurant.

"He was my Commander," Bob continued. "He was one great Commander," he said.

"Thanks," Cat said and turned her head, as a hint that she didn't want to talk about it there.

Bob took the hint and said, "Well, it was good to meet you all. I have to get back to my table, now."

During their meal, several more of Mark's team members saw him and came by and wanted to know how he was doing.

Suddenly, Mark put down his fork, grabbed his crutches and got up. "Will you excuse me," he said. "I have to go do something." Then he hobbled out of the restaurant as fast as he could.

He had hardly touched his plate, so Cat figured something was wrong. She took some money out of her purse and handed it to Carol. "Here's money for Mark and me. I'm going to go check on him," she said, and then she followed Mark outside.

When she caught up with Mark, he was leaning against a post that held up the porch roof. "Are you all right, Mark?" Cat asked.

"No, not really," he answered. "Are you ready to go?"

"Almost," Cat said. She had gotten the keys to Skip's car so she asked if he would like to sit in the car until they were ready to go.

"No, I just needed some air," he answered.

"You didn't eat much of your food," Cat said.

"I wasn't hungry," he answered.

"Mark, what's wrong?" she asked, as she gave him a worried look.

"Nothing, I just wasn't hungry," he answered, raising his voice.

Soon Sherry came skipping up to Mark with Carol and Skip following her. She was carrying a small stuffed kitten. "Wook, Mista Mok," she said as she held it up for him to see. "See my pwetty kitty," she said.

"Yes, Sherry Rene," he said. "That's really a pretty kitty."

"I gonna call her Pwetty Kitty," Sherry said.

"That's a good name for her," Mark said.

"Come on, Sherry," Carol said, as she took her hand. "Let's go get in the car. We have to go home now."

"Oh, us don't go home yet," Sherry said.

"Yes, we have to go home, now. Mr. Mark doesn't feel well," Carol said, as she led Sherry to the car.

"You sic, Mista Mok?" Sherry asked, as she turned around to look at Mark.

"Yes, Sherry Rene. I don't feel well," he answered.

"I sorry you don't feel well, Mista Mok. I kiss you. Make you feel bedda," she said, as she stopped and turned back to walk with Mark.

"I just need to go home, Sherry. I'll feel better when I get home," he said.

They hurried on to the car and got in and Skip drove back to the church to pick up Cat's car.

Skip helped Mark get into the car, then asked, "Cat would you like for me to go with you and help Mark get into the cabin?"

"Yes, thanks, Skip. That would be nice," she said, as she got into the back seat and fastened her seat belt. Then Skip got into the driver's seat of Cat's car. Carol drove their car and Sherry on to their cabin. Mark leaned his head back and went to sleep.

When they got to Cat's cabin, Skip helped Mark get inside and onto the sofa in the den. "Is there anything else you need?" Skip asked.

"Not that I can think of right now," Cat answered.

"Well, call me if you need me," Skip said. "Oh, here's a carry-out. Carol noticed that Mark didn't eat anything, so she fixed him a carry-out."

"Thanks, Skip. Tell Carol I said thanks, too."

"Will do," Skip said, as he started out the door. "You be sure and call if you need something," he said and then he walked on over to their cabin.

"Cat, I need my pain medicine," Mark said when she walked into the den to check on him.

"Sure, Mark, I'll go get it."

She handed him a glass of water, one pain pill and the rest of his medicine, because it was time to take it.

"Cat, I need more than one pain pill," he said.

She opened the bottle and took out another pain pill and handed it to him. He tossed the handful of pills into his mouth and swallowed them all at once. Then he lay back down on the sofa.

"I need to go to sleep, now," he said, and he closed his eyes.

Cat still hadn't had a chance to look at the birthday information that Carol had given to her, so she went into the kitchen and sat down at the table with the brochure.

About 6:00 p.m., she began to get hungry and went to see if Mark would like to eat something from his carry-out or something else.

She tried to awaken him, but he just opened his eyes and went right back to sleep. "Mark, do you want something to eat?" she asked him when she caught his eyes opened for a few minutes.

"No. Leave me alone," Mark said and shut his eyes again.

Cat began to get worried and decided that it wasn't good for Mark to be asleep that long, especially since he hadn't eaten anything.

"Mark, Mark, wake up," she said, as she shook him hard.

"No," he said. "Leave me the hell alone," he said angrily, and he turned away from her and closed his eyes again.

Then she spotted the bottle of pain medicine that she had set down on the coffee table. It had been half full when she set it there. Now it was almost empty.

"Mark, Mark," she said shaking him again. "Did you take more pain medicine?

Mark, did you take some more of these pain pills?"

"Yes," he said and closed his eyes again.

"How many?" she asked.

"How many, Mark?" she asked hysterically.

"Mark, how many of these pills did you take?"

"Don't know, maybe six," he mumbled.

She ran to the phone and dialed Carol's number. "Carol, I need to talk to Skip," she said when Carol answered the phone.

"What's wrong, Cat?" she asked.

"Just let me talk to Skip," Cat screamed.

He was immediately on the phone. "What's wrong, Cat?" he asked.

"It's Mark," she cried. "He's taken too many pain pills. Please help me get him to the hospital."

"I'll be right there," he said.

"What's wrong?" Carol wanted to know.

"It's Mark, I gotta go," he said, as he ran to the car and sped over to Cat's cabin.

They loaded Mark into Skip's car and headed to the hospital.

As soon as they arrived and told them that Mark had taken an overdose of pain medicine, he was rushed into an examination room. Cat followed, but they stopped her.

"We'll have to pump his stomach," the nurse said. "You wait in the waiting room. We'll come get you."

When she went to the waiting room where Skip was sitting, he was on the phone talking to Carol.

"I'm sorry, Honey, but I didn't have time to explain. I had to get Mark here as soon as I could."

Cat stood at the window and cried. "This can't happen again. Please God, don't let it happen again. I can't lose someone else that I love. I just can't."

After a couple of hours, the nurse came and got Cat and Skip. "You may go in to see him now," she said. "The doctor wants to talk to you."

"This is Doctor Polanski," the nurse said, as she took them to an office and asked them to sit down. Then she left.

"Mrs. Fuller?" the doctor asked.

"No, I'm Mrs. Ryan," Cat said. "Mr. Fuller is a friend of mine."

"Oh, I'm sorry," he said. "I was under the impression that you were his wife."

"I'm his fiancée," Cat said hesitantly. She could see his reluctance to tell her anything about Mark, since she wasn't his wife, so she decided to lie a little. Well, it really wasn't a lie. Mark had asked her to marry him. She just hadn't made it official yet.

"You were listed as his nearest of kin," Dr. Polanski said, as he looked at Mark's chart. "This is not my level of expertise, but I can tell you, Mr. Fuller is very depressed. In my experience with patients who are this depressed, once they try suicide and fail, they try again. They usually succeed the second time.

"I see that he is a Unit Commander with the FSC. They have an excellent therapist on staff there. If I were you, I would get him an appointment as soon as possible.

"As I said, this is not my field of medicine, but to me, he is presenting symptoms of PTSD, which means post traumatic stress disorder. I want to watch him for another hour and if he does all right, I'll send him home."

"Thank you, Dr. Polanski. I'll see about getting him an appointment with the therapist," Cat said.

So, Cat and Skip sat in the waiting room until Dr. Polanski released Mark. Mark was still pretty out of it when they arrived back at home. Skip helped him into the cabin and onto the sofa in the den and he lay down and closed his eyes.

"I gotta go home, Cat," Skip said after he got Mark settled. "Call me if you need me and I'll be right over. Do you need me to take off from work Tuesday to help get him to the surgeon?"

"I don't know, yet. I don't know how he'll be by then. I'll probably need some help, though," Cat said.

"Just let me know in time to get a substitute for my class," Skip said.

"I tell you what, Skip," Cat said on second thought. "I'll manage without you. There's no need for you to take off work. We'll make it OK."

"Are you sure?" Skip asked. "I'll be glad to do it if I have time to get someone to take my place."

"That's OK," Cat said, as she walked Skip to the door. "We'll manage."

After Skip was gone, Mark opened his eyes and called, "Cat, come here."

When Cat went into the den to see what Mark wanted he said, "Cat, I need a pain pill."

"No, Mark, you don't need a pain pill. They gave you something at the hospital just before we left."

"Cat, I need a pill," Mark insisted.

"Mark, I just brought you home from the hospital because you had an overdose of pain medicine. I'm not going through that again."

"Cat, give me the damn pill," Mark clenched his teeth and raised up and angrily looked Cat in the eyes.

"No, Mark," she said and then she ran upstairs. She had never seen Mark like that. He was always so sweet and even-tempered.

There had to be something really wrong for Mark to act like that. Maybe Dr. Polanski was right and Mark did have PTSD. "I'll call tomorrow, as soon as I can and get him an appointment," she thought.

She cautiously opened her door and walked to the head of the stairs. She could see the sofa, but Mark wasn't lying on it anymore. Then she heard him in the kitchen banging cabinet doors. She was glad that she had put the pills in a drawer and locked it. She didn't know what to do. Was Mark dangerous in his current frame of mind? Would he harm her or do some other harm to himself? Soon, his search exhausted him and he hobbled back to the sofa and lay back down. Cat slowly went down the stairs and into the den. Mark was lying back with his eyes closed.

"Cat, please give me something," he said almost in a whisper, without opening his eyes.

"I can't, Mark," Cat said, as she walked over to the sofa. "They gave you something at the hospital before we left. It's too soon for you to have anything else."

"I can't stand the pain," Mark said with his eyes still closed.

"Where do you hurt, Mark?" Cat asked. Mark didn't answer at first. Then he said, "I feel so guilty, Cat. I can't stand it any longer."

"Why do you feel so guilty, Mark?" Cat asked. She was confused as to why he would feel so guilty that it would make him act that way.

"They told me none of my men were seriously hurt. Just

superficial cuts. I believed them. Then, I find out today that they lied to me," Mark said.

"Who lied and what did they lie about?" Cat wanted to know.

"Tim Lane," Mark said, as he began to cry. "He was only 19. He had only been in my unit for four months. He was hurt bad. He, he just died."

"Oh, Mark, I'm so sorry," Cat said, as tears began to appear in her eyes, too.

"He was an only child. His parents are older people. They'll never have another child. They want me to say something at Tim's memorial. How can I do that, Cat? It was my own stupid mistake that killed him. How can I face them?"

"Mark, I know how bad guilt hurts," Cat said. "I felt so guilty after Jim died. It ate me up inside. If I hadn't insisted on going on the assignment when Jim didn't want me to go, he would still be alive. Because of me, the person I loved most in the whole world was killed. That's why I had to blame you for Jim's death. It hurt too much to blame myself. I hated myself. I couldn't stand to look at myself in the mirror. The guilt ate me up from the inside and there was nothing left, but a hard empty shell on the outside. There was nothing left to live for, but I couldn't die. I died a little every day, but I still couldn't die. I had to live with that horrible gnawing guilt every day. I couldn't eat. I couldn't sleep. And all through the pain of the guilt, I wanted Jim. I wanted him so badly I couldn't stand it.

"Then one day, when I thought I had finally reached the end of my rope, a wonderful, caring friend came and asked me to go to church with him. I didn't want to go to church, because I hated God as well as hating myself, but this wonderful friend insisted that I go to church with him.

"You saved me, Mark. I will always be eternally grateful to you for that. It took three years before I could repay you, but I'm going to do all I can to help you the same way you saved me. I'm not going to let you go down as deep into that pit as I went. I love you, Mark. I'm going to try to keep you from going through what I went through. Now, you sit up and stop blaming yourself for Tim's death. You had no way of knowing that there was a trap there. It happened. There's no way you can go back and change that. I know, I wished over and over that I could go back and bring Jim back to life, but it doesn't happen that way. You just have to learn to forgive yourself and go on with your life. Tomorrow morning, I'm going to make an appointment for you with the staff therapist and you're going, if I have to drag you. You're going to get well and I'm going to marry you, Mark Fuller. I lost one man that I loved. I don't intend to lose another one."

"After that, what can I say, Cat," Mark said. "You don't know how long I've wanted to hear you say that you love me, but you wait until I can't even like myself to say it. I don't even know whether you really mean it or if you're just saying it to keep me from killing myself."

"I mean it, Mark," she said and she leaned down and kissed him. At any other time, he would have grabbed her and returned her kiss, but this time, he just sat there with no emotion. He was drained of any feeling. He only wanted to go to sleep and never have to think about Tim Lane's dying ever again. He knew he would have to eventually face Tim's parents, but he was unable to do that right now. Would he ever have the strength to face them? He didn't know. At least now he knew that Cat would be by his side. Maybe her love would give him the strength he needed to make it. He could only hope and pray that it would.

CHAPTER 6

Early Monday morning, Cat called the number for the staff therapist, Doctor Lindstrom. Then she was connected to the person making appointments. When she explained that she was calling for Unit Commander Mark Fuller, she was given an appointment in two weeks. "Do you have anything sooner than that?" Cat asked. "He's really in bad shape."

"I'm sorry, but that's as soon as we can get you in to see Dr. Lindstrom. He'll be out of town until then. If you need a therapist before that, here's a number you can call," she said, then she gave Cat the number.

Cat wasn't happy waiting two weeks to get help for Mark, but she knew there was nothing she could do. She just hoped that, after they saw Doctor Sanders and his cast was removed, Mark would be in a better frame of mind.

Mark had had a fairly quiet night and was calmer that morning. Cat fixed a good breakfast and Mark came to the table and ate a small but sufficient amount.

After Cat had cleaned up the kitchen, she asked Mark if he would like for her to wash his clothes so he would have something clean to wear the next day.

"Whatever you want to do," Mark said, without any feeling in his voice. "I don't want to wear any more of Jim's clothes, though. You can go through my stuff and get out what you think is appropriate."

So Cat picked out some shirts and pants and a sport jacket.

She washed the shirts and pants and hung the jacket up to air out, hoping that the wrinkles would fall out. If they didn't, she would run the iron over it.

About 10:00 a.m., there was a knock on the door and Cat went to answer it. She was surprised to see Jason standing there. "May I come in?" he asked.

"Certainly," Cat said, as she stepped aside to let him come into the room.

"You know where Mark is," she said, pointing toward the den.

"Hi, Mark," Jason said, as he walked up to the sofa where Mark was lying.

"Sit down, Jason," Cat said, indicating a chair in front of the sofa.

"Thanks, Cat," he said and sat down. "Some of the guys told me about Tim," Jason said. "I was sorry to hear that."

Mark took a deep breath and said, "Thanks."

"I heard that his parents wanted to see you," Jason continued. "I thought you might like to have some company when you go see them."

Mark was shocked that Jason would offer to go with him. "I would appreciate that, Jason," Mark said. "I was really dreading it, but I knew I had to go."

"Cat, do you need someone to help get Mark to the doctor tomorrow?" Jason asked.

"Well, yes," she answered. "My brother-in-law had planned to go, but he would have to take off work to go. Are you busy tomorrow?"

"Not that I know of," Jason said. "Would you like for me to come and help?"

"I would if Mark would like for you to help," she answered. "Mark, would you like Jason to help me get you to see Dr. Sanders tomorrow?"

"If he wants to come, it doesn't matter to me," Mark answered, again without any hint of feeling in his voice.

"His appointment is at 2:00 p.m.," Cat said. "I wanted to leave about 1:00 so we would have plenty of time."

"I'll be here by 1:00, then," Jason said. "Oh, I have Mark's stuff in my car. May I bring it in?"

"Yes, of course," Cat said. Then she showed Jason where to put Mark's things.

"I need to go now," Jason said, as he waked to the door. "I'll see you tomorrow, Mark. Bye, Cat."

"Bye, Jason. Thanks for your help," Cat said, as she walked with him to the door.

"I appreciate your offering to help Mark, Jason," Cat said, as she took his hand and squeezed it. "He really needs a friend like you right now."

"I kind of figured that," Jason said. "We're not taking on an assignment right now. You know we're short-handed. Since I don't have anything to do anyway, I thought I might be of use to Mark and you."

"Thanks, again, Jason," Cat said. "I'll see you tomorrow."

After Jason left, Mark drifted off to sleep and Cat busied herself with different chores. She got Mark's clothes ready to go for the next day. Then she sat down at the kitchen table to look, again, at the birthday information that Carol had left.

A knock on the door brought Sherry Rene, followed by Carol. "Mista Mok," Sherry squealed and ran and jumped into his lap.

"Not today, Sherry," Mark said, as he lifted her up and set her back onto the floor. "Mr. Mark doesn't feel like playing with you today," he said.

"Mista Mok, I make you feel betta," she said and she kissed his cheek.

"Not today, I said," Mark said gruffly and pushed her away.

"It sounds like my child is irritating Mark," Carol said, "I better go get her."

"Sherry Rene, come here," Carol said, as she walked into the den.

"No, I make Mista Mok feel betta," she said and she sat down on the floor next to the sofa.

Carol came and took her hand and led her into the kitchen. "Mr. Mark said he doesn't feel like playing with you today. You'll just have to wait until he feels better."

"I kin make him feel betta," Sherry said and she ran back to the den and hugged Mark. Then she sat down on the floor beside him again.

"I read you story, Mista Mok. You go sleep. Den you feel betta," Sherry said, as she pulled out her book and started reading.

Soon, Mark was chuckling. After a while, he was laughing. Then he picked Sherry back up and set her on his lap.

"I make you feel betta," Sherry said, as she smothered him in kisses.

"Yes, Sherry Rene, you made me feel much better. Thank you so much."

"You welcum, Mista Mok," Sherry said. Then she and Mark read her book together.

While Sherry and Mark were reading her book, Carol and Cat were discussing the birthday party.

"About the cake," Cat said. "I don't think it's a good idea to have a cake with Mark's badge and gun on it. Not in the frame of mind he's in now. Just get one cake and decorate it with Strawberry Shortcake or whatever you want on it, and just put Sherry's and Mark's names on it. That's all it needs. I don't think we should say anything about the unit on the birthday cake."

"OK, Cat," Carol said. "Whatever you say. You know how Mark might react and if you think he would have a bad reaction, I think we should do as you said."

The next morning, Cat fixed breakfast early because she wanted to leave about 1:00 for Mark's appointment with Dr. Sanders. Mark ate a little bit because Cat insisted. "It'll be late when we eat lunch, so you need to eat now, so you won't fall out on me," Cat told him.

About 15 minutes until 1:00, there was a knock on the door. When Cat opened it, there stood Jason, just as he had promised.

"Come on in, Jason," Cat said, as she opened the door wider. "Mark's in the den. I really appreciate your doing this."

"I was glad to do it," he answered. "I wasn't doing anything else, anyway."

"We're just about ready to go," Cat said. "I just have to help Mark get his shoes on."

Jason helped Mark into the front passenger seat and Cat got into the back. Then Jason drove to the doctor's office. Mark and Cat were taken to an examination room while Jason waited in the waiting room.

"We need to get an X-ray of your shoulder and leg first," the nurse said. She had Mark sit down in a wheelchair and she took him to get the X-ray while Cat waited in the examination room.

After Mark was back in the examination room, Doctor Sanders came in carrying Mark's chart. "Hello, Mr. Fuller," Dr. Sanders said, as he sat down on a stool. "How is your eyesight now?" he asked

"My eyes feel better, but I still have this hazy mist and I still can see only shadows," Mark answered.

"OK, let me take a look," Dr. Sanders said. He examined Mark's eyes, then he said, "I want to see how well you can see. Put this over your left eye and tell me what you can see on the chart down there."

Mark read off a few letters and then Dr. Sanders told him to change eyes and do the same thing for the right eye.

After Dr. Sanders completed his examination of Mark's eyes, he said, "Dr. Nix will come see about your arm and leg. After he's finished, I want to see you across the hall in my office. Dr. Nix will be in here shortly. He's looking at your X-rays now." Then he left Mark and Cat alone in the examination room.

Shortly, a young man in a white lab coat entered the room and introduced himself as Dr. Nix. "Your arm is doing nicely," he said. "I think you can go without the sling now. If it starts to bother you, though, I would put it back on. I want you to use moist heat on it about four or five times a day. Here's a list and description of some exercises I want you to do four times a day. I've made an appointment for you to come to the hospital once a week for some extensive exercises. If you don't do these exercises, your arm will get stiff and you'll lose the use of it. So it's important for you to do these exercises at home between visits.

"As for your leg, it looks really good. I'm going to take this heavy cast off and put on what we call a walking cast. It's lighter weight and you'll be able to get around a lot better. Just remember, your leg isn't completely healed. You still have to be careful with it. After we get this new cast on your leg, I want to see you again in four weeks. Hopefully, it'll be completely healed by then."

Then he went out and came back with an instrument for removing the cast and applied the new cast.

"Now, just sit here for a few minutes while the new cast sets. Then Dr. Sanders wants to see you in his office."

When the cast was ready, the nurse came and took Mark and Cat to Dr. Sanders' office. Mark was amazed at how much lighter the new cast was.

"I almost feel human again," he said, as he walked over to Dr. Sanders' office.

"Come in and sit down," Dr. Sanders said, when the nurse opened the door for them. "Please close the door," he told the nurse, as she was leaving.

"The reason I asked you to come to my office is because I wanted to present two options to you," Dr. Sanders began.

"The first option is to do nothing and hope that eventually your eyesight will get better or you'll get used to your vision the way it is and be satisfied that you can see that well.

"The second option is a little riskier. There's an experimental surgery that's similar to cataract surgery, where the lens is peeled off and a new lens is inserted. If it works, you'll be able to see again. If it doesn't, then you'll not be able to see at all.

It's a 50/50 chance. You don't have to give me your answer today.

I want you to go home and think about it. See if you're willing to take that chance. Of course, we'll only do one eye at a time to make sure that you don't lose sight in both eyes at the same time. Here's a brochure that explains the procedure. Do you have any questions?"

"Yes," Mark said. "Are there any other options? I need to be able to see better than what I'm seeing now. I can't even go back to my job like I am now. What will I do if this surgery doesn't work?" Mark was beginning to get very agitated, so Cat took his hand and squeezed it.

"It's OK, Mark," she said. "We'll just pray about it. God will take care of it. Just calm down."

"Calm down," Mark said, as he pulled his hand out of Cat's hand. "It's not your eyes. How would you act if it was your eyes?" Then he stood up and paced the floor.

"I understand how you feel, Mr. Fuller. We just have to give it a little more time. Your eyes may get better by themselves. You may not even need the surgery. I just wanted to give you your two options and let you think about it. When you've made your decision, you can let me know. If you have no more questions, then, I'll wait to hear from you."

Then the doctor walked over to the door and opened it. Cat realized that Dr. Sanders was dismissing them, so she took Mark's hand and urged him out of the office and into the waiting room where Jason was nervously waiting.

"Wow," Jason said. "Looks like you got rid of some of that weight you were carrying around."

"Yeah," Mark said. "Come on, let's get out of here."

Jason helped Mark get into the front seat and Cat got into the back again. Then Jason got into the driver's seat. He turned and looked at Mark and said, "What did he say?"

Mark took a deep breath and said, "I may never get my eyesight back."

"Is that all he said?" Jason asked.

"Isn't that enough?" Mark asked angrily.

"Yes, I guess it is," Jason said, as he started the engine and pulled off of the parking lot.

"Mark, do you feel like going by the funeral home for a few minutes?" Jason asked. "It might be better to go there today instead of waiting and getting a shock tomorrow."

"I don't really feel like it, but maybe you're right. I should get it over with today, since everything is already messed up, anyway," Mark answered.

At the funeral home, Jason parked the car and helped Mark get out. Then he helped Cat out. Jason hurried to the door and opened it for Mark and Cat, since Mark still had to rely on his crutches until he got used to his new cast.

Jason signed the book and then Cat signed it for Mark and herself. Then they walked slowly down to where the casket was resting among numerous plants and sprays of flowers.

Mark stopped just before reaching the casket. He took Cat's hand and squeezed it before walking the rest of the way to the casket. When Mark looked at the face of the young man lying in the casket, he started to weep.

"Tim, I'm so sorry," he cried. "I didn't mean for this to happen. Please forgive me."

Jason walked up to Mark and put his arm around his shoulders. "It's OK, Mark. It wasn't your fault. You have to believe that. Come on, let's sit down for a while," Jason said, as he led Mark to a bench and urged him to sit down. They sat there for a while and Mark cried softly. Cat sat on one side and held his hand and Jason sat on the other with his arm around his shoulders.

Soon, an elderly man and woman came in and walked up to the casket. Cat assumed that they were Tim's parents. They stood there crying for a long time and then they turned and saw Mark. They walked over to Mark and Mrs. Lane held out her hand to Mark.

"You're Commander Fuller aren't you?" she asked.

"Yes, Ma'am," Mark said, as he took her hand and squeezed it. "I'm so sorry for your loss."

"I'm so glad you came," she said. "Tim always spoke so highly of you. He really respected you. He thought you hung the moon. He didn't think you could ever do anything wrong. He said one day that he would follow you anywhere. That's why he was injured so badly. He just wanted to be as close to you as he could get."

"I'm sorry that I led him into a trap, Mrs. Lane. I know you'll probably never be able to forgive me, but I would appreciate it if you could find it in your heart to try," Mark said with tears in his eyes.

"How could I not forgive you," Mrs. Lane said. "You gave my son the happiest four months of his life. He died doing something he loved. He loved working with you.

He had always wanted to be a Federal Agent and you gave him that opportunity. No one else would take a chance on him because he was a little clumsy, but you did. I'll never forget what you did for him."

Then Mr. Lane stepped up and shook Mark's hand. "What my wife said, that goes for me, too. She's more articulate than I am, but I feel the same way."

"Commander Fuller, would you say something at Tim's memorial?" Mrs. Lane asked. "It doesn't have to be anything elaborate. It doesn't even have to be very long. I would just like for you to say that you liked him and was proud to have him in your unit. Would you do that?"

"Of course, Mrs. Lane," Mark said, as he stood and put his arm around her. "I was proud of Tim and I would be honored to be able to say something at his memorial."

Mark stood holding Mrs. Lane for a few minutes and let her cry on his shoulder while he cried with her. After a while, he said, "Mrs. Lane, I'll be here tomorrow. I really need to go now, though. I've just come from the doctor's office and I'm getting kind of weak."

"I'm sorry, Commander Fuller," she said, stepping back away from him. "I didn't realize you were so badly injured. Of course you need to get back home and rest. I'll see you tomorrow."

"I'll see you, then," Mark said, as he took her hand again and then he took Mr. Lane's hand. "Again, I'm so sorry for your loss."

Jason and Cat shook their hands and told them who they were and added their own words of comfort. Then Jason helped Mark out to the car and drove them toward home.

"Jason, would you please stop at KFC? I'd like to get some chicken and things for dinner," Cat asked.

"Sure, Mrs. Ryan, I mean Cat. I'd be happy to stop," Jason said, as he pulled into the parking lot and Cat got out and went into the restaurant.

When they got home, Cat started putting the food on the dinning room table. She called Carol to see if she wanted to come and get some for their dinner.

In a few minutes, the front door opened and Sherry ran in, followed by Carol. Sherry ran into the kitchen and hugged Cat and then she ran to the den in search of Mark.

"Mista Mok," she said, as she climbed up into his lap. "Mama sed you saw dat docta today. Did he make you well?" she asked.

"No, but he changed my cast," he answered. "See? It's better."

"Oh, yeah," she said, as she touched his new cast. "It wuks bedda. Will it make you feel bedda?"

"Yes, Sherry Rene, it makes me feel a lot better," he said.

Then Sherry saw Jason. "Hey, you," she said pointing at Jason. "You make my Mista Mok feel bad. You wid that mean man. Dat man make my Mista Mok feel bad."

"I didn't make Mr. Mark feel bad, Sherry Rene. The man I was with made him feel bad, but I helped him. I'm his friend," Jason said.

"That's right, Sherry Rene. Mr. Jason is a friend of mine. He helps me. He isn't mean to me like that other man. Now you be nice to Mr. Jason," Mark said.

"He's a good fwend?" she asked.

"Yes, Sherry Rene," Mark said. "He's a real good friend."

Then Sherry jumped down and ran over to Jason and hugged his legs. "I wik you den, Mista Jason," she said.

Carol and Cat were in the kitchen getting the food ready and Cat asked, "Carol, why don't you call Skip and tell him to come over here and eat. It would be a lot simpler than trying to carry it over there?"

"OK," Carol said and she called Skip. "He said he'll be over in a few minutes," Carol said.

A few minutes later, he knocked on the door and came in.

When the food and dishes were on the table, Cat said for everyone to come to the dinning room. They all held hands and Skip blessed the food. While they were eating, Mark told them about his new cast and the condition of his arm. He didn't mention his eyes and no one asked him about them. They knew that if he had gotten some good news about his eyes, he would have said something. No one wanted to cause him any more grief than he had already been through.

After they had eaten, the men went into the den and Cat and Carol cleaned up the dishes and put the extra food into the refrigerator.

"What about Mark's eyes?" Carol asked Cat. "I noticed that he stayed away from that subject."

"Well, it doesn't look good," Cat said. "Dr. Sanders told him that there was an experimental surgery that could be done on his eyes, but it was really risky. The doctor wants him to think about it and let him know if Mark wants to have the surgery.

"What does Mark want to do, then?" Carol asked.

"I don't know," Cat answered. "He needs to really think about it. Dr. Sanders said he may get to where he can't see at all if he has the surgery."

"Gee, that's not good," Carol said. "I guess he does need to really think about it."

After a while, Skip said that he needed to go on home. He had papers to grade and lessons to prepare.

"Yeah, I do, too," Carol said. "I guess I'd better get my child and head on home."

"Did you order the cake?" Cat asked.

"Oh, yeah, I forgot to tell you," Carol said. "I ordered the cake with the Strawberry Shortcake motif and only put Sherry's and Mark's names on it like you said. I'll pick it up the day before the party. I also bought all of the other things that we'll need. They're all over at our cabin."

"Carol, are you coming?" Skip called from the front door. He was carrying Sherry and was ready to leave.

"Yes, I'm coming," Carol said. "See you later, Cat."

"Bye," Cat said and she blew a kiss at Sherry.

"Bye, Aunt Kitty. Bye Mista Mok," Sherry said.

"I guess I had better be going, too," Jason said, as he stood up and got ready to go. "I'll see you in the morning, Mark. Don't worry about what Dr. Sanders said this afternoon. God is still in control. He always has the last say. I'll see you tomorrow, Cat. Good night."

"Good night, Jason," Cat said, as she let Jason out the door and shut and locked it.

The next morning, Cat fixed a good breakfast, but Mark refused to eat anything.

"I'm too nervous, Cat," he said. "I was awake all night trying to think about what I'll say at Tim's memorial. I just don't know what to say. I'm sorry, everyone. If I hadn't been so stupid, Tim would still be alive. I don't think that would go over very well, do you?"

"No, Mark," Cat said. "I don't think that's what Tim's parents had in mind when they asked you to speak at his memorial. Didn't you like Tim?"

"Yes, I liked him," Mark said. "He was a great kid. He always obeyed my commands without arguing or hesitating. I wish I had a whole unit of young men like Tim."

"Then that's what you need to say," Cat said. "That's what the Lanes want to hear you say. Then they can let him go, knowing that he died doing what he loved with the Commander that he loved. That's what they want from you, Mark. To know that you loved him as much as he loved you, and that he didn't die in vain."

"Thanks, Cat," Mark said. "That's what I needed to know."

Shortly, there was a knock on the door. When Cat opened it, she expected to see Jason, but Jenny Long was standing there instead.

"Hi, Cat," she said. "I heard that Mark Fuller was here. Is that correct?"

"Yes, come on in," Cat said, as she stepped aside to let her come in. "He's in the den. You remember where it is, don't you?"

"Yes, of course," Jenny said, as she walked up to the sofa. "Hello, Mark," she said.

"Jenny," Mark said, surprised.

"I heard what happened and that Cat was taking care of you. How are you feeling?" she asked.

"Like a bomb blew up in my face," Mark said sarcastically.

"If that was supposed to be funny, it wasn't," Jenny said.

"It wasn't meant to be funny," Mark said. "How did you know I was here?"

"There was a unit meeting and the Director said that you were injured and was staying with Mrs. Ryan, who was nursing you back to health. He also told about Tim Lane's dying. I'm so sorry to hear that. I know you must be devastated," Jenny said.

"Yes, as a matter of fact, I am," Mark said. "His parents want me to say something at his memorial service today. I'm having a hard time with that."

"May I hitch a ride with you?" she asked.

"You'll have to ask Jason. He's driving me. I still have a cast on my leg and I still can't see," Mark answered.

Just then, there was a knock on the door and when Cat opened it, Jason was standing there. "Hello, Jason," Cat said. "Mark's about ready to go."

"Good," Jason said. "I came early, so I could get Mark into the funeral home before the crowd gets there. It'll be easier if there aren't a lot of people there when we arrive."

"Let me help him get his shoes and jacket on and tie his tie and he'll be ready," Cat said.

"Jason, have you met Jenny?" Mark asked.

"I don't think I ever have," Jason answered.

"This is Jenny Long," Mark said. "Jenny, this is Jason Hall. Jason, Jenny would like to ride to the funeral with us, if that's OK with you."

"Sure, that's fine with me," Jason said. "Nice to meet you, Jenny."

"Aren't you going?" Mark asked when he saw that Cat still had on her jeans.

"No, I don't think I'll go," Cat said. "I still avoid funerals."

"Well, we'll be back after while," he said, as he kissed her goodbye.

As Jason helped Mark to the door, Jenny followed. At the door, she stopped and asked, "Mark, you and Cat are not an item or something are you?"

"If by an item, you mean are we getting married, yes we are," Mark said.

"Oh, I thought she was only taking care of you," Jenny said. "I guess my information was in error."

"What information was that, Jenny?" Mark asked.

"Never mind," she said. "I think I'll go on to the funeral by myself. I'll see you there. Thanks, anyway, Jason. It was nice meeting you."

As Jenny drove off, Mark watched her go and said under his breath, "You had your chance, Jenny, and you blew it."

"What did you say, Mark?" Jason asked, as he was helping Mark into his car.

"Nothing, Jason. Nothing at all," Mark said.

While Mark and Jason were at the funeral, Cat was busy cooking. She put a beef roast on to cook, and when it was tender, she peeled carrots and potatoes and put them around it. She peeled apples and cut them up and put them into a frozen pie crust. She sprinkled sugar and cinnamon on top of the apples and then sliced some stick margarine on top of that. After she put a top crust on the apples, she spread margarine on that and sprinkled it with more sugar and cinnamon. Then she stuck it into the oven to bake while she finished the roast.

Carol and Sherry came by on their way home from school. "Why don't you and Skip bring Sherry and come over here to eat again?" Cat asked, when Carol came in and commented on the delicious aroma of the roast and pie cooking.

"Sure, I'll call Skip when you're ready," Carol said. "Is there anything I can do to help?"

"You can set dishes and silverware on the table if you would like," Cat said.

As Carol busily put place mats, plates and napkins on the table, Cat casually mentioned that Jenny came by.

"Jenny Long came by?" Carol asked. "Why did she come by?"

"She heard that Mark was here and she came by to see him," Cat said.

"I wish I had been here," Carol said. "I would have liked to have seen her. I haven't seen her in years. Didn't she and Mark date for a while?"

"Yes, I think they did," Cat said. "She seemed like she wanted to get back together with Mark, but when Mark kissed me goodbye, she changed her mind."

"Well, she might as well change it," Carol said. "He's in love with you now, anyway."

"Yeah, that's right," Cat said a little unsure of herself. She wondered if Jenny could still take Mark if she wanted to.

Her thoughts were interrupted by the noisy arrival of Mark and Jason. They had been gone three hours and Cat had begun to worry. She breathed a sigh of relief, as they walked into the kitchen and Mark came over and kissed her on the neck.

"Did you think we had gotten lost?" Mark asked.

"No," Cat said. "I knew you would come home when you were ready."

"Mista Mok, I need kiss, too," Sherry said, as she pulled on his pants leg.

"Yes, Ma'am," he said, as he picked her up and gave her a big hug and a kiss.

"I gots sumptin fo you, Mista Mok," Sherry said and she put her hand into her pocket and pulled out a small red heart.

"I gots a heart fo you," she said.

"Why, thank you, Sherry Rene. I'll treasure it forever," Mark said. "What is that wonderful aroma I can smell? It smells like apple pie. That's my favorite."

"It is apple pie," Sherry said. "Aunt Kitty made it."

"How did Aunt Kitty know it was my favorite?" he asked. "Have you been reading my mind, Aunt Kitty?"

"No, I figure it was just a lucky guess," Cat answered. "I have dinner almost ready. You guys go wash up. Carol call Skip and tell him to come on over," Cat said, as she shooed everyone out of the kitchen.

When Skip arrived, everyone gathered at the table, held hands and Skip said the blessing on the food.

After they had all eaten their fill of roast and the fixings, Cat cut everyone a piece of apple pie. Mark declared it was the best apple pie he had ever eaten.

Then the men went into the den while Cat and Carol cleaned up the kitchen. "I wonder how everything went at the funeral," Carol said. "It must have gone well, since he is apparently in such a good mood."

"Cat, will you please come here for a minute?" Mark called from the den.

When Cat went into the den, Carol followed her to see what Mark had wanted with Cat.

"Sit here, Cat," Mark said, as he motioned for her to sit in a chair in front of the sofa.

"Now, if Jason will help me," he said, as he attempted to get down on his knee, "I would like to ask you a question."

Cat caught her breath. She knew what was coming and she didn't know what her answer would be.

"Catherine Rene Reynolds Ryan, will you do me the honor of becoming my wife?" Mark asked, as he produced a beautiful engagement ring.

Cat hesitated for a moment wondering what to say. Then she said, "Yes, Mark. Yes I'll marry you."

Mark tried to stand and pull Cat up to him, but he fell over and pulled her on top of him. They both laughed and he hugged her tightly and kissed her.

Everyone laughed at Cat and Mark trying to get up from the floor and falling down again. "Here, let me help you," Jason said, as he pulled Cat up and Skip helped Mark get to his feet.

"Congratulations," everyone said, as they hugged Cat and shook hands and patted Mark on the back.

"Cat, that's the exact same spot where Skip asked me to marry him. It's been really lucky for us. Maybe it will be for you and Mark, too," Carol said.

"I hope so," Cat said.

Now, they tackled the chore of cleaning up the kitchen while everyone tried to talk at the same time. They wanted to know when he had purchased the ring and when the wedding would take place.

"I decided that if I had nerve enough to say what I did at Tim's memorial service, then I could have nerve enough to ask Cat to marry me," Mark said. "I asked Jason to take me by the jewelers after the memorial. Cat, if you don't like it, or it doesn't fit, we can exchange it."

"I love it, Mark, and it fits just fine," Cat said, as she held it up to admire its beauty.

"Aunt Kitty, now you kin help Mista Mok get the widdle gul fo me to pway wid," Sherry said, as she hugged Cat and examined the beautiful ring.

Cat and Mark both laughed and Cat said, "I guess you're right, Sherry Rene, now I can help Mr. Mark get that little girl."

They all sat down in the den and visited for a while until Skip said, "Carol, I need to get home. I have more papers to grade and other things to do."

"OK, I'm coming," Carol said. "Come on Sherry. Tell everyone bye and let's go."

She hugged and kissed Cat and said, "Bye Aunt Kitty." Then she hugged and kissed Mark. "See you lata, awagata," she said.

"See you later, alligator," Mark said, as he hugged and kissed her.

"Bye, Mista Jason," she said, but he didn't get a hug and a kiss. Then she ran over to Skip, who was standing at the door. He picked her up, said good night, then he and Carol left.

"I guess I need to be going, too." Jason said. "They turn the lights out at 10:00 p.m. and I want to get back before that. Is there anything you need before I go, Mark?"

"There is one thing you can do for me, if you don't mind," Mark said. "Would you carry my things upstairs. I think I can make it up to my bedroom now. I think my bed would be more comfortable than this sofa."

"Sure, just show me where and I'll be glad to take them up," Jason answered.

So Jason picked up Mark's case and Mark led the way upstairs. It was a little difficult at first, but it didn't take long for him to master going up the stairs. When they reached his bedroom, Mark opened the door and Jason carried his case inside.

"Where do you want this?" Jason asked.

"Just throw it over there in the corner," Mark answered. "When I feel like it, I'll put things away. Thanks for your help. I really appreciate what you've done for me. I don't think I could have made it to Tim's memorial if you hadn't gone with me."

"I hope everything goes well with your eye surgery," Jason said, as he walked to the door. "I won't be able to come back for a while, since we're going out on assignment tomorrow. I'll really miss you. I know the guys will, too. They really admire you."

"Thanks again, Jason," Mark said, as he shook his hand. "You don't know what that means to me."

"Oh, before I forget," Jason said, as he walked out the door and hesitated. "Director Halbert wants you to come by his office when you feel better. He said to tell you there was no rush. He would just like to talk to you."

"Thanks, I'll do that," Mark answered. Then they walked down the stairs together and to the door. "Well, I guess I'll see you whenever I can," Jason said. "I'll check on you when I get a chance. Bye for now."

"Goodbye, Jason. Thanks again. I guess I already said that, but I guess I can't tell you enough how much I appreciate everything you've done for me," Mark said.

Then Jason left and Mark closed the door and started to go back into the den. Cat had gone back to the kitchen to finish cleaning up, so Mark went into the kitchen instead of going into the den. He walked up behind her, put his arms around her waist and kissed her on the neck. "I love you, Cat," he said and turned her around to face him.

"When will you help me make the little girl that Sherry wants?"

"Not yet, Mark," Cat said, as she pulled away from Mark. "I just can't marry you until after the first of the year. I thought we had already talked about that and you understood."

"I understand, Cat," he said. "I just have trouble waiting. I need you now, Cat. I think Jim would understand. You're still holding on to a dead man. I'm alive, Cat. Do you want me or do you want a dead man?"

"Mark, please don't do this to me," Cat said, as she began to cry.

"Make up your mind, Cat. It's me or Jim. You need to make a decision. I couldn't have you when he was alive, but he's dead now, Cat. You have to accept the fact that he isn't coming back. If you love me, then forget about Jim and marry me."

"Mark, I can't believe you said that," Cat said, as the tears ran down her cheeks. "I thought you understood me. What has happened to that wonderful man I thought you were?"

"I'm tired of waiting, Cat," he said, as he grabbed her arm. Cat pulled her arm out of his grip and ran upstairs in tears.

She flung herself onto the bed and wept. What had happened to Mark all of a sudden? He had always been so kind and understanding. She didn't like this new Mark. Did he think that just because she had accepted his ring and said she would marry him, that now he owned her? She might need to rethink her decision to marry him.

"Cat, may I come in?" Mark said, as he knocked lightly on her bedroom door.

"No, Mark. Please go away," she answered.

"I really need to talk to you, Cat," he said. "Please let me come in."

"Go away. I don't want to talk to you," she answered.

"Cat, I'm sorry for what I said and the way I acted," he said. "I don't know why I did what I did. Sometimes, I just can't help myself. Please let me come in. I promise I'll behave, if you will."

"No, Mark. I'll come out," Cat said, not willing to let him come into her bedroom. "You go on down to the den and I'll be down shortly."

"OK, Cat. I'll meet you in the den," he said. Then he walked slowly down the stairs.

Cat cautiously opened her bedroom door and saw that Mark had gone. She went to the top of the stairs where she could see him sitting on the sofa in the den. She took a deep breath and went to join him.

"Cat, I apologize," Mark said, as she walked into the den. "I know I was way out of line. I just wanted to wake you up to the fact that Jim is gone and he's never coming back. I'm offering you a chance to live again. If you don't want it, just say so and I'll leave and forget the whole thing. If you still want me, I guess I'll just have to wait until you're ready. I've waited this long, I guess I can wait a few more months. I just hate to keep competing with a dead man. I know he'll always win because the longer he's dead the more perfect he'll become. I bet you can't even remember anything bad about him now, can you?"

Cat didn't answer that, but she felt that Mark may be right. Jim was becoming more and more perfect every day. She couldn't remember anything that had irritated her about him when he was alive.

"Mark, why are we having this argument now, right after you just gave me this beautiful engagement ring?" she asked.

"Because, my love," he said. "I want to know before we get married that I am the only one that you love. I don't want to get married and find that I am still competing with Jim Ryan. Yes, Cat, he was my best friend, but I was jealous of him. He had everything that I wanted, the job as Unit Commander, the love and respect of all the men in the unit and the woman I loved.

"Then when he died, I got the job of Unit Commander, the respect of the men in the unit and the love of the woman I loved, but Jim is still there. He still has the love of the woman I love, and she still loves him more than she loves me. Not only that, I'll probably never be able to be Unit Commander again."

"Mark, I don't know what to say," Cat said sadly. "I love you, but I can't help it if I still love Jim. How long have you been in love with me, anyway?"

"I loved you the minute I first laid eyes on you, but you were engaged to that Matt fellow. Then, Jim got rid of him and married you, so I lost out again. When Jim died, well, I thought I could finally get you, but you still belong to Jim. I guess you will always belong to Jim."

That night, Mark slept on the sofa in the den again. He still wasn't ready to move to his bedroom upstairs.

CHAPTER 7

The next morning, Mark asked Cat to call the Director for him. He told her that Jason said that Director Halbert wanted to see him. She called and was told that Mark could come by the Director's office any time that day, so, after breakfast, she and Mark went downtown to the FSC office.

When Director Halbert's assistant told them that the director was ready to see him, Mark took Cat's hand and headed into the Director's office.

"You remember my fiancée, Catherine Ryan, don't you Director Halbert?" Mark said, as he walked into the Director's office.

"Yes. Hello Ms. Ryan, you may wait out in the waiting room while Mark and I talk," Director Halbert said.

Cat started to leave, but Mark grabbed her hand and pulled her back into the room and said, "No, Cat." Then to the Director he said, "Anything you have to say to me, you can say in front of her. We're going to be married, so whatever you have to say concerns her, as well."

"OK, she can stay, then," Director Halbert said. "I heard that you went back to the doctor for a check-up. How are your injuries coming along?"

"My shoulder is about healed," Mark said. "My leg will be well in a few weeks."

"What about your eyesight?" the Director asked.

"Not so good," Mark answered.

"What did the doctor say about your eyesight?" Director Halbert pressed Mark for an answer.

"He said there's an experimental surgery that could give me my eyesight back," Mark answered.

"How long before you can see again, then?" Director Halbert wanted to know.

"I would have to have the surgery on one eye, wait until it heals and then have the other one done," Mark said.

"How long?" the Director asked.

"I don't know. He didn't say for sure. I guess two weeks for each eye, maybe a month," Mark replied.

"I need to get your unit active again," the Director said. "Right now, Ted Ames is acting Unit Commander."

"Ted Ames?" Mark asked incredulously.

"Is there something wrong with that?" the Director asked. "After all, he's been commanding part of the unit for years now. Why not make him Commander of the whole unit? Do you have something against Ted?"

"No, Sir," Mark said sullenly.

"Good, because I've been thinking about giving him that unit."

"You can't do that, Sir," Mark said jumping to his feet. "I've been with that unit ever since I started here. That's my unit. You can't give it to Ted."

"I'm the Director, Commander Fuller. I can do anything I want to do."

"No. You can't give away my unit," Mark was across the room and leaning over the Director's desk in a flash. "I worked hard to make that unit what it is. I can't let you give it to someone else."

"Commander Fuller, sit down," Director Halbert said. "I can do anything I want to do and you can't stop me. Now, sit down and calm down."

Cat jumped up and grabbed Mark's arm and tried to pull him back to his seat, but he just shook her hand off and stayed where he was. "Are you not even going to wait to see if I can come back or not?" Mark asked.

"I'll give you one month," the Director said. "You said it would take at least one month to see if you get your eyesight back. If you're not able to perform the duties of Unit Commander at that time, you'll go on permanent disability."

"No!" Mark said. "You're not going to do that to me;. not after what I've been through for FSC." Then he grabbed Cat by the arm and stormed out the door. Cat tried to apologize to the Director, but Mark just kept pulling her forward until he was out in the hall.

"Take me home, Cat," he said, as he headed for the car.

"Mark, wait a minute," Cat said, as she stopped moving. "What are you doing? Do you realize who you were talking to? You need to go back and apologize."

"No, I don't, Cat. Now, get in the car and take me home," Mark shouted.

Cat got into the car, but she didn't start the engine.

"Take me home, Cat," Mark shouted again. "I'm not going back in there."

"Calm down, Mark," Cat said. "You're scaring me."

"Start the damn car," Mark shouted again. "If you don't start the damn car, I'll get out and walk."

Cat started the car and slowly moved out of the parking lot.

"Stop the car, Cat," Mark said. "I'll walk home. I don't want to ride with you anyway."

"You can't walk home, Mark," Cat said, as she kept on driving. "It's 20 miles to the cabin. You can't walk one mile with that cast. Now, calm down. I'm taking you home."

"I said stop the damn car," Mark said again, as he opened the car door. Cat slammed on the brake, so Mark wouldn't fall. "Get back in the car, Mark," Cat said, as she tried to hold back her tears. Mark just ignored her and started walking down the road.

Cat began to cry. She didn't know what to do. Mark was becoming more than she could handle. She drove slowly for a while hoping he would get back into the car, but he wouldn't, so she just drove on home. She hoped that someone they knew would come by and pick him up and bring him on home.

After Cat arrived home, she sat on the sofa in the den crying. She debated about calling the police. Shortly, she heard a car pull into the driveway and a car door slammed. Then she heard the front door open and close with a bang. She turned around in time to see Mark making his way up the stairs and into his bedroom. Then Carol came into the cabin with a worried look on her face.

"Cat, do you know where I found Mark?" she asked.

"Walking down the road, I suppose," Cat answered.

"Yes, walking down the road. He was way up town," Carol said. "What happened?"

Cat started crying again and between sobs, she told Carol the whole story. "He didn't like it when I said he should apologize to Director Halbert," Cat said. "He really lost it then."

"Didn't you say that you had the number for another therapist you could call while Dr. Lindstrom is out of town?" Carol asked. When Cat said she did, Carol said, "Why don't you call him?"

Cat called the number that was given to her from Dr. Lindstrom's office. Dr. Albert Wise answered her call. "May I help you?" he asked.

"Yes, I'm calling for Unit Commander Mark Fuller. I was told you could help us while Dr. Lindstrom is out of town," Cat stated.

"What seems to be your problem?" Dr. Wise asked.

"It's Commander Fuller," she answered. "He's very agitated. He needs some help as soon as possible."

"Can you come to my office in the morning?" Dr. Wise asked.

"Yes. What time?" Cat answered.

"Can you come around 10:00 a.m.?" Dr. Wise asked.

"Yes. We'll be there. How do I get to your office?"

Dr. Wise gave directions to Cat and she wrote them down so she wouldn't forget them.

"Cat, will you be all right?" Carol asked. "If Mark is in that bad a shape, maybe You'd better come over to our place tonight."

"I'll be OK, Carol," Cat said. "I don't think he'll hurt me. He'll probably calm down after while and apologize."

"Well, you call if you need us," Carol said, as she went out the door. "I'll send Skip over. Maybe he can handle Mark."

After Carol left, Cat went into the kitchen to prepare a light meal. She didn't feel like eating, after what she had gone through with Mark, and she figured he probably wouldn't eat either. After she got it ready, she went up the stairs and tapped lightly on Mark's door.

"Mark," she called. "I have dinner ready."

There was no answer, so she knocked again a little louder. "Mark, I have dinner ready," she said.

There was still no answer, so she opened the door slightly. Mark was lying on the bed. He was fully dressed with his shoes still on and he was just lying there staring at the ceiling.

"Mark, are you OK?" she asked, as she hurried over to the bed.

"I'm OK, Cat," Mark answered. "Just leave me alone."

"Mark, please let me help you," Cat begged.

"Cat. Just leave me the hell alone," he said through clenched teeth. Cat inched her way backward toward the door. She was afraid of Mark when he was like that. He wasn't even the same person.

When she got back downstairs, she called the barracks where Jason was staying.

When a man answered, she asked if Jason was there.

"I'll see," the man said and was gone for a while.

"Hello," Jason finally said.

"Hi, Jason, this is Cat Ryan," Cat said when Jason answered.

"Hi, Cat. Greg said there was a sweet-sounding lady on the phone for me. What can I do for you?" Jason asked.

"I hate to bother you, but I really need you," Cat said, as she began to cry.

"What's wrong, Cat?" Jason was alarmed by Cat's tears.

"It's Mark," she said. "He's really bad again. I have an

appointment for him tomorrow, but I need someone to help me with him. I thought maybe he would go if you helped me with him."

"Cat, we're supposed to go out on assignment tomorrow, but I'll see what I can do," Jason answered.

"Please try hard," she begged. "I really do need you."

"Let me check and I'll call you right back," Jason said.

Cat hung up and waited for about an hour. She was beginning to think that Jason wasn't going to call when the phone rang.

"Hello, Cat," Jason said. "OK, I'll see you tomorrow. What time is his appointment?"

"It's at 10:00 a.m., but we'll need to leave by 9:00," Cat said.

"OK. I'll see you in the morning," he said and hung up.

The next morning, Cat told Mark that she had gotten him an appointment with Dr. Wise.

"I'm not going, Cat," Mark said.

"You need to go and get well, Mark," Cat said.

"Just leave me alone, Cat. I just want to be left alone," he said angrily.

About 9:00 a.m., Jason knocked on the door. Cat opened it and let Jason come in and led him to the den, where Mark was lying on the sofa.

"Hey, Mark, up and at 'em," Jason said, as he walked into the den.

"Go fly a kite," Mark said. "I'm not going to any shrink. You just wasted your time coming here."

"Yes, you are, Mark," Jason said. "You're going if I have to hog tie you and drag you there."

They wrestled for a while, but eventually Jason got Mark up off the sofa and into the car. Cat crawled into the back seat and Jason drove to the doctor's office. At the doctor's office, Dr. Wise took Mark into his office and asked Cat and Jason to wait out in the waiting area.

"Sit down, Commander Fuller," Dr. Wise said. "You are a Unit Commander, I was told. Is that correct?"

"I'm no longer a Commander," Mark said sullenly. "Not since the accident."

"Tell me about the accident," Dr. Wise said.

"There's nothing to tell," Mark said sullenly. "I made a stupid mistake. It cost one of my men his life and me my eyesight. End of story."

"I don't believe that's the whole story," Dr. Wise said. "Why don't you start at the beginning and tell me the whole story."

"I don't wanna talk about it," Mark said moodily. He sat there silently for a few minutes and just glared at Dr. Wise.

"The lady and gentleman who came in with you," Dr. Wise said. "Is she your wife?"

"No," Mark said.

"What's she to you, then?" Dr. Wise asked.

"None of your business," Mark answered.

"OK, then. Is she a friend or a relative?" Dr. Wise asked.

Mark didn't answer. He just sat sullenly in the chair.

"OK. Let's go another route," Dr. Wise said. "What would you like to talk about?"

"Nothing," Mark said. "It wasn't my idea to come here. I just want everyone to leave me alone."

"OK. We'll just sit here and say nothing until you're ready to say something," Dr. Wise said.

"All right. I messed up," Mark finally said. "Is that what you wanted me to say?"

"I want you to say whatever you want to say, Commander Fuller," Dr. Wise said.

"Don't call me Commander. I'm not a Commander any more," Mark said.

"OK," Dr. Wise said. "What do you want me to call you?"

"Just call me Mark."

"OK, Mark, tell me about the accident," Dr. Wise said.

"We were called out on an assignment. It was a bombing suspect. Jim, our Unit Commander, had told us over and over again to make sure there were no traps before we stormed into an area. I was in too much of a hurry. I didn't take the time to check it out. There was a trap. I tripped it and it went off. A young man, only nineteen, was killed. Most of my men were injured in some way and I lost my eyesight as well as having a dislocated shoulder and a broken leg. There was no excuse for that. I had been trained to do better."

"So, do your men blame you for injuring them?" Dr. Wise asked.

"No, I don't think so. At least no one has said he does," Mark said slowly.

"Then why do you blame yourself? Couldn't that have happened to anyone?" Dr. Wise asked.

"Yes, it could have, but it didn't happen to anyone. It happened to me," Mark said loudly.

"Because it happened to you, you can't forgive yourself. Is that right?" Dr. Wise asked.

"Yes. I don't deserve to be forgiven," Mark said. "I killed a 19-year-old boy. His parents are elderly and he was their only child. How can they ever forgive me?"

"How do you know they blame you?" Dr. Wise asked.

"They don't. That's just the thing. They don't blame me. They should, but they don't. Maybe it would be easier if they did," Mark said with his head in his hands.

"The lady with you. How does she feel about it?" Dr. Wise asked.

"What do you mean?" Mark asked.

"I mean, does she blame you for the accident that took your eyesight? Do you feel like less of a man with her since the accident?" Dr. Wise asked.

"No. She didn't have anything to do with it," Mark said.

"Are you sure?" Dr. Wise asked.

"I don't understand what you mean," Mark said.

"I think you understand, Mark," Dr. Wise said. "How did she act before the accident and how does she act now?"

"You're wrong, Dr. Wise," Mark said. "She didn't want anything to do with me before the accident. Now, she's taking care of me."

"Why don't you tell me about that, Mark," Dr. Wise said.

"Tell you about what?" Mark asked.

"About your relationship with the lady. What is her name?" Dr. Wise asked.

"Cat, Catherine. Catherine Ryan. She has nothing to do with this," Mark said.

"I disagree, Mark. I think she has everything to do with this. Tell me about her and your relationship," Dr. Wise said.

Mark sat silently again. There was no way he was going to try to explain his relationship to Cat with this prying person. After all, Cat had nothing to do with why he was so angry all the time now.

"Mark, I'm waiting," Dr. Wise said.

"You'll wait till Hell freezes over, then," Mark said. "My relationship with Cat is none of your business."

"How did you meet her?" Dr. Wise asked.

Mark sat silently and didn't say a word.

"Did you know her before the accident?" Dr. Wise asked, trying to get Mark to open up about Cat.

Mark still didn't say anything.

"Do you love her?" Dr. Wise was going to get something out of Mark any way he could and he felt that Cat held the key to Mark's anger.

"Yes, I love her," Mark finally said. "I love her more than anything else in my whole life. I love being Unit Commander, but I love her even more than that."

"Tell me about her, then, Mark," Dr. Wise said. "I'd like to know about her."

"There's not a whole lot to tell about her," Mark said. "I loved her from the minute I laid eyes on her, but she belonged to someone else," Mark said.

"Who did she belong to?" Dr. Wise knew he was getting somewhere now, but Mark gave him the silent treatment again.

"Was she the wife of a friend of yours?" Dr. Wise continued to probe.

Mark took a deep breath and said, "Yes. She was."

"And," Dr. Wise urged Mark to continue.

"And he died and now she belongs to me. End of story. I've had enough of this. I'm leaving," Mark said.

"Not yet, Mark," Dr. Wise said. "Tell me how her husband died."

"You're going to pull it all out of me aren't you?" Mark asked.

Then he was silent for a long time while Dr. Wise waited for him to open up.

"We were on an assignment," Mark started. Then he stopped. "Cat and Jim were on an assignment. I wasn't with them. Cat got captured and Jim had to leave her behind. He called me and begged me to go back with him and get Cat. He knew I would go. He knew I loved Cat and would do almost anything for her."

Then Mark stopped again. It was hard for him to go on, now.

"After we got Cat, we had to fight our way back out," Mark started again. "Jim told me to take Cat to the chopper and he'd stay behind and cover us. He was already injured, but he insisted that I take her and go. Cat and I got to the chopper and Jim caught it just as we were taking off. He was a sitting duck, though. He was hanging outside the chopper while I tried to pull him inside. I don't know how many times he was hit, but he was losing a lot of blood. He stopped breathing and I did CPR on him, but he was losing blood faster than I could do CPR. I did the CPR until I was exhausted, but he never regained consciousness."

Then Mark broke down and cried. "I did everything I could to save him. I really did. He just had too many wounds. He lost so much blood. There was nothing I could do to save him. I tried, but I couldn't save him."

Then Mark wept. He wept deep, bitter tears. Dr. Wise sat quietly until Mark had finished. Then he said, "You did everything you could to save him, so why do you feel so guilty?"

Mark sat silently for a few minutes and then he softly said, "I wanted his job and his wife. Mostly his wife. I didn't want him to die, though. Believe me. I didn't want him to die. I just wanted Cat to be mine."

"I believe you, Mark," Dr. Wise said. "When you begin to believe it yourself, then you'll begin healing."

"I loved Jim like a brother," Mark said. "I didn't want him to die. It just happened that way."

"So, you got his wife and I assume you got his job, too. Did that make you happy?" Dr. Wise asked.

"No." Mark said. "I can hardly look at Cat or touch her without feeling guilty.

Now, since my accident, I've lost the job that I wanted so badly, too. I'm miserable."

"Is that why you had the accident?" Dr. Wise asked. "You felt guilty because you didn't feel you deserved Jim's job?"

"I guess. You're the doctor. You tell me," Mark answered.

"OK. Here's how I see it," Dr. Wise said. "You finally got what you wanted, but the price was too high, so now you don't feel that it was worth the price you had to pay for it. Is that about right?"

Mark just sat and looked at Dr. Wise for a few minutes before saying anything.

"I don't know, doc. I thought Cat was worth anything I had to do to get her. I guess I was wrong," Mark finally said.

"It's hard living with that kind of guilt, isn't it, Mark?" Dr. Wise asked.

"Yes, it is," Mark said slowly.

"When you can finally accept the fact that you did everything you could to save Jim, then you can begin to forgive yourself. When you can forgive yourself, you can get rid of the guilt. When you get rid of the guilt, you can learn to live and love again. You have to love yourself before you can learn to love Cat or anyone else for that matter. What you've done here today should put you on the road to recovery. You can never be whole as long as you keep all that guilt bottled up inside of you. How do you feel now?" Dr. Wise asked.

"I feel better," Mark said.

"I think we made a breakthrough," Dr. Wise said. "Now that you have begun to open up, don't shut back down again. You need to continue to open up. Dr. Lindstrom will be back next week. I see you have an appointment with him. You need to continue with your treatment," Dr. Wise said.

"Can't I see you again?" Mark asked.

"Yes. If you would like," Dr. Wise said. "Would you rather see me instead of Dr. Lindstrom?"

"Yes, I would," Mark said.

"Then you can make an appointment at the desk as you go out," Dr. Wise said.

"Be sure to cancel your appointment with Dr. Lindstrom, though."

Then he rose and walked Mark to the door. "I'll see you next week, then."

"OK," Mark said, as he walked out to where Cat and Jason were waiting.

"Dr. Wise, this is Cat, Catherine Ryan and Jason Hall," Mark said.

"Nice to meet you both," Dr. Wise said, as he shook hands with Cat and Jason. "Ms. Ryan, I have given Mark a prescription. I want him to take one every night at bedtime. Will you see that he takes them?"

"Yes, Sir. I will," Cat said.

"I'll see you next week, then," Dr. Wise said, as he walked back into his office.

"We have an appointment with Dr. Lindstrom," Cat said.

"That's all right, Cat," Mark said. "I'm canceling that appointment and I need to make one for Dr. Wise for next week."

"Whatever you say, Mark," Cat said. She certainly didn't want to cause any trouble over a doctor's appointment.

Mark got an appointment for 2:00 p.m. the following Wednesday. That would be two days before the birthday party. Cat hoped that things would go well with that appointment and nothing would go wrong with the party. Carol had worked so hard on it. Cat really prayed that everything would work out all right.

When they got to the car, Mark sat in back with Cat. "I want to talk to you, Cat," Mark said after Jason started the car. "I'm sorry for the way I've been acting. I know I've been a pain. Dr. Wise has really helped me to see some things that I couldn't see before. I know you were upset with me because you wanted me to see Dr. Lindstrom, but I've already started with Dr. Wise and I want to stay with him. Some day, when I'm well, I have some things I want to tell you, but I can't tell you now. Maybe some day I'll be able to tell you. I just want to tell you how sorry I am for causing you so much grief. Will you forgive me?"

"Of course I will, Mark," Cat said. "I love you, Mark. I just want you to get well and be the man I fell in love with again."

"With your love and Dr. Wise's help, I think I'll be able to be that man again some day. Just be patient and stay with me. Please stay with me, Cat. I need you."

"I need you, too, Mark," Cat said. "I may need you even more than you need me."

CHAPTER 8

Mark was getting better mentally. He was beginning to control his temper. After talking to Dr. Wise, he was able to come to grips with his guilt over Jim's death. Even though he had secretly coveted Jim's job and wife, he finally realized that he wouldn't have done anything to get them while Jim was still alive. He also realized that he had done everything humanly possible to save Jim. His shoulder was adapting to the therapy and was becoming stronger each day. Jason had given him a neat three-pronged cane to use and he was getting around a lot better. He was even looking forward to his next visit with Dr. Wise. He wanted to tell him how much his life had improved since his last appointment.

The day of Mark's appointment had arrived and he was disappointed that Jason wasn't going to go with them. Jason said that he probably could get out of going on the assignment, if Mark and Cat needed him, but he really needed to go with the team. Mark said that he was pretty sure that he and Cat could handle it this time, since he was so much better than he had been before.

"Thank you, Jason, for all that you've done for Cat and me. We probably wouldn't have made it without you. You are a true friend," Mark said.

"I was happy to do it," Jason said. "Just let me know if you ever need me again."

So Cat and Mark made the trip to Dr. Wise's office without an escort. Cat sat in the waiting room and waited while Mark went into Dr. Wise's office for his appointment.

"How has your week been?" Dr. Wise asked.

"It's been great," Mark answered. "It's the first time since Jim's death that I haven't been consumed with guilt. My arm and leg are better, also. I just have to have the surgery on my eyes and then I'll be whole again."

"When do you have your eye surgery?" Dr. Wise asked.

"I haven't made an appointment yet," Mark answered.

"Why haven't you?" Dr. Wise asked.

"I'm afraid," Mark said.

"Why are you afraid?" Dr. Wise asked.

"I'm afraid it will be a failure. There's a 50 percent chance that I'll be completely blind if it doesn't work," Mark answered.

"So you haven't made a decision yet?" Dr. Wise asked.

"If I have the surgery and it doesn't work and I go blind, I can't marry Cat," Mark said.

"Why is that?" Dr. Wise asked.

"Do you know how hard it is to measure up to Jim Ryan? Even before my accident, I couldn't measure up to him. Do you think that I could even get close to Jim, If I was blind?"

"If she really loves you, it won't matter if you're blind or not," Dr. Wise said.

"I can't take that chance," Mark said. "She stays with me now because she thinks maybe I'll get better, but if she knows I definitely will never be able to see, she'll leave me."

"Do you really believe Ms. Ryan is that fickle?" Dr. Wise asked.

"I don't know," Mark said. "I love her so much, I can't take the chance."

"Why don't you give her a chance to prove that she really loves you?" Dr. Wise asked.

"I'm afraid of what she'll say," Mark said.

"Then I don't think you're as well as you think you are," Dr. Wise said.

"What's that supposed to mean?" Mark asked, getting angry.

"When you feel strong enough to ask Ms. Ryan if she would be with you if you were completely blind, then you're strong enough to accept her answer. No matter what it is," Dr. Wise said.

"I don't understand," Mark was confused.

"When you can accept rejection and not lose it like you've been doing, you're getting well. Why don't you just ask her and see what she says. Then come back next week and let me know her answer," Dr. Wise said.

"Maybe I don't want to know her answer," Mark said, as Dr. Wise walked him to the door.

"Be sure and make an appointment before you leave," Dr. Wise said. Then he walked back into his office.

"Let's go home, Cat," Mark said, as he took her arm and headed toward the exit.

Mark was quiet all the way home. Cat wondered what had happened to Mark in Dr. Wise's office. He seemed to be in such a good mood before his appointment. She had thought that he was getting better, but now she didn't know. When they arrived at the cabin, Mark went into the den and Cat went into the kitchen to prepare dinner.

"Cat, can you come here for a few minutes?" Mark called.

"Sure. What do you need, Mark?" Cat asked.

"Sit down, here," Mark said, as he patted the seat next to him. "I want to talk to you about something."

"What is it, Mark?" Cat asked.

"I've been thinking about having that eye surgery that Dr. Sanders told me about. What do you think?"

"Well, he said there is a chance that you'll be able to see again," Cat said.

"He also said I might be completely blind, too," Mark said.

"I guess you would just have to take that chance and trust that God will make everything be OK," Cat said.

"How would you feel about having a blind husband?" Mark asked.

"I love you, Mark. It wouldn't matter to me if you were blind or deaf or whatever. I would be happy just to be your wife," Cat said. Then she leaned over and kissed him.

"I was hoping you'd say that because I want to try the surgery," Mark said. "In the morning, will you call Dr. Sanders' office and set it up?"

"Sure, I will, if you're sure you want to try it," Cat said.

"I'm sure," he said.

The next morning, Cat called Dr. Sanders' office and made an appointment for the surgery. That was also the day before the birthday party. Charlotte and Tyler were going to arrive that afternoon. Cat was excited to see them again. She hadn't seen them since she and Mark had become engaged. She had called Charlotte and told her, but Charlotte didn't seem too happy about it. Cat was hoping that Charlotte was more receptive to the engagement now than she had been.

Carol left Sherry Rene with Cat and she and Skip went to the airport to pick up Charlotte and Tyler. Skip took them to their cabin first to unload their luggage and then he drove back over to Cat's.

Cat hugged Charlotte and Tyler when they came into the cabin. Sherry didn't remember them from the last time, so she cautiously walked over to them. "This is your Aunt Charlotte and Uncle Tyler," Carol said. Sherry shyly said "Hewo, Aunt Char-let and Unka Tywer."

"Hello, yourself, Sherry," Charlotte said. "Can I get a hug?"

Sherry gave Charlotte a quick hug and then ran back and jumped into Mark's lap. Mark had stayed on the sofa while Cat had greeted Charlotte and Tyler.

"Dis is my Mista Mok," Sherry said, as she patted his chest. "He got hurted, but I made he betta. Din't I Mista Mok?"

"Yes, you did Sherry Rene," Mark answered. "You made me a lot better. Hello Charlotte, Tyler."

"Hi, Mark," Charlotte and Tyler said in unison.

"Everyone, sit down. I have dinner just about ready," Cat said. Then she went into the kitchen to finish getting it ready and Carol followed her.

"What can I do to help?" Carol asked.

"You can go ahead and set the table and put ice into the glasses," Cat said.

"Everything's almost ready."

When everything was on the table, Cat asked everyone to come sit at the dining room table. They all joined hands and Skip said the blessing on the food.

After everyone had finished eating, the men went into the den and the women cleaned up the kitchen. Then Carol got out the birthday party decorations.

As Cat, Carol and Charlotte hung party decorations, Charlotte asked Cat, "Cat, you told me that you and Mark were engaged, but you never did tell me how you two ever got together. I thought you said that he's the reason Jim died. How did that happen?"

"I was wrong. Mark tried to save Jim," Cat said. "I'll tell you about it some time, but not now."

"Sherry sure does like him, it seems," Charlotte said.

"Yes, she's crazy about him and he's crazy about her, too," Carol said. "She's always wanting to come over and see Mista Mok. That's what she calls him."

"Well, if I was you, I wouldn't want her to get too close to him," Charlotte said. "What happens if he suddenly decides to leave?"

"He isn't going to leave, Charlotte," Cat said angrily. "We're going to be married."

"I don't understand that, either," Charlotte said. "Isn't that a little sudden?" How long have you known him, anyway? Has he been staying here all this time, just the two of you?"

"Yes, Charlotte." Cat was really biting her tongue to keep from saying something she knew she would regret. "He's been staying here all the time he has been recuperating, just the two of us."

"That's enough, Charlotte," Carol said. "I don't think it's any of your business, anyway. Mark is a very upstanding and moral person. I wouldn't be afraid to leave Sherry with him all day. I don't like what you're insinuating and I know Cat doesn't, so you might as well stop it now."

"I just hope you don't regret it, is all I've got to say," Charlotte said, as she walked off in a huff.

"It's OK, Cat," Carol said, as she put her arm around Cat's shoulders. "I think she's just angry because Sherry likes Mark better than she does her. She doesn't realize how long it's been since Sherry has seen her. She's probably forgotten her by now. Charlotte will come around after a while. If she doesn't, then it's her loss and not ours."

After all of the decorations were put up, Cat and Carol went into the den. Charlotte had already gone there and was trying to get Sherry to sit in her lap.

"Why don't you come sit with me, Sherry Rene?" Charlotte asked, trying to coax Sherry over to her lap.

"I gots to stay here wid my Mista Mok," she said.

"You can see Mr. Mark all the time, but you can't see me very often," Charlotte coaxed. "Why don't you come over here and tell me what you want for your birthday?"

"I want Mista Mok to get well. That's what I want." Sherry said. Then she hugged and kissed him.

"Why don't you go see Aunt Charlotte for a few minutes?" Mark whispered into Sherry's ear. "Then you can come back and sit in my lap."

"No. I wanna stay here," Sherry pouted. "Why can't I stay here?"

"You can stay here, if you want to," Mark said. He certainly didn't want to get Sherry upset. If she was forced to go to Charlotte, she probably would never have anything to do with her. So he just let her stay in his lap and read her book to him.

The next day was the birthday party. It was scheduled for 6:00 p.m. There was a lot that still had to be done, so Cat fixed a quick breakfast and the others came over and they all had breakfast together. Sherry had gotten to know Charlotte a little better, so Charlotte was in a better mood. She still looked a little peeved when Sherry turned loose of her hand and ran over to Mark and hugged him. Mark picked her up and hugged and kissed her and took her over to the table and sat down.

"Happy buttday, Mista Mok," Sherry said, as she gave him a gift-wrapped package.

"Thank you, Sherry Rene. Happy birthday to you, too," Mark said, as he gave her a small gift-wrapped package.

"You open youas fust," Sherry said.

He opened it and found a beautiful picture of Sherry in a gold frame. The frame had hearts on each corner and "I love you, Mr. Mark" was written at the bottom of the picture.

Mark looked at the photograph and tears came into his eyes.

"Don't you wik it Mista Mok?" Sherry was afraid he didn't like it because he was crying.

"I love it, Sherry Rene," he said, as the tears ran down his cheeks. "I'll treasure it always."

"Now, I open mine," Sherry said, as she tore into her package. "Oh," she said, as she carefully took out a delicate gold chain with a beautiful small gold heart in the center. In the center of the heart was a small diamond. "Oh, I wuv it, Mista Mok. It's butiful."

"I'm glad you like it," Mark said with a lump in his throat. "Here, let me help you put it on."

Sherry turned around and Mark fastened it. Then he gave her a hug and a kiss.

Sherry hugged and kissed Mark in return and said, "I wuv you Mista Mok."

"I love you, too, Sherry Rene," he said. "You'll never know just how much."

"OK, now that's over, let's eat so we can get busy," Charlotte said.

They sat down and ate their meal quickly and cleaned up the kitchen.

"I have to go get the cake and some other things now," Carol said. "Charlotte would you like to go with me?"

"Sure," she said. "I don't know what to do here, anyway."

After they left, Mark took Sherry into the den and Skip and Tyler followed them. Cat busied herself with making punch and getting paper plates and cups out and arranged. She had everything ready by the time Carol and Charlotte arrived with the cake. The cake was beautiful. It had little Strawberry Shortcake girls in each corner and flowers and other decorations. In the middle it said, "Happy Birthday Sherry Rene and Mr. Mark."

"Oh, It's beautiful," Cat said. "I want to get some pictures of it."

So there were pictures made of the cake by itself; the cake with Sherry; the cake with Mark and the cake with Sherry and Mark together.

By 5:00 p.m., the guests started arriving. Jason was the first to arrive. "I know that the invitation said no gifts, but I wanted to give you something, anyway. He gave Mark a gift-wrapped package and said, "Open it right now." So Mark opened it. Inside was a coffee cup and on it was printed, "Number One Hero."

"Jason, I don't deserve this," Mark said.

"Yes, you do," Jason said. "That's how I see you."

"Thanks, I appreciate that, Jason. You don't know how much I appreciate it," Mark said with tears in his eyes.

"I think I do, Mark," Jason said. "I need to find Sherry. I have something for her, too."

"Here she is," Mark said, as Sherry came running up to Jason and hugged him.

"Hi, Mista Jason," she said.

"Happy birthday, Sherry Rene," Jason said. "Here, this is for you."

"Thank you, Mista Jason," she said and ran to show Carol what Jason had given her.

Most of the men from the unit began to arrive soon and they all shook Mark's hand and told him how much they missed him in the unit.

Next to arrive were Sherry's friends from day care and their parents. Sherry's gift table was beginning to fill up with presents. Carol told her she needed to wait until later to open them, so she was beginning to pout and Mark picked her up and said, "Sherry Rene, you don't look like my pretty, little princess when you pout like that. You need to look real happy on your birthday so you can be my pretty princess."

"OK, Mista Mok. I sorry. I be happy," she said. Then she wiggled out of his arms and ran to play with her friends.

Carol was watching the drama between Sherry and Mark and she leaned over and whispered to Charlotte, "That's why I love Mark. He knows just how to handle my child when she's fussy."

"Well, I still think you need to keep an eye on him," Charlotte said. "Did you ever find out why Cat brought him here, anyway?"

"No," Carol said. "I never asked. I figured it was none of my business." She didn't want to give Charlotte the satisfaction of knowing that she had had misgivings when Cat first brought him home, but she soon got over them. After all, Sherry didn't take up with just anyone and she had loved Mark from the very beginning.

Ted was the last to arrive. Cat was secretly hoping that he wouldn't show up, but he did. Mark was standing by the door greeting everyone who came in. He was standing there alone when Ted came in. Cat was on the other side of the room, but she was watching the interaction between Mark and Ted. She couldn't tell what they were saying but she could tell by Mark's frown that he didn't like what Ted had to say.

"The invitation said, No gifts, but I thought you might like to have this. I have no use for it and I found it in some of the FSC stuff that was taken from here."

Mark took the gift-wrapped package and carefully opened it up. It was the picture that was taken when Cat had gotten her FSC badge. There was a smiling photograph of her between the equally smiling photo of Jim and Mark. Mark immediately remembered when the photograph was taken. He also remembered how he felt that day. He was so proud of Cat and his heart was so full of love for her. When Ted had taken the photograph, he had guessed how Mark had felt about Cat. He had even made a snide remark about coveting something that he could never have. Cat and Jim didn't know what Ted was talking about, but Ted knew that Mark knew exactly what he meant.

Mark gave Ted an angry look and took the picture and walked away. Ted just followed him. Mark walked into the kitchen and into the pantry. He knew he was going to have to confront Ted and he didn't want anyone else to hear what he had to say.

"Thank you for your gift, Ted," Mark said. "I, more than anyone else, would appreciate this gift. I don't know why you decided to give it to me today, though. It would have been best if you had waited until we were alone."

"You think you're so smart, don't you, Mark Fuller," Ted said. "Well, you may have gotten Jim's job for a while, but you couldn't keep it. You may be getting his wife, also, but let's just see how long you can keep her. Do you think she'll want a blind man. She'll get tired of having to lead you around some day and then you won't have her either."

"You shut your mouth about Cat," Mark said angrily. "You don't even know her. She would never desert me. Even if she didn't love me, she's loyal enough to stay with me, anyway."

"So she doesn't love you, but she's staying with you out of pity, then. Is that what you're saying," Ted said sarcastically.

"No, I didn't say that," Mark denied it. "Get out of here, Ted Ames. You're not welcome here."

"You aren't the one who invited me and this place doesn't belong to you, so you can't order me to leave. You're not a Unit Commander any longer, so you can't order anyone to do anything," Ted sneered.

Mark clenched his teeth and grabbed Ted by the arm and pushed him out the back door. "I said leave, and don't you ever come back here," Mark said, as he slammed the door in Ted's face.

Mark leaned against the wall and slowly slid down to the floor and wept. "How could someone you thought was your friend be so cruel," he thought.

"Mark, are you in here?" Cat said, as she looked in the kitchen for Mark. She had seen him and Ted head that way and she was afraid of what might take place there.

Mark quickly wiped his eyes and took a deep breath. "I'm here, Cat," he said, as he quickly stood up.

"What were you doing in the pantry?" Cat asked, as he walked out of the pantry and toward her.

"I just needed a little quiet time. It was getting too noisy for me," he said. As he walked by the table, he lay the photograph face down on the table. He decided to leave it there until he had time to retrieve it.

"Sherry's going to open her gifts and she wants you to be there," Cat said. She saw him place the photograph on the table and picked it up and looked at it. It felt like a knife stuck into her heart as she looked at it. Jim was so handsome. He was so proud of her that day. She was so proud of herself and Mark...how did Mark feel? He was looking down at her with a wide grin on his face. Cat had been looking at the camera, so she didn't know that Mark had been looking at her. Did she see something in Mark's eyes that she had never noticed before?

She took the photograph and wrapped a piece of newspaper around it and took it into Jim's office and locked it in his desk drawer. No one else needed to see that photograph. That was why Mark had been so angry with Ted. Ted saw something in Mark's eyes as he looked at her, too; something that shouldn't have been there.

Then she went back into the living room where Sherry was opening her gifts. She had Mark help her open them. She sure did love Mark. He loved her, too. "I think they've been good for each other," Cat thought. "Mark is a really good man. I'm lucky to have him, really lucky."

After everyone had gone home, Cat and Mark cleaned up the mess and got the cabin back in order. Then they sat on the sofa in the den to rest.

"What did you do with it?" Mark asked.

"What did I do with what?" Cat asked.

"You know what," Mark said.

"You mean the photograph?" Cat asked.

"Yes, the photograph. What did you do with it. I know you had to have gotten it. It was gone when I went back for it," Mark said.

"I put it away," Cat said. "Does it matter where I put it?"

"No, not really. I just didn't want everyone to see it," Mark said. "As long as it's put away. That's all that matters. You're not going to ask me why are you?"

"No. I think I know why," Cat said. "What I don't know is why Ted hates you so much," Cat said. "Why does he hate you?"

"Because Jim made me his Second-in-Command. Ted thought he should have gotten it. Jim and I worked so well together, though. He didn't even have to tell me what he wanted. I just knew. He had to tell Ted over and over again. Ted wanted to do things his way and Jim wanted it done the way he wanted it done. Jim and I were so close. Ted was jealous of our closeness, too."

Cat wiped a tear from her eyes. Just thinking about Jim brought back the hurt and the longing again. Mark put his arm around her and drew her to his chest. He kissed her gently at first and suddenly his pent up desire took over and his kisses became urgent, passionate kisses.

"No, Mark," Cat said, as she pushed him away. "I can't. Not yet," she said.

"When, Cat," Mark said. "I can't wait much longer. How strong do you think I am? I know you need me as much as I need you. I can feel it when I kiss you. When Cat? How much longer?"

Cat just got up and walked to the stairs. "Not tonight, Mark," she said and walked up the stairs to her bedroom, leaving Mark alone to wonder when or if she would ever really be his. "Damn that Ted for bringing that photograph. How could he have ever let Ted take a photograph like that when he was so vulnerable," Mark thought.

CHAPTER 9

The surgery for Mark's right eye was scheduled for October 18. Dr. Sanders deadened Mark's eye and lay him back on his back and strapped his hands down. The surgery took only 30 minutes. Dr. Sanders put a thick patch on Mark's eye and said that he needed to come back the next day.

The next day, Dr. Sanders took the patch off of Mark's eye and put some drops into it. He waited for a few minutes and told Mark to cover his left eye and look at the chart in front of him.

"Can you read any of the lines on the chart?" Dr. Sanders asked.

"Yes. Yes I can," Mark said excitedly. Then he read off one of the smaller lines of letters.

"Good," Dr. Sanders said. "How does it feel?"

"It burns," Mark said.

Then Dr. Sanders put some more drops into his eye. "I want you to put these drops into your eye four times a day. I want to see you back here next week. Be sure and make an appointment before you leave."

Mark made the appointment on the way out and he and Cat headed for the car. Mark was so excited. "Cat, I can see," he said. "I can really see. God answered my prayer."

"I'm so glad, Mark," Cat said. "I knew He would."

"Let's stop by and tell Sherry," Mark said. "She'll be wanting to know how I'm doing."

When they walked into Carol's and Skip's cabin, Sherry ran up and hugged Mark.   "Mista Mok," she shouted. "How you eye, now?" she asked.

"My eye is great," Mark said, as he lifted Sherry up and hugged and kissed her. "I can see your beautiful face, Sherry Rene. I can see you."

"Me so happy," she said. "Now you be happy, too?"

"Yes, Sherry Rene. Now I'll be very happy," Mark said.

"I have dinner fixed," Carol said. "You two might as well stay for dinner."

So the dinner conversation was centered around Mark's eye surgery and its success. After dinner, Cat helped Carol clean up the kitchen and then she said, "I guess we'd better get on home. We have to put drops into Mark's eyes again soon. He has to go back next week for a check-up. Hopefully, we'll be able to get his second surgery done soon."

That night, as Cat lay in bed looking at the ceiling, Mark knocked softly on her bedroom door. "Cat, may I come in?" he asked.

Cat was silent at first until Mark knocked again a little louder. "Cat, please let me come in."

Finally, Cat gave in and said, "Come on in, Mark."

"Cat, I have to talk to you," Mark said. "Cat, I have to know. I can't sleep. I have to know," Mark said. "I have to know. Are you going to marry me or are you just stringing me along?"

"Yes, Mark. I told you I'll marry you, but not right now. I thought you understood why," Cat said.

"Cat, I know you don't want to get married on your and Jim's anniversary, but there are other days. It doesn't have to be Novembver 21. It can be November 18 or December 20 or any other day. Please, just set a date. At least give me a date to look forward to. I was afraid I would be blind and maybe you wouldn't want to be saddled with a blind man, but I can see, Cat. I can see."

Cat sat silently on the side of the bed and listened to Mark pour out his heart before saying anything.

"Mark," she said. "I would have married you even if you couldn't see, but I can't marry you until after the first of the year. I just can't. I owe it to Jim's memory. OK, if you just have to have a date. What about January 16? That's in the middle of the month. That would be a good time for a wedding."

Mark gave a relieved sigh and pulled Cat up and into his arms. "OK," he said. It's January 16. In the morning, we'll start planning our wedding. You can't back out now. I love you, Cat. I've waited for so long." Then he kissed her and said, "Good night. I'll see you in the morning."

The next morning, Mark was excitedly writing on a pad when Cat came down to the kitchen. Mark had already made coffee and the wonderful aroma permeated the kitchen.

"Good morning, Mark," Cat said, as she poured a cup of coffee and stirred sugar and creamer into it.

She took her coffee over to the table and tried to see what Mark was working on.

"What are you doing?" Cat asked.

"I'm making a guest list," Mark said, as he continued writing.

"You're serious about starting our wedding plans, then," Cat said.

"Of course," Mark said. "It gives me something to do while I'm waiting."

Cat gave a short chuckle and started fixing breakfast.

"Mark, I really need to get back to work," Cat said after breakfast. "I haven't been since you've been so sick. If I don't go back, I'll probably lose my job. I don't want to lose it. Will you be OK with my going in to work this morning?"

"Sure," Mark said. "I'll find something to keep me occupied. You go and do what you have to do."

So Cat went to the newspaper office and worked until 1:00 p.m. On the way home, she stopped at KFC and got some chicken and vegetables for their lunch. When she arrived at the cabin, she said, "Mark, I'm home," but there was no answer. She went through every room, but there was no one there. "Where can he be?" Cat asked herself. "Sherry isn't home, so he wouldn't be down at Carol's."

Soon, the front door opened and closed and there was Mark. He was out of breath and his clothes were wet with sweat.

"Mark, what have you been doing?" Cat asked.

"I've been jogging," he answered between gasps for breath.

"How can you jog with a cast on your leg?" Cat asked.

"It wasn't easy," Mark answered. He went to the refrigerator and got a bottle of water and drank half of the bottle in one drink.

"Why?" Cat asked.

"Why not?" Mark replied. "I need to build up my strength and endurance."

"Why?" Cat asked again. She knew Mark had something in mind and he didn't want her to know. That was why he was evading her questions.

"Did you have a good day at the newspaper office?" Mark asked again, evading her question.

"Yes, I did, but you're evading my question. Why do you need to build up your strength and endurance?" Cat asked.

"Because I'm a Unit Commander with the FSC," Mark said. "I'm going to be again. I will not let Ted Ames cheat me out of what is rightfully mine," Mark said through clenched teeth.

"Do you really think they'll let you be Unit Commander again?" Cat asked.

"I can see, Cat," he answered. "When I have the surgery on my left eye, I'll be able to see well again. My shoulder is well and my leg soon will be. All I need to do is build my strength and endurance back up. Then they'll have no excuse to take my position away from me."

Cat hoped Mark wasn't building himself up for a big let-down. Director Halbert had given him a month to get well. Would he be able to accomplish all that in the two weeks he had left?

When Mark made his follow-up appointment, Dr. Sanders gave his right eye a close examination. Everything looked good, so Dr.

Sanders said he could do surgery on his left eye, if Mark was ready for it.

"Ready," Mark said. "I've been ready for a long time. When can you do it?"

"If you're ready, I can do it next week," Dr. Sanders said.

Mark made an appointment for the next week to have surgery on his left eye. He was so optimistic that everything would go well that he was already planning on going to see Director Halbert the following week.

Things don't ever go as we plan, though, and the surgery on Mark's left eye didn't go as well as the right eye had gone. He developed an infection in his left eye that was excruciatingly painful. He couldn't stand any light, so he shut himself up in his room with the drapes drawn and he lay on the bed in complete darkness. Dr. Sanders prescribed an additional drug for Mark to put into his eye four times a day. Cat tried to get him to eat, but he refused to eat and only let Cat into his room to put the drops into his eye. Besides the pain from the infection, Mark was deeply depressed. He had been looking so forward to seeing again, that when he had the problem, he felt that he would never be able to see again.

"Cat, I'm not going to make Director Halbert's deadline. He won't let me go back to my Commander's position. What am I going to do?" Mark moaned.

"You don't know that, Mark," Cat said. "Just have faith and let God take care of it."

"Sometimes I don't think God likes me," Mark said.

"Don't say that, Mark," Cat said. "God loves you. He has taken care of you so far and He can keep on taking care of you."

"I'm sorry, Cat. I just feel so depressed. I hurt so bad. I just don't think I'll ever get well."

Cat kissed him and said, "You'll get there, Mark. It just won't be as fast as you thought it would be."

By the time Mark had to go back for his follow-up, the pain had subsided and Mark was able to tolerate light again. When Dr.

Sanders checked Mark's eye, he said that the infection was gone, so he had Mark cover his right eye and read the eye chart. He read one of the lower lines on the chart as he had done with his right eye.

"That's good, Mark," Dr. Sanders said. "I think your eyes will be all right now. If you have a problem, just call and make an appointment. I really don't think you'll have any more trouble now, though."

"That's great news," Mark said. He could hardly contain his excitement. Now all that prevented him from getting his position back was his leg. He called Dr. Nix's office and made an appointment for the next day.

"Dr. Nix," Mark started when the doctor entered the examination room where Mark and Cat were waiting. "I need to know how soon I can walk without this thing on my leg."

"Well, Mr. Fuller, we have to get another X-ray first. After that, I should be able to tell you. Now, I'll get the technician to take you to X-ray."

Mark was taken to X-ray and, when he returned, he and Cat waited some more. After about 30 minutes, Dr. Nix came in carrying the X-rays. He put them up on the light table and showed Mark where the break was.

"Here's the break," Dr. Nix said. "You can see that it's healing nicely. Maybe about two more weeks in the cast and we should be able to take it off."

"I don't have two more weeks, doc," Mark said. "Can't you take it off now?"

"If we take it off now, it will not be completely healed and may break again when you use it," Dr. Nix said.

"It looked to me like it was healed," Mark said.

"Well, it wasn't," Dr. Nix said. "Just give it two more weeks. Then we'll take the cast off."

"Then there's no way you'll take it off before that?" Mark asked.

"No, Mr. Fuller," Dr. Nix said. "There's no way I'll take that cast off before it's completely healed."

Mark wasn't very happy with the doctor's decision, but he knew he would have to abide by it. He made an appointment to come back in two weeks then said, "Come on, Cat. Let's go."

The next week was the last week of the month that Director Halbert had given Mark. Mark called the Director's office and made an appointment to see him. He hoped that he could talk the Director into giving him some more time.

On the day of his appointment with the Director, Mark was so nervous he couldn't eat. His appointment was at 9:00 a.m., so he told Cat he wanted to go ahead and leave about 8:00 and maybe he would eat something after his appointment.

"Come in Mark, Ms. Ryan," Director Halbert said, as he opened the door to admit them into his office. Mark and Cat entered the Director's office and he indicated a couple of chairs to them. "Please sit down," he said.

"I see you still have a cast on your leg," Director Halbert said. "How about your eyesight?"

"My eyesight is good," Mark answered. "The surgery was a success. I have to wear this cast for at least two more weeks, though."

"Then, you're not physically able to return to work. Is that correct?" Director Halbert asked.

"Yes, Sir. That's correct," Mark answered.

"Then I have no other alternative but to give your position to Ted Ames. He's been waiting for a month. It isn't fair to make him wait any longer," the Director said.

"It's just two more weeks, Sir," Mark said, getting angry. "Can't you just give me two more weeks?"

"What if you're still unable to carry out your duties as Unit Commander?" the Director asked. "Do you think I should wait some more? How long do you think I should wait, Mark?"

"Two more weeks, Sir," Mark said. "Just two more weeks. I'll be able to perform my duties in two more weeks."

"I don't know, Mark," Director Halbert said. "It isn't fair to Ted to keep putting him off. You also have that mental problem."

"Sir, I'm seeing Dr. Wise, the therapist. I've gotten better mentally as well as physically. Just give me two more weeks. I'll be completely well by then," Mark argued.

"I'm sorry, Mark," Director Halbert said. "I have to do what I think is best for the unit. Maybe when you're well, another unit might become available. Then you would be first in line to be Unit Commander of it."

"I don't want another unit, Sir," Mark said. "I want my unit. Jim and I trained those men the way we wanted them. They do everything the way I want it done. I don't want to have to train another unit from the beginning."

"Well, I'm sorry, Mark, but that's the deal. You can either take it or leave it. When you're completely well, come back and we'll see what we can do," the Director said.

Mark gave the Director a hate-filled stare. "To hell with you," he said, and he grabbed Cat's hand and headed for the door. "Come on, Cat, let's go home," he said as he almost dragged Cat to the door. He didn't stop dragging her until he reached the car. He got into the car on the passenger's side and let Cat get into the car by herself.

"Let's go," Mark said impatiently. Cat hadn't even had time to fasten her seat belt or start the engine.

Cat knew it was best to do as Mark said, so she started the engine and drove all the way home without saying a word. Mark sat silently and just stared ahead.

When they arried home, Mark stomped over to the sofa in the den and flung himself down onto it. "He didn't even try to give me a chance," Mark said. "I think he already had his mind made up before we got there. Even if I had been completely well, he probably wouldn't have given me my job back. He had to bring up my mental problem. Does he think I'm mentally unbalanced? Do you think I'm mentally unbalanced, Cat?"

What could Cat say? Here he was ranting about not getting what he had wanted and he asked her if she thought he was mentally unbalanced.

"Mark, I think you need to learn to control your anger," Cat said cautiously.

"What does that mean, Cat?" Mark asked sarcastically.

"It means that you need to learn to count to ten before you blow up like you do," Cat said. "Do you realize what you just said to Director Halbert?"

"I didn't say anything wrong to him," Mark said.

"Mark, I can't believe you," Cat said. "Would you have taken that if one of your team members had talked to you the way you talked to Director Halbert?"

"I would have been more understanding with my men," Mark said. "He could have given me at least two more weeks. He just didn't want to. I've put most of my life into that unit. Jim and I trained them together. That unit is a part of Jim and me," Mark began to sob.

Cat couldn't help it; she began to sob with him. She sat down on the sofa beside him and started massaging his neck and his shoulders and then his back. He began to calm down at her touch. He took her hand and kissed it. "You don't understand, Cat," Mark said, as he looked deeply into her eyes. "That unit is my last tie to Jim. If I lose it, I've lost my contact with Jim."

"You still have a contact with Jim, Mark," Cat said. "I'm your contact to Jim."

"I can't use you, though, Cat," Mark said. "I feel guilty." Then he stopped. He almost said something he didn't want her to know. He didn't want her to know how he had wanted to take her away from Jim, how he had thought he would have been better for her than Jim was. No, there was no way he could use her as a contact to Jim. Even though Jim had asked him to take care of her when he was dying, he still felt guilty when he thought about Jim and Cat together.

"Why do you feel guilty, Mark?" Cat asked.

"Never mind, Cat," Mark said. "I didn't mean to say that. You're right. You are a tie to Jim. Now, just leave me alone for a while will you? I need to think. I need to accept what Director Halbert said. I need to let it go. It's best if I just sit here by myself for a while."

Cat went on into the kitchen to fix something to eat, but Mark wasn't alone for long. Sherry burst into the cabin with Carol following her. "Mista Mok," she called. When she saw him on the sofa in the den, she ran to him and jumped up onto his lap.

"How is you eye now?" she asked.

"My eye is a lot better, now, Sherry Rene. Thank you for asking," Mark answered.

Cat and Carol went into the kitchen to talk while Sherry entertained Mark in the den. "How did it go?" Carol asked.

"His eye is a lot better," Cat answered. "He still has to wear the cast for two more weeks, though. It was really bad in the Director's office. Director Halbert doesn't want to hold Mark's position until he's able to go back to work. Mark asked him to give him at least two weeks. The Director refused and Mark cussed him out and dragged me out of his office. He may not even have a job at all now."

"Oh, Cat, I'm so sorry," Carol said. "Does Mark think he'll be able to do what he does in two weeks?"

"He thinks he can," Cat said. "He's been out jogging with his cast on. He got some weights and he's been working out with them. He really is building up his muscles. I can feel them getting harder and firmer."

"He does look like he's filling out, I noticed," Carol said.

"If he would just learn to control his temper, he would be a lot better off," Cat said.

"Why aren't you in school, anyway?" Cat asked.

"Oh, they're having the fair parade and they let us go early so we could attend the parade," Carol said.

"When is the parade?" Cat asked.

"It's at 2:00 p.m.," Carol answered. "I don't know if we'll go or not. There'll be so many people there. Do you want to go if we go?"

"I don't know. I'll have to see if Mark wants to go," Cat answered.

"If Mark wants to go where?" Mark asked from the doorway.

"Carol says they're having a fair parade at 2:00. Would you like to go?" Cat asked.

"Sure, if Sherry Rene is going. I haven't been to a parade since... well, I don't guess I've ever been to a parade. Do you want to go Sherry Rene?"

"Yes, Mista Mok. Let's go to a pawade," Sherry said, as she wiggled with excitement in Mark's arms.

"Tell Aunt Kitty to stop yaking and fix us something to eat. We're hungry," Mark told Sherry.

"Aunt Kitty, top aking and fis us somptin ta eat. We hungry," Sherry said.

"Yes, Ma'am," Cat said with a laugh.

Mark and Sherry went back into the den and Cat said, "It's amazing. Mark can be all angry and moody and Sherry can come in and jump into his lap and he becomes an altogether different person."

"Cat, why don't you go ahead and marry him and get him that 'widdle gul' that Sherry wants? You know he loves you. I can see it every time he looks at you. What are you waiting for?" Carol asked.

"You know why I can't marry him right now," Cat said, with tears in her eyes. "It's too close to our anniversary. You of all people should understand."

"Cat, Jim's gone and he isn't coming back. It's not like you're being unfaithful to him," Carol said.

"I just can't. Not now," Cat said, wiping away a tear. "I told him January 16."

"So, you've finally set a date," Carol said. "That's still two months away. Why can't you make it sooner?"

"Just leave me alone, Carol. I told you I can't do it yet. You should understand," Cat said, as she got out bacon and eggs and cooking utensils.

"OK, I'll leave you alone, but I don't think you're being fair to Mark," Carol said.

At the parade, Skip held Sherry up so she could see everything.

"I want Mista Mok to hol me," she said and she squirmed down and ran over to Mark. She held her little hands up to Mark and said, "Hol me Mista Mok." He, of course, picked her up and sat her on his shoulders.

"I think Mark is trying to steal my daughter from me," Skip said with a frown.

Cat looked at Mark's happy face and Sherry happily sitting on his shoulders and said, "You have to watch out for Mark. He'll steal all the females' hearts."

"Well, he won't steal mine," Carol said. "My heart belongs to only you, Skip."

"Cat, why don't you marry the guy and give him a daughter of his own, so he'll leave mine alone?" Skip tried to sound light-hearted, but Cat could see that he was hurt.

"I am going to marry him, soon," Cat said. "In January."

"Why wait so long?" Skip asked.

"Maybe I just want to start the new year out right," Cat said.

"Well, I'll be glad when you do get married," Skip said. "Then maybe he'll be occupied with you instead of Sherry. I'd kinda like to see him without that tortured look on his face, too. Everytime he looks at you, he looks so pitiful."

"Now you're teasing is getting too personal, Skip," Cat said, a little peeved at what Skip was getting at.

"I wasn't teasing," Skip said and he moved away from Cat before she could hit him.

CHAPTER 10

The next two weeks went by fast and it was soon time for Mark's appointment with Dr. Nix.

"If he doesn't take this thing off my leg this time, I'm taking it off myself," Mark said on the way to the doctor's office.

"No, you're not," Cat said. "You know what he said. It might break again unless it's completely healed."

At the doctor's office, Mark was taken to have an X-ray before seeing Dr. Nix. Then he and Cat were put into an examination room to wait.

"Well, you're in luck, Mr. Fuller," Dr. Nix said, as he entered the examination room carrying the X-ray. "Everything looks good. I'll take the cast off now, if you want me to."

"Of course, I do," Mark said.

"I thought you might," Dr. Nix said, as he produced the instrument for removing the cast.

In the car on the way home, Mark said, "Now I'll show that pompous, old fool. I'm just as good now as I ever was. Let me out a mile from home. I want to jog the rest of the way home."

"I don't think you better do that yet, Mark," Cat protested.

"I said stop the car and let me out, Cat. Do what I said."

So Cat stopped the car and Mark got out and started jogging. Cat waited for a while to let Mark get a head start and then slowly drove behind him.

Just a short distance from the cabin, she could tell that Mark was having trouble. He was beginning to limp on his right leg. She held her breath and hoped that he would be able to make it the rest of the distance to the cabin. He did finally make it. When she drove into the driveway, he was leaning against the post gasping for breath.

"Are you OK?" she asked, as she ran up to him.

"I'm OK," he answered. "I'm just a little out of shape. I feel good, though. I just have to get out and work out some more. I'm going to make it, Cat. I know I can do it. You just watch me. I'm going to get my job back, somehow. I know I can do it."

So, for the next few weeks while Cat was at work or volunteering at the children's hospital, Mark was either jogging or working out. He was slowly building up his muscles and his endurance. Cat could see changes every day when she returned home. She was secretly proud of Mark for his determination, but she felt like he really didn't have a chance at getting his old unit back. She stopped by the barracks one day on her way home from work and talked to Jason.

"I'm sorry, Cat," Jason said. "I know you want Mark to be able to come back to his old unit because he wants it so much, but I don't think that's going to happen. We've moved on and he's only stood still. We've adopted some new tactics. Mark would have to go through training all over again and I know Mark, and I know he wouldn't like it. How's he doing, anyway?"

"He's great," Cat said. "He's almost back to his old stamina and endurance. He's building up his muscles. His attitude is a lot better. Why don't you come by and visit him some day? I know he would enjoy seeing you."

Jason sighed and slowly said, "I might do that. Don't tell him I'm coming, though. Just in case I don't get a chance."

Cat took that to mean that he probably wouldn't be coming. Therefore, she was surprised when she answered a knock on the door several days later and there stood Jason.

"Hello, Jason, come on in. It's good to see you again." Then she called to Mark, who was in the den watching TV. "Look who's here, Mark."

"Hey, Jason. Come on in, Pal," Mark said, as he stood up and shook Jason's hand. "What brings you out our way?"

"I just got lonesome for you and thought I would come pay you a visit," Jason said.

"I know you better than that, Jason," Mark said, as he motioned for Jason to be seated. "What do you have on your mind?"

"You just get right to the point, don't you, Mark?" Jason said.

Cat didn't want to eavesdrop, so she went on into the kitchen. If Jason was going to give Mark some bad news, she didn't want to see Mark's reaction.

"Cat said that you were better," Jason started.

"Cat said. When did you see Cat?" Mark asked suspiciously.

"We bumped into one another the other day," Jason evaded his question.

"Cat didn't say anything to me about bumping into you," Mark was beginning to get angry. He felt that Cat had somehow stepped over the line and was messing in something that wasn't any of her business.

"Well, that doesn't matter, anyway," Jason said, trying to get Mark to calm down again. "Anyway, she said you were back in shape again," Jason said as quickly as he could to avoid any other unpleasantness.

"I heard that Don Gardner had to retire and they're looking for a replacement for him. I just thought I would mention it to you; just in case you're interested," Jason said.

"Why would I be interested in that bunch of losers?" Mark said through clenched teeth.

"I don't know. I just thought you might want to get back as Commander of a unit," Jason said.

"I don't want to be Commander of just any unit. I want to be Commander of MY unit." Mark was getting loud and Cat stepped out of the kitchen to see what was going on.

"I'm sorry, Mark, but I don't think that's going to happen," Jason said, as he stood up and started toward the door.

"Wait a minute, Jason. Where are you going?" Mark asked, as he followed him to the door.

"I came here to talk to you because I thought we were friends, but you're treating me like your enemy. I'm not your enemy, Mark. I just thought I could help. I'm sorry I came," Jason said.

"Wait a minute, Jason," Mark said, as he put his arm around Jason's shoulders. "I apologize. You're right. You're not the one I should be mad at. Come on back and sit down. Let's talk some more. Cat, would you get us something to drink?"

"Sure, Mark," Cat said, as she went back into the kithen and put ice and Coke into two glasses and brought them back into the den. Then she decided to stay and see what was going to happen next.

"OK, Jason. Now that I've calmed down. Tell me about the position," Mark said.

"Like I said, Don Gardner is retiring in a few weeks. They've already begun looking for his repladement. They're having a hard time beause no one wants it. No one wants their name associated with, like you said, 'a bunch of losers'," Jason said.

"So that's what you think I am now? A loser?" Mark asked.

"No, of course not, Mark," Jason tried to explain. "I just thought it would be a way for you to get back in. Then maybe you could transfer later on."

"You don't think I'll get my unit back then?" Mark asked.

"I'm sorry, Mark, but I don't think that's going to happen," Jason said.

"Why?" Mark asked

"Well, for one thing, we're doing some new tactics. You'd have to go back to the training facility and learn them. For another thing, Director Halbert doesn't want you back," Jason said.

"OK, I understand why Director Halbert doesn't want me, but why can't you just show me the new tactics?" Mark asked.

"It's not that simple, Mark," Jason said. "It's a new rule. You have to go through training. There's a new training academy in Jonesboro and everyone has to take two weeks of training and be certified."

"Why wouldn't I need to go through training if I take Don's team?" Mark was confused.

"Because they're not going to use the same procedures that we do," Jason said.

"So, that's what everyone thinks of me now, huh? They think I'm just a broken down old horse that isn't good for anything but to lead a bunch of losers into...what? What would I even be doing?" Mark asked.

Jason sighed, "I don't know, Mark. It wouldn't be much, though. The only reason FSC keeps them on is because some of them are getting close to retirement. It wouldn't look good if they got rid of them just before their retirement."

Cat could hardly sit still. She wanted to go to Mark and put her arms around him and kiss away the hurt she knew he was feeling. He had worked so hard to get back his strength. Now he would probably just quit. She wished there was something she could do, but she knew that Mark had to work it out for himself.

"OK, Jason," Mark said after a few minutes. "What do I need to do? Do I need to get the training first or do I need to put my application for the unit in first?"

"I think you need to take the unit first before they do give it to someone else," Jason said. "I'll help you with the training whenever I can. Maybe you can send some of your men to the training academy and then they can train the others."

"All right, Jason. It's a deal. I'll go to Human Resources first thing in the morning and put my application in. Thanks for letting me know. Thanks for coming by. You are a good friend. I'm sorry I gave you a hard time," Mark said.

"It's OK, Mark," Jason said, as he walked toward the door. "I know about how you feel. I know how close you were to those guys. They still think a lot of you. They're sorry that you won't be their Commander any more."

"We'll see about that, Jason," Mark said. "We'll see about that. Thanks again for coming."

Cat let out a sigh and relaxed. She had been so tense and had clenched her teeth so tightly that her jaw as well as her head ached.

"Well, I guess I know what the Director thinks of me now, don't I?" Mark said, as he came back into the den and sat down.

Cat sat down next to him and put her arm around his shoulders. "I'm proud of you, Mark," she said. "You're learning how to control your temper."

"Is that what you call it?" Mark asked. "Whatever you call it, it feels like a rock in the pit of my stomach," Mark said. "Well, what do you think? Should I take that unit of losers and try to make something out of them or do I forget the whole thing?"

"I say you take those losers and make them winners, Mark," Cat said. "I know you can do it."

"If you say so, Cat," Mark replied.

"I do say so," Cat said and then she kissed him.

The next morning, after breakfast, Cat drove Mark to the FSC building. He was nervous as he walked into the Human Resources Office. It was just like he was beginning all over again.

"I'm Mark Fuller. I was Unit Commander until I was injured a few months ago. I've recovered from my injuries and now I'd like to apply for the Unit Commander position that's open," Mark told the receptionist.

"Do you have a form from your doctor stating that you're able to return to work?" she asked.

"No, I didn't know I had to have one," Mark answered.

"I'm sorry, but you do have to have one before you can return to work," she said.

"I'll get one, but I need an application, anyway," Mark said.

"OK, here's an application, but you need to bring the doctor's form first. Then you can apply for a transfer."

"What do you mean apply for a transfer?" Mark asked.

"When you come back, you'll come back to your unit. Then you can apply for the other position. If you're given the new position, you'll have to be transferred to the other unit," she said.

"Thank you for the information," Mark said. "Do I bring the doctor's form to you?"

"Yes, you can bring it to me and I'll take care of putting you back on the active list. Then you will need to report to your Unit Commander."

"Thanks," Mark said. Then he took Cat's hand and said, "Come on, Cat. Let's go."

When they got to the car, Mark said, "Damn, I thought it would be simpler than that. You know what that means? It means I have to report to Ted Ames before I can go back to work. Do you know how hard that's going to be?"

"I can imagine how hard it'll be, Mark, but I know you can do it. You're just going to have to be humble. Do you know how to be humble?"

"No, Cat. You know I'm not a humble person," Mark said sarcastically.

"Well, the first thing we have to do is go to Dr. Nix's office and get a form," Cat said. "I guess we'll need one from Dr. Sanders, too. Don't you think?"

"I guess so," Mark answered. "It's best to get them both. That way I won't have to do it all over again before I can go back to work."

So they got a form from both doctors and took it back to FSC. While they were there, they went up to the Director's office and hoped that they would be able to see him without an appointment.

"Come on in and sit down, Mark, Ms. Ryan," Director Halbert said. "What can I do for you?"

"I'm ready to go back to work," Mark said. "I just turned my doctor's forms in down at Human Resources."

"Are you sure you're able to perform your duties properly?" the Director asked.

"Yes, Sir, I am," Mark answered.

"You realize that I had to give your unit to Ted Ames, don't you?" the Director asked.

"Yes, Sir, I realize that," Mark said, as he tried to keep the anger out of his voice.

"Then, what do you expect to do?" Director Halbert asked.

"I've been informed that Don Gardner's Unit will be available soon. I want it," Mark said.

"You want to be the Unit Commander of Don Gardner's Unit? Is that what I understood you to say?" the Director asked incredulously.

"Yes, Sir. I want to be Unit Commander of Don Gardner's Unit," Mark answered.

"Well, I never expected that," the Director said. "I thought I would have to fight you over Ted's Unit."

Mark had to bite his tongue to keep from saying something when the Director said Ted's Unit, but he knew he was only baiting him.

"I would appreciate whatever you can do to get Don Gardner's Unit for me," Mark said.

"OK, if that's what you want," Director Halbert said. "I'll see that you get it."

"So, when and where do I report?" Mark asked.

"You can report to Ted Ames on Monday morning," Director Halbert said. "You know where to report."

"Thank you, Sir. I appreciate your help," Mark said. "Come on, Cat. Let's go."

As they walked out the door, Mark turned to Cat and said, "I guess I do know how to be humble after all."

"It's a good thing you do," Cat said with a giggle. "Now you're going to have to continue to be humble when you see Ted."

"Now, that's what's going to be hard," Mark said. "You're really going to have to pray for me before I see Ted. I don't know how much more humble I can get."

"If you can just be humble long enough to get transferred to Don Gardner's Unit, that's all you need to do. Once you get out of Ted's Unit, you won't have to be humble to him any more," Cat said.

"Let's stop at the restaurant and eat lunch before we go home," Mark said. "I don't want to go home just yet."

CHAPTER 11

Shortly after Cat and Mark arrived home from seeing Director Halbert, Carol and Sherry came bursting through the door. Sherry, of course, ran to Mark and jumped up into his lap.

"Hewo, Mista Mok," she said. "How you feel?"

"I feel great, Sherry Rene," Mark answered. "How do you feel?"

"I feel gwat, too. Mommie said we gonna hab a big Thanksgibin dinna soon. We drawed piktures ob turkeys. See my turkey?" Sherry answered.

"What a pretty picture of a turkey," Mark said. "Now you made me hungry for turkey."

"Come into the kitchen, Cat, I want to talk to you," Carol said, as she led Cat into the kitchen. "You know the 21st is almost here. I know you do by the way you're acting. Anyway, Skip and I are going to take a short trip to celebrate our five-year anniversary. I was wondering if you would be able to take care of Sherry while we're gone? If you don't think you can, I was going to ask Skip's mom and dad if they'll come and stay at the cabin while we're gone. I really don't want to ask them, though, if you think you can handle it."

"I don't know, Carol," Cat said. "It has really been hard this year. This thing with Mark has really brought everything back so vividly. What if I tell you I can handle it and then when the day gets here, I can't do it? I hate to say no, because Mark is so crazy about Sherry and that would give him more time with her, but I just don't know."

"Well, I don't want you to say you'll do it, if you don't think you can," Carol said.

"How soon do you need to know?" Cat asked.

"Well, I'd like to know by next week," Carol said. "That would give me enough time to see if Skip's parents can come and to call and make our reservations."

"Mark starts back to work Monday," Cat said. "I'm afraid he's going to have problems. Let me get through that and see how his attitude is. Then I'll let you know. Is that OK?"

"Sure, just let me know before the week's out," Carol said.

That night, Cat dreamed of Jim. She dreamed that she was being pulled away from him and he was trying to get to her. He would get close and she would reach out her hand to him. Sometimes their fingertips would touch, but then she would be pulled away again. Finally, she was pulled so far away from him that she could barely see him anymore. She started to cry. She cried softly at first. Then she cried deep, anguished sobs. Her heart was breaking and she couldn't stop the sobs. Her whole body was wracked by the anguished sobs. "Jim, Jim," she cried.

Suddenly, Jim was there. "I'm here, Hon," he said, as he enfolded her in his warm, comforting arms. He kissed her neck. He kissed her cheek. He kissed her lips. She felt his warm body against her. He felt so real. The kisses on her lips felt so real. She leaned against him. He was there. He had come back for her. "Oh, Jim, I've missed you so," she said. "Why did you leave me? I needed you so much."

As she lay in Jim's comforting arms, she drifted off to sleep. When morning arrived, Jim was gone. She cried and got up and dressed. It had only been a dream. Jim was still gone. He was never coming back. No matter how she prayed and wished it to be so, Jim was never coming back. She had thought she had gotten over it, but this new thing with Mark and the unit just brought it all back. Now, Carol was making it worse by telling her about her plans, plans for a five-year anniversary that she could celebrate with Skip, but Cat would never celebrate with Jim. Then she started to cry again. She prayed, "Please, God. Help me make it through this. I miss him so much. Please help me make it through it."

Finally, she was in control enough to go downstairs. Mark was already downstairs and had made a pot of coffee. He was sitting at the kitchen table drinking a cup of coffee when Cat walked in.

"Good morning, Cat," he said. "Did you sleep well?"

"No, I didn't," Cat said, as she poured a cup of coffee and stirred sugar and creamer into it. "I dreamed about Jim last night," she said, as she sat down at the table next to Mark. "It was so real. I thought he was there with me." She had to choke back another sob. "I thought I was getting to where I could handle it, but the closer it gets to November 21, the harder it is to bear," she said.

"I thought I heard you crying last night," Mark said.

"You didn't come into my room by any chance, did you?" she asked thoughtfully.

"No, I didn't want to disturb you," he said. Then he thought to himself, "Yes, Cat, I was the one who was there, but I can't admit it to you."

"I just thought…never mind what I thought," she said and then she got up and walked toward the den. She unlocked Jim's office and went into it. She went over to his desk and unlocked the desk drawer. The photograph was still there. She picked it up and looked at it again. "Yes," she thought. "I definitely saw in Mark's eyes what I thought I had seen when I looked at it before. He must have been in love with me way back then. I'll need to be more careful around Mark, now, or he might try to talk me into getting married sooner than I can do it," she thought. "How did I ever let myself get into such a mess," she wondered. "I guess you can't help who you fall in love with. Sometimes your heart has a mind of its own." When she went back to the kitchen, Mark was still sitting at the table nursing a cup of coffee.

"Mark," Cat said, and then hesitated before going on. "What did you and Jim argue about? You know, the reason you left the unit. I never did find out why you left."

"I don't even remember," Mark said, as it became more difficult for him to breathe. "That was a long time ago, Cat. How do you expect me to remember that?"

"You two were having problems when that photograph was taken weren't you?" Cat asked matter-of-factly.

"What photograph?" Mark tried to pretend he didn't know what she was talking about.

"The one that Ted brought for your birthday," Cat said.

"I'd like to kill that Ted," Mark thought.

"Cat, why are you bringing this up now? It's been a long time. A lot has happened to me since then. How do you expect me to remember that?" he asked.

"It must have been very important back then. It broke up a really good friendship and an even greater partnership," Cat said.

"It must not have been much because Jim still called me to help him rescue you and I came didn't I?"

"I just wanted to know what could be so bad that you had to leave the unit," Cat said.

"I don't know, Cat. I don't remember and Jim's gone, so you can't ask him," Mark said. "Why is it so important that you know what Jim and I argued about, anyway? It doesn't matter now."

"I just thought it had something to do with why Jim died," Cat said.

"No, it didn't have anything to do with why Jim died, not really, anyway," Mark said.

"Mark, I need to know," Cat cried. "Please tell me why you and Jim broke up such a good friendship."

"Do you really want me to tell you?" Mark said, exasperated that Cat wouldn't leave it alone. "OK, I'll tell you the whole story, but you won't like it. It's not a very pretty story. You may not even like me after I tell you. Do you want to risk that?"

Cat sat down and lay her head on the table and cried. "Did you let Jim die?" she asked.

"No, I did not let Jim die. He died because he wanted to be a hero. That's what usually happens to heros. They die being heroic. Jim died saving your life. That should satisfy you. The man you loved, loved you so much, he was willing to die for you. Now, are you satisfied or do you want the whole story?"

Cat was really sobbing now. She was sorry that she had ever opened this discussion. She didn't understand why it was so hard for her to face Jim's death this year. She had gotten through it better last year. Mark had brought back all those terrible memories, though. Now that he was going to be the Unit Commander again, it really brought back memories. That photograph was the last straw. Why did she have to go look at it again? How would she ever make it through the rest of this month? How would she ever make it through the rest of this year?

"Cat, I'm sorry," Mark said. "I shouldn't have said that. I know that this time of year is hard on you. I'll leave if it will make it easier on you. Maybe having me here, just makes it harder on you. I can get a bed at the barracks. I can see and I can walk now. It won't hurt me to live in the barracks."

"No, Mark," Cat said. "I don't want you to leave. I need you here. I don't want to be alone right now. Please stay."

"I won't leave if you don't want me to go," Mark said. Then he stood behind her and kissed the top of her head. "I love you, Cat. I'd give almost anything to keep you from hurting like you are now. I would have exchanged my life for Jim's if I could. I tried to get him to let me stay and for him to take you and go, but he wouldn't. I've hated myself every time I see you look at a picture of Jim or say his name and cry. I should have died and Jim should have lived. Is that what you want me to say? Well, I said it. Does that make it better? Did it bring Jim back? No, it didn't. Neither would my telling you what we argued about. I love you, Cat, and I want to marry you, but if marrying me only makes your pain worse, then I'll leave and never bother you again. I don't want to see you hurt. It hurts me to see you cry and beg Jim to come back to you. I can't stand it any longer, Cat. If you're going to continue to mourn for Jim, then you have no room for me in your heart. I know why you keep putting me off. You're still married to Jim and you always will be. Goodbye, Cat." Then Mark stormed out the front door, slamming it behind him.

Cat began to cry and she cried until there were no more tears to cry. "Have I lost Mark, too?" she asked herself. "Am I as blind as Mark has been?" Mark had offered her the most precious thing he possessed and she had taken it and stomped on it until there was nothing left of it. Why had she done that? Was she afraid to love someone again? Was she capable of loving Mark like she had loved Jim? Mark was right. She felt like she was still married to Jim and she was being unfaithful to him every time Mark kissed her. "I hope I haven't lost Mark, too," she said, as she got up and took their cups to the sink and washed, dried and put them away.

Cat busied herself around the house, hoping that Mark would return. At lunchtime, she fixed a sandwich and ate a bite or two and then threw it away. At dinnertime, she ate a container of yogurt. She was a little hungry, but didn't feel like eating very much. About 10:00 p.m., she decided that Mark wasn't coming back, so she went to bed.

It didn't do her any good to go to bed, she just lay there awake wondering where Mark was. She wondered if he had gone to the barracks. She got back up and dialed Jason's number.

"Jason, this is Cat, Cat Ryan," she said. "I'm sorry to call you so late, but I have to know. Is Mark there?"

"Why?" he asked.

"We had a fight and he left," she said. "I just thought he might have gone there."

"Yeah, he's here," he answered. "He didn't want me to tell you."

"May I talk to him?" she asked.

Jason was gone for a few minutes. When he came back, he said, "He doesn't want to talk to you."

"Tell him I need to talk to him," Cat said.

"Cat, just leave it for a while," Jason said. "He doesn't want to talk to you tonight."

"Thank you, Jason," she said, and hung up.

Cat lay back down again and cried into her pillow. It was going to be a long, lonely night.

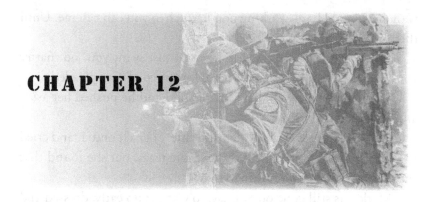

CHAPTER 12

After a sleepless night of tossing and turning, just before daybreak, Cat decided she might as well get out of bed. She hadn't slept at all, and she was sure she wouldn't sleep now. She went downstairs and made a pot of coffee. When it was ready, she poured a cup and stirred sugar and creamer into it.

How long was Mark going to punish her, she wondered. He was supposed to start his new job Monday. Was he going to go through that without her help. "I wish I'd never asked him about that argument he had had with Jim," she thought.

About 10:00 a.m., there was a knock on the door. When Cat opened the door, Mark was standing there.

"I need to get my stuff," he said, as he walked past Cat and toward the stairs. Then, without saying anything else, he went on up the stairs and into his bedroom. He gathered up his things and came back down the stairs.

"Please don't go, Mark," Cat said, as she grabbed his arm.

Mark picked up her hand and took it off his arm. "I think it's best if I leave for a while," he said. "Now that I'm better, it's too hard to keep my distance. This is best for both of us."

"I don't want you to go, Mark," she said. "Please don't go."

"Cat, I love you, but I can't compete with a dead hero. I thought I could, but I can't. I'm not a hero. I've never done anything heroic. What's more, I don't think I ever will. When you decide that you want a plain old hard-working non-hero, then you can call me. Until then, I'll be at the barracks."

"Please don't go, Mark. I love you. I just want you, no matter whether you're a hero or a non-hero. I want you," Cat pleaded.

"You know where I'll be, Cat," he said and he pushed her aside and walked out the door.

Cat ran to the sofa in the den and threw herself onto it and cried again. She didn't think she had any more tears, but she found that she still had many more tears to cry.

Mark was still gone on Sunday, so Cat got up early, dressed and called Carol to see if they were going to church.

"We're taking Sherry to Sunday School and staying for church," Carol answered. "Are you and Mark going?"

"I'd like to go with you if I may," Cat said. "Mark isn't here."

"Oh, did Mark go somewhere?" Carol asked.

"He's staying at the barracks," Cat answered. "What time will you be leaving?"

"Probably about 9:30 a.m. We'll come by and pick you up," Carol said. She wondered why Cat cut her off so abruptly when she asked about Mark, but she knew better than to ask any more questions.

"I'll be ready," Cat said. "Just pull up and blow the horn."

So about 9:30, when Skip blew the horn, Cat ran out and got into their vehicle.

"Wheas Mista Mok?" Sherry asked.

"He isn't here, Sherry," Cat answered.

"Whea is he?" she asked.

"He's with some friends of his," Cat answered. She wished now that she hadn't gone with Carol and Skip. She didn't realize that Sherry would want to know where Mark was.

"When will he be back?" Sherry was persistent.

"I don't know, Sherry," Cat said.

"Sherry, quit asking so many questions and leave Aunt Kitty alone," Carol said.

She noticed that Cat was on the verge of tears and that one more question about Mark would probably start them. She could hardly wait until she could get Cat alone and find out what happened to Mark.

At church, Cat didn't get a lot out of the sermon. She was thinking about the last time she was there. Mark had been with her and he was in love with her.

After church, Skip asked if she wanted to go with them to the restaurant. "I might as well go with you," Cat answered. "You would just have to back track to take me home first."

While they were eating, Jason came over to their table. "Hi, Cat, everyone. I'd like to introduce you to my girlfriend. This is Debbie Allen. Debbie, this is Cat Ryan and her sister, Carol, Carol's husband, Skip and daughter, Sherry."

"Hello, Debbie. It's nice to meet you," they all said.

"I won't disturb your meal," Jason said. "I just wanted to say hello and introduce you to Debbie."

"Jason, wait a minute," Cat said, as she grabbed his arm. "How is Mark doing?"

"He's fine, Cat. I wouldn't worry about him, if I was you. He's doing just fine. See you later," he said. Then he and Debbie went back to their own table.

"Well, you know he's OK," Carol said, as she squeezed Cat's hand.

"Yeah, I guess so," Cat said, but she had lost her appetite. "I think I'll go on outside and wait for you."

"It's kind of chilly, Cat," Carol said. "It might be a while. You know how Sherry is. She likes to play with her food."

"I'll be OK," Cat said. "I have a warm coat on."

"Here, take the car key and wait in the car, then," Carol said handing her the key.

Cat sat in the car and cried. Why was this year so hard? It had to have something to do with Mark and his trouble. Maybe she was beginning to let go of Jim, but she really didn't want to. Mark was forcing her to let go before she was ready, but would she ever be ready? Had she given up her last chance of ever finding happiness again? She knew right then and there that she would some day have to make a decision. She would have to choose either Jim, who was never coming back, or Mark, who was alive and well. She just hoped it wasn't too late and that she would make the right choice.

Soon, she heard the happy voice of Sherry and looked up to see Sherry running toward the car. Cat dried her eyes and tried to smile.

"Aunt Kitty," Sherry said, as she crawled into the car beside Cat. "Wook what I gots?" she said. It was a small stuffed puppy. "It so sof and cudwey. Feel Aunt Kitty," Sherry said, as she held it against Cat's cheek.

"Yes, it is Sherry," Cat said.

"I gonna call him Mista Mok," she said.

"I don't think you should call him Mr. Mark," Cat said.

"Why?" Sherry asked.

"I just don't think Mr. Mark is a good name for a little puppy," Cat said.

"But I wik Mista Mok," Sherry argued.

"Why don't you name it something else, like Fluffy or Candy or something else?" Cat insisted.

"No," Sherry said, getting mad. "I wik Mista Mok. I gonna name him Mista Mok," she said.

"OK, Sherry," Carol said. "We'll find a good name for your puppy. Let's not decide right now."

Then the trip home was made in silence. When Skip pulled up in front of Cat's cabin, Carol got out, too. "Skip, take Sherry on home with you. I want to visit a while with Cat," Carol said.

As they entered the cabin, Carol said, "OK, Cat, let's go into the kitchen. I want to know what's going on. Sit down here at the table and tell me everything. First off, I want to know where Mark is."

"He's at the barracks," Cat said.

"Go on," Carol said. "Tell me the rest of it. Why is he at the barracks?"

"Yesterday, we had a fight and Mark left. He took his things and said he was staying at the barracks," Cat answered.

"What did you fight about?" Carol asked.

At first, Cat wasn't going to tell Carol, then she changed her mind.

"It was about Jim," Cat said. "It's always about Jim."

"What do you mean, Cat?" Carol asked.

"I don't know. I think Mark feels like he doesn't measure up to Jim and I'm having a hard time letting him go," Cat said, as she began to cry.

Carol got up and put her arms around Cat. "I know it must really be hard for you, especially since our anniversary is so close. I can only guess what you're going through, but don't give up on Mark. I think he's a keeper. I know, I was against him at first. I thought he was just taking advantage of you, but I don't think Sherry would be so crazy about him if he wasn't a pretty good fellow."

"Oh, Carol, I think I've already messed things up. When I call and ask to talk to him, he refuses to talk to me. What can I do if he won't even talk to me?" Cat asked.

"Why don't you just give him some time," Carol said. "He says he loves you. If he really does, he'll be back. Just give him a little time."

"I guess I'll have to," Cat said.

"Do you still want to keep Sherry while Skip and I are gone, or does this change your plans?" Carol asked.

"Yes, I'll still keep Sherry," Cat said. "It may even be better for me. At least I won't be so lonesome and Sherry may keep me busy enough to forget what day it is."

"OK, I'll tell Skip's parents that you're going to keep her. That way they can make their own plans," Carol said. "Are you OK now?"

"Yes, I'm OK. You go on home. I'll be all right," Cat said, as she stood up.

"Thank you for your concern. When will you and Skip be leaving?"

"We'll leave on the 19ᵗʰ and return on the 22ⁿᵈ. That way, we'll have two full days to celebrate," Carol said.

"OK, just bring her and her things on over when you're ready to go," Cat said.

"Thanks for keeping her, Cat," Carol said, as she went out the door. "I really hated to ask Skip's parents. They already had other plans and they would have had to change their plans to take care of Sherry. I'll see you later."

Now, Cat was left alone with her thoughts. It was her own fault she knew. If she hadn't bugged Mark about his fight with Jim, he wouldn't have left. It still bothered her, though. What did they argue about that was so bad they let it come between them? Well, it was best that she leave it alone. If she wanted Mark back, she would have to forget it.

The rest of the day dragged by and finally it was time for her to go to bed. She undressed and put her nightgown on and lay down on the bed, but she couldn't go to sleep. She kept thinking about Mark. She hoped it wouldn't be too hard on him to have to work under Ted Ames. Ted used to be such a nice person. He and Jim had been good friends. At least they were until Mark came and Jim made him his Second-in-Command. That's when Ted changed. I guess it would have made me mad, too, if I had been working for someone and a new person came in and was put over me. I guess that was how Ted felt. Oh, well, that wasn't her problem. She just hoped that Mark could at least hold his temper until his transfer went through. She finally drifted off to sleep and the morning sun woke her when it peeped through a space in the window blind.

She got up, dressed and went downstairs. The cabin was so quiet. She had gotten used to seeing Mark on the sofa in the den and she automatically looked over at it, as she walked toward the kitchen. She gave a sigh and continued on into the kitchen. She automatically made coffee and poured a cup. She stirred sugar and creamer into the cup without even thinking. She seemed to be working on auto-pilot. "Is this how it's going to be from now on?" Cat asked herself.

"Well, I'm glad I have my job at the paper. If I didn't have that, I would really be in a bad fix."

After she finished a light breakfast, she grabbed her purse and car keys and headed for the newspaper office. On the drive downtown, she kept wondering how Mark was making out with Ted Ames. She prayed that God would help him hold his temper. She knew that, if he smarted off at Ted, he would never be able to get his Commander's position again.

At the newspaper office, she still remained on auto-pilot. She did everything as a mechanical robot. At the end of the day, she felt that she had wasted the whole day. She would probably have to rewrite everything she had written. "Oh, well," she thought. "Maybe I'll feel better tomorrow."

That was about the way her whole week went. She was glad when the week ended and she could stay huddled up at home on the sofa in the den. She felt close to Mark when she lay on the sofa. She could even smell the scent of his cologne, as it still lingered on the pillows and cushions he had lain on. She wanted to call the barracks and see if he would talk to her, but she didn't want to be rejected again. Maybe Jason was right. Maybe after he cooled off, he would come around. She just had to wait.

CHAPTER 13

The 19th of November finally arrived and Carol brought Sherry and her belongings over that morning. Sherry already knew that her mother and father would be going on a short trip and that she would be staying with Aunt Kitty, but when it came time for Carol to leave, she started to cry.

"No, Mommie, don't go," she cried. "Don't weve me. Pwese don't weve me."

Cat tried to console Sherry, but she wouldn't be consoled. "Oh, how I wish Mark was here," Cat thought. "He would be able to handle her."

"Look, Sherry," Cat said. "I'll read a book to you. Mommie and Daddy will be back soon. We'll have fun while they're gone. Please don't cry."

Carol finally left in tears herself and Cat was left with a crying, unhappy Sherry Rene. "If you'll be good, Sherry, we'll have some ice cream after while. Would you like that?" Cat asked.

Sherry brightened at the thought of getting ice cream and stopped crying. She was good the rest of that day and the next day, because it was exciting to be staying with Aunt Kitty. Cat had a lot of fun activities for Sherry to do and Monday and Tuesday passed quickly, but on the morning of Wednesday, November 21, Carol called and Sherry started crying for her all over again. The only way Cat could get her to stop crying was to promise to take her shopping for a new book.

"If you be good and stop crying, Sherry, after breakfast, we'll get you a new book and we may even get some more ice cream," Cat said.

"I be good, Aunt Kitty," Sherry said. Then she stopped crying and ate her breakfast.

After Cat had cleaned up the kitchen, she dressed Sherry in some warm clothes and put a coat and cap on her and carried her out to the car.

"We'll go to the park first and feed the squirrels," Cat said, as she started the engine. "Would you like that?"

"Yes, I would," Sherry answered.

They spent a few hours at the park feeding the squirrels and then got to Simmons Drug Store about noon. Since it was so close to lunchtime, the store was pretty crowded with people who came in on their lunch break.

Cat and Sherry were standing in front of a display of children's books. "Here's one I think you'll like, Sherry," Cat said, as she picked up one and held it down for Sherry to see.

"Mista Mok," Sherry said and she started running toward the door.

"Sherry, come back," Cat called and started after her, but she stopped suddenly, as she saw why Sherry was running away.

"Hello, Sherry Rene," Mark said, as he picked her up and hugged and kissed her.

"Hello, Cat," he said, as he walked over to where Cat was standing.

"Hello, Mark," Cat said with her heart racing. "How have you been?"

"I'm OK," he said.

"How is the job going?" Cat asked.

"It's terrible, but I'm making it. I think Ted has given me the worse jobs he can find. He would make me clean the toilets, but he isn't in charge of them."

"How are you doing?" Mark asked.

"Lonely," Cat said.

"Sorry about that," Mark said.

"Mista Mok, I gotta git sumptin fo my Mommie and Daddy fo they anibursary," Sherry said.

"What do you want to get for them?" Mark asked.

"Go ova dere," she said and pointed to the jewelry counter.

Mark carried Sherry over to the jewelry counter and Cat followed.

"I wik dat," Sherry said, as she pointed to a beautiful, delicate gold necklace with a single diamond on a pendant.

"Yes, Sherry, that's a beautiful present for your mother. What about your dad. What would he like?" Mark asked.

"Dat wing," Sherry said. "He wud wik dat wing."

Mark told the lady at the jewelry counter to gift wrap the items that Sherry had picked out and he handed her his credit card. "Here, put them on this," he said.

"No, Mark," Cat said, as she walked up beside him. "I'll pay for them. You don't need to."

Mark turned around and looked at Cat and said, "I've got money, Cat. I have a job now. It may not be much of a job, but I do have a job."

"I'm sorry, Mark," Cat said, stepping back. "I didn't mean to insult you. I just didn't want you to feel obligated to pay for what Sherry wanted."

"Do you have a book you want, Sherry Rene?" Mark asked. When she handed him the books that Cat had picked out for her, Mark put them on the counter with the other items. "Add these to the total," he told the clerk.

"May I walk you to your car?" Mark asked, still carrying Sherry Rene.

"Yes, of course," Cat said. Her heart was beating so fast she could hardly breathe. Being so close to Mark again had her heart racing.

At the car, Mark put Sherry into her car seat and put his hand against the car next to where Cat's head was. He leaned into her and lightly kissed her lips. "I've missed you, Cat," he said.

"I've missed you, too," Cat said.

"Do you know what today is?" he asked.

"Yes, of course, I know what today is. I've been dreading it for so long." Cat said.

"Did anything disastrous happen?" Mark asked sarcastically. "I mean, did the world come to an end? Did Jim suddenly come back?"

"That's not fair, Mark," Cat said almost in tears. "You know that wasn't what I meant."

"Well, I guess I'd better go now," Mark said abruptly. "My lunch break is about over. I don't want to be late getting back to work. I might get chewed out again."

"Mark, I'm sorry," Cat started, but Mark put his finger to her lips and said, "You have nothing to be sorry about. This was my choice. I'll make it. It's just a few more days. Now, I really have to go." He gave Cat one last kiss and turned to Sherry. "See you later, alligator," he said to her.

"See you lata, awagata," Sherry said, as she waved goodbye to him.

Cat watched as Mark strutted off down the street. At the corner he got into his parked car. He drove by and waved again. Then he turned the corner and was gone from Cat's sight.

She stood leaning against the car watching the corner where Mark had turned. Her heart was still beating so fast she had a hard time breathing.

"Aunt Kitty, let's go get ice cweam," Sherry said. That brought Cat out of her trance. "OK, Sherry, just a minute."

As she turned to open the car door, a hand reached around her and opened it for her.

"Hello, Cat," Ted Ames said.

"Oh, hello, Ted, you startled me," she said.

"Fancy meeting you here," he said.

"Yeah, it is a coincidence, isn't it," Cat said, trying to inch away from his arm.

"I haven't seen you for a while. How are you getting along?" he asked.

"I'm OK," Cat answered. "Excuse me, but I have to go. Sherry's in the car and I don't want her to get cold."

"It is kind of chilly isn't it," Ted said, as he put a hand on Cat's waist and pulled her to him. Then he kissed her hard on the lips.

Cat pulled away and slapped him. Ted held a hand to his face and said, "You'll be sorry you did that. I thought, since you let Mark kiss you and didn't slap him, I could do the same. You know, for old times sake."

"I don't let just anybody kiss me," Cat said.

"You weve my Aunt Kitty awone," Sherry said. "You a mean man. We don't wik you. Now go away."

"I'll go, but you'll be sorry," he said. "I can make it real hard on Mark Fuller. You seem to like him quite a bit. How would you like it if I make it really hard on him?"

"I wouldn't like it," Cat said. Then she got into the car and started the engine. "I have to go now. I could make it hard for you, too. Just remember that." Then she drove off. Her hands were shaking so badly that she could hardly hold the steering wheel.

"He was watching when Mark kissed me," she thought. He had probably guessed that they were in love. She hoped that her love for Mark didn't cause him anymore trouble than it already had.

"I don wik dat man," Sherry said. "He a mean man."

Cat agreed, but she couldn't tell Sherry that. She didn't want Sherry doing something that might cause Mark problems. As long as Mark was under Ted Ames' control, she would have to try to be nice to Ted.

"Let's go get a hamburger and a milk shake, Sherry. How about that?" Cat said, as she drove to the McDonald's down the street.

Cat placed their order and then found a table for Sherry and herself. It was pretty hard to do, since the restaurant was full with the lunch crowd. As she was getting Sherry settled, she heard her name called. She looked up to see Jason standing beside her table.

"Hi, Jason," Cat said.

"Hello, Cat, what a coincidence, meeting you here," Jason said.

"I was thinking the same thing," Cat said. "Would you like to sit down and share our table?"

"Yes, I would like that very much," Jason said.

"Hewo, Mista Jason," Sherry said. "We just seed that mean man, too."

"What mean man?" Jason asked.

"Never mind her," Cat said. Then she tried to get Sherry to hush, but she was determined to tell Jason who she saw.

"Dat mean man wid you. Dat day you made Mista Mok mad," Sherry said.

"Hush, Sherry," Cat said.

"Oh, you mean Ted Ames?" Jason asked. "Where did you see him?"

"Ova dere," Sherry pointed toward the street. "We seed Mista Mok, too."

Cat was becoming exasperated with Sherry. She really didn't want everyone to know about her chance meeting with Mark.

"Oh, you did?" Jason asked. "Where did you see Mr. Mark?"

"In dat dwug stoa," Sherry said.

"Sherry eat your hamburger and drink your milk shake," Cat said.

"That's OK, Cat," Jason said. "If it's supposed to be a secret, I won't tell anyone."

"It isn't supposed to be a secret, Jason," Cat said. "I just don't want it broadcast all over town."

"I won't tell anyone," Jason said. "That's really strange that you ran into three FSC personnel in just a few minutes, isn't it?"

"Yes, it is," Cat agreed. "I guess you all eat lunch at the same place and we just happened to be here when you were eating," Cat said.

"I guess that solves that then," Jason said, as he gave a slight chuckle.

"Jason, tell me the truth," Cat said, as she leaned close to Jason. "How is Ted treating Mark?"

"Well, Cat, you didn't hear it from me, if anyone asks you, but it's bad. If I was in Mark's place, I wouldn't put up with it. He has more self-control than I would have. I guess knowing that you're going to be out of it in a few days helps you to cope, but I don't know if I could, even under those circumstances."

"Is there anything I can do to help?" Cat asked. "I could go to Director Halbert, if you think it would help."

"No, I wouldn't do that, Cat," Jason said. "That would just make it worse. He'll be out in a few days. I'm sure he can take it for a few more days. Well, I guess I'd better go. I sure don't want to get on Ted's bad list. I have longer to go than Mark does. If he knew I was talking to you, he'd punish me in some way. I'll see you around. Bye. Bye, Sherry Rene."

"Bye, Mista Jason," Sherry said. "I wik Mista Jason, but not Mista Ted."

"Well, hurry up and finish eating," Cat said. "We need to get out of here."

Cat was thankful when they finally got back home. She spent the rest of the day entertaining Sherry. She loved Sherry, but she had really tried her nerves. She felt bad that Mark had paid for Carol's and Skip's gifts. She would have to find some way to repay him. She knew he probably wouldn't let her, but she thought she needed to do it, anyway.

About 6:00 p.m., Carol called. "How's it going?" she asked.

"It's going," Cat answered. "We went to town. She got two new books and we had a hamburger and a milk shake. You do let her have ice cream don't you?"

"Yes, she gets ice cream occasionally," Carol said. "Has she been bad?"

"No, not really," Cat said.

"May I speak to her?" Carol asked.

"Sure, here she is," Cat said, then she handed the phone to Sherry.

"Mommie, I saw Mista Mok," Sherry said, as soon as she got the phone.

"You did?" Carol asked. "Where did you see Mr. Mark?"

"At da dwug stoa," Sherry said. "He put me on he shodas and he byed me two books."

"He did?" Carol was all ears. She wanted to hear more. "What else did he do?" She asked.

"He byed you and Daddy a gif," Sherry said.

"Why did he do that, Sherry?" Carol asked.

"I don know," Sherry said. "Cause he wiks you, I guess. I awso saw Mista Jason and dat mean Mista Ted," Sherry kept on going and Cat felt like crawling under the table.

"May I speak to Aunt Kitty again?" Carol asked.

When Cat took the phone, Carol asked, "What was that all about? Where were you?"

"No, Carol, before you ask, I didn't plan it. It just happened," Cat said. "We were in Simmons Drug Store and Mark walked in. He was on his lunch break. I guess he saw us go into the drugstore and followed us in. I guess Ted must have seen us, too, because he came up and harassed me after Mark left. Then we ate lunch at McDonald's and ran into Jason. It was just a coincidence."

"How is Mark making out with Ted?" Carol asked.

"He says he's OK, but Jason said Ted was riding Mark pretty hard," Cat said. "I wish there was something I could do, but Jason said it was best if I just stayed out of it. He said Mark only has a few more days to go. He should be able to make it for just a few more days."

"Well, I hope it works out OK for Mark," Carol said. "Sherry is so crazy about him. I would really like to see him succeed. Oh, by the way, Skip and I are going to a fancy night club tonight and going dancing. If you need me, I'll have my cell phone.

"One more thing I want to ask about and then I want to say goodby to Sherry," Carol said. "I was just wondering how it's going with you. You haven't said anything about it."

"I'm OK," Cat said. "Mark made a comment that hurt a little, but Jim and our anniversary is still a sore subject with him. I really thought he understood, but I guess he doesn't."

"I guess he just wants you to go on and get past it, Cat," Carol said. "I probably would be the same way, if anything happened to Skip, so I can't chide you for something I might have done myself. Just hang in there, Kid. Mark loves you. He'll come around. You only have about a month and a half to go. We need to get together when I get home and start some planning, too."

"We'll talk about that when you get home," Cat said.

"OK," Carol said. "Now, let me say goodbye to my child."

Cat handed the phone to Sherry and walked off. She didn't want Sherry to see her cry. This had been harder than she let on. She certainly didn't want Mark to know how much his remark hurt. "Oh, well," she thought. "It'll be better tomorrow."

CHAPTER 14

On Thursday afternoon, Carol and Skip arrived back home. When Skip pulled into the driveway, Sherry ran out to meet them. Cat had put the gifts that Sherry had gotten for them on the bar in the kitchen and Sherry ran and got them as soon as they came into the cabin. "Happy anibursary," Sherry said, as she handed them their gifts.

"Thank you, Sherry," Carol said, as she opened hers. "Oh, it's beautiful," she said, as she saw the delicate necklace. "You picked this out by yourself?" she asked.

"Mista Mok helped," Sherry said. "You wik it?" she asked.

"Yes, Sherry. I love it," Carol said, as she fastened it around her neck.

"Thank you for my gift, too, Sherry," Skip said. "I really like it. It just fits, too. Did Mr. Mark help you pick this out, too?"

"Yes. Mista Mok helped," Sherry said.

"Cat, I hate to rush, but we really need to get home and unpack. I have to do laundry, too, so I guess we had better get Sherry and her stuff and head home," Carol said.

"Sure. I understand, Carol. You go on home," Cat said. "I'll see you later."

"See you lata, awagata," Sherry said.

"See you later, alligator," Cat said, and she hugged and kissed Sherry goodbye.

Now the house was really quiet. Cat wandered through the

house, picking up things and straightening up. Having Sherry there for a couple of days had gotten everything out of order. Cat hadn't realized how having a four-year-old in the house could disrupt everything. It had been a good disruption, though. At least she had company. Now she was all alone. She was left with her lonely thoughts, things she had no business to be thinking. "Will this terrible feeling ever end?" she wondered. "Well, I might as well go to bed," she thought. "There's no reason to keep staying up trying to get interested in something when all I can think of is Mark."

She didn't even realize that she said Mark instead of Jim. Thoughts of Mark were slowly pushing thoughts of Jim out of her mind and she hadn't realized it yet.

Carol was busy all day Friday and Saturday, so Cat was alone all week-end. She called Carol on Saturday night to see if she could ride with them to church on Sunday.

"Sure," Carol said. "You know that we take Sherry to Sunday School and then stay for church, don't you?"

"Yes," Cat said. "I still want to go with you. Will you pick me up at 9:30 in the morning?"

"Yes," Carol said. "We'll see you about 9:30 in the morning, then."

As Cat sat in the pew at church, Sherry came running out of her Sunday School class and sat down between Cat and Carol.

"Mista Mok," Sherry said, as Mark walked up behind Cat and sat down next to her.

"Hi, Sherry Rene," Mark said, as she came over and jumped up onto his lap.

"I miss you, Mista Mok," Sherry said.

"I miss you, too, Sherry Rene," Mark said.

"Hi, Mark," Cat said, as she took his hand. Her heart was racing so she could hardly breathe. "I miss you, too," she said breathlessly.

Then the service started, and they were quiet until the service ended. As they filed out the door, Carol asked if Mark would like to go to the restaurant with them.

"Sure, I'll go, but I'll take my car and Cat can ride with me," Mark answered. "Would you like to ride with me, Cat?"

"Yes, of course," Cat said, as her heart raced.

"We'll go on and meet you at the restaurant," Carol said, as she fastened Sherry in her car seat.

Before Mark opened the door for Cat, he pulled her to his chest and kissed her. "I've really missed you, Cat," he said.

"I didn't tell you to leave, Mark," Cat chided. "You're welcome to come back at anytime."

"I can't come back yet, Cat," he said. "I have something I have to prove to myself first."

"How is it going with you and Ted?" Cat asked.

"My transfer has finally come through," Mark said. "I start in Don Gardner's unit on Monday morning. Since Thanksgiving is on Thursday, Don's last day will be Wednesday, so I'll take over as Unit Commander when we come back after Thanksgiving."

"Speaking of Thanksgiving," Cat said. "You are coming for Thanksgiving, aren't you?"

"If nothing happens to prevent it, I'll be there," Mark answered.

"I guess we had better get going," Mark said. "They'll be wondering what happened to us." Then he opened the door and helped Cat get into the car. When they got to the restaurant, Carol, Skip and Sherry were sitting at a table and had already begun eating.

"Come sit by me, Mista Mok," Sherry said, when she saw Mark and Cat walk in, so Cat and Mark sat down for a few minutes and gave their drink orders to the waitress. Then they went to the food bar and filled their plates.

As they ate, several of Mark's old unit members came by and said hello and that they were glad to see that Mark was able to be back at work. Jason stopped by for a few minutes, also.

"I heard that your transfer came through," Jason said. "When will you be leaving?"

"I start in Don's unit tomorrow," Mark said.

"Good luck, Mark. You'll need it," Jason said.

"Thanks, Jason," Mark replied.

Carol and Skip finished eating and said that they needed to go on home. "I'll see you later, Cat," Carol said. "Bye, Mark. It was good to see you again."

"See you lata, awagata," Sherry said and waved goodbye.

"See you later, alligator," Mark said to Sherry. "Bye Carol and Skip."

Cat and Mark sat at the table for a while talking about Mark's new job. Then all of a sudden, Jason hurried over and said for Mark to come outside. Carol needed him. He and Cat rushed outside to find a frantic Carol and Skip. "She's up there, Mark. It's Sherry. I was talking to Jason and I looked around and she was gone. I don't know how she got up there," Carol cried, as she pointed to a scaffold 50 feet in the air.

Mark didn't waste any time. He jerked off his jacket and tie and threw them in Cat's direction. He hoped that she caught them. "Jason, do you have any gear in your vehicle?" Mark asked, as he ran to the bottom of the platform.

"I've got some rope and tackle in the trunk," Jason replied. "I'll go get it."

"Mommie, Daddy," Sherry cried. "Get me down."

"I'm coming, Sherry Rene," Mark shouted up to her. "You just be still. I'll get you down."

"Mista Mok, get me down," Sherry wailed.

"I will, Sherry. Just be patient," Mark said, as he tied the rope around his waist. Jason tied the other end to a steel girder attached at the side of the platform.

Mark wasted no time in climbing up the side of the tower. Once his foot slipped, but he caught himself and continued to climb. Cat's heart sank when she saw him slip. "Please, God," she prayed. "Help him get Sherry and bring her down safely."

Sherry had gotten into a basket that was attached to the side of the tower. The basket was used by the workers to carry them up to the top of the tower. Sherry had found the button that raised the basket up and had pushed it. The basket had then continued all the way to the top.

When Mark reached the top where Sherry was, he grabbed her and held her tightly as he pushed the button and lowered the basket to the ground. A large crowd from the restaurant had gathered at the bottom of the tower and everyone cheered and clapped when Mark grabbed Sherry.

When Sherry was safely in her mother's arms, everyone slapped Mark on the back and congratulated him on a good rescue. Several of the onlookers were filming the incident with their phone cameras. One man in particular said that he couldn't wait to get home and put it on You Tube. That night, it was on the news, also.

"Thank you, Mark," Carol said through her tears. "I don't know how to properly thank you, but believe me, I'm going to try."

Skip gave Mark a big hug and said, "Mark, I'll forever be grateful to you. I didn't know what to do. I'm so glad you were here. Thank you so much."

Cat kissed Mark and said, "Thank you from me, too, Mark. Now you can't say you've never done a heroic deed. You're definitely a hero now."

"That wasn't so heroic," Mark said. "I knew Jason wouldn't let me fall. I just did what anyone would have done." Then he took Jason by the hand and said, "Thanks, Jason. I appreciate your help. I couldn't have done it without you."

"You're welcome, Mark. I was glad to do it," Jason said. Then he turned to Cat. "He's more of a hero than he thinks. The tackle wasn't working properly. If he had slipped off that girder, I wouldn't have been able to have kept him from falling."

Cat trembled when she heard that. "Please don't let Mark know that. It might affect him in an adverse way."

"Don't worry, Cat," Jason said. "I won't. He'd chew me out, anyway. He'd tell me to take better care of my equipment."

"I guess I'd better go pay for our meal," Mark said. "I rushed out without paying."

When he went into the restaurant to pay, the owner didn't want to charge him. "You did a great thing by saving that little girl," he said. "I don't want you to pay."

"I want to pay, though," Mark said. "Besides, that was my fiancee's niece. I was almost obligated to save her."

The owner wouldn't accept Mark's money, anyway, and Mark finally gave in and accepted a free meal for a heroic deed. When he got back to where Cat and the others were standing, Carol said that they were going on home. "I'll see you later, Mark. Thanks, again for rescuing my daughter."

"You're welcome, Carol. I was glad to do it," Mark said. Then he took Cat's arm and said, "Come on, Cat. Let's go, too."

When they were in the car, Mark asked, "Are you in a hurry to get home?"

"Not really," Cat answered. "Do you have somewhere you want to go?"

"Yes, I do. I want to show you something," Mark said.

He drove toward the cabin, but he went on past it. He drove past the hunting lodge, where Cat and the others stayed when Olga Kinski was chasing them. Cat wondered where Mark was going. They were going way past the lodge.

Finally, Mark pulled into a secluded spot next to a peaceful-looking lake. The lake was surrounded by trees ablaze in vibrant fall colors. It was so beautiful, Cat caught her breath. "Mark, it's beautiful," she said.

"I thought you might like it," he said, as he put his arm around her shoulders and pulled her to him. "I found it when I was staying at the lodge protecting you and your sisters. There were times when I had to come here to be by myself and think." Cat wondered if she had been the subject of some of those thought sessions, but she refrained from asking. She lay her head on Mark's strong shoulder and relished his warmth.

"Cat, I think working under Ted has helped me to mature," Mark started. "It was a great shock to my ego at first, but I've learned how to be humble. Maybe that was what I needed all along. I think that if I had been humble when Jim was alive, we never would have had that argument.

"I now understand why you wanted to wait to marry me. You may not have known yourself, but I realize now that I wasn't ready to marry you yet. You can take all the time you need. I'll not rush you anymore. Just assure me that you will eventually marry me and I'll be satisfied. I know that I was trying to compete with Jim when there was really no need to try to compete with him. I was egotistical enough that I thought if I could get you to marry me before you were over Jim, then I would have beaten Jim. I have to apologize to you for that. I think now whenever you're ready, I'll be ready, too. We can start our marriage out with no ghosts from the past to destroy the love we have for each other. I hope you can see the change in me, because, Cat, I have changed. That's what I wanted to tell you. I hope you still love me and want to marry me some day, but I want you to know that I'll abide by your decision whatever it is."

Then he kissed her and waited silently for her to finish crying and give him an answer. She sat silently for a few minutes and then she wiped her eyes and said, "Mark, that was the most beautiful marriage proposal I have ever heard. Yes, I've noticed a change in you and I like the change. You do know how to be humble don't you? I'm glad you finally understand me and why I have to wait. We can still get married on January 16 or whatever day you choose. I love you more every day and I'm ready to be your wife anytime after the first of the year."

Mark gave a little chuckle and said, "As long as it's after the first of the year. OK, Cat, you've already said January 16, so if that suits you, it suits me, too. Let's shoot for that, OK? Now, I need to get you home. I have to get back to the barracks and get ready for tomorrow. I may have to be humble again."

So, Mark started the car and drove back to Cat's cabin. He walked her to the cabin door, kissed her, then he left. Cat felt so lonely when he left. She could hardly wait for Thanksgiving to be able to see him again. "Yes, things are getting better," she thought. "Maybe the new year will be a lot better than this one has been." She really hoped that marriage to Mark was the answer to her problems. It seemed like it was beginning to be, anyway.

CHAPTER 15

On Monday morning, Mark reported to Don Gardner's unit. "Well, I see you got my position," Don said, as he shook hands with Mark. "You're going to have some resentment."

"I'm used to resentment," Mark said.

"Cassidy is my Second-in-Command," Don said. "She feels like she should have gotten it. I heard that you pulled some strings to get it. That really made her mad."

"Well, she'll just have to get glad again," Mark said. "How about the rest of the team? Do they all feel that Cassidy should have gotten it?"

"I don't know if they feel that Cassidy should have gotten it, but they sure don't like the idea of working under you," Don answered.

"Why is that?" Mark asked.

"They didn't like the fact that Jim took you over Ted Ames," Don answered. "Come on into my office. We have things to discuss that I'd rather not say in front of my team."

When they were settled in Don's office, he said, "You know Cassidy. You might as well expect trouble from her. She'll give you trouble in more ways than one."

"I can handle Cassidy," Mark said.

"Well, there's also Dave Hightower," Don said. "He'll probably give you trouble, too. He's already been griping about your coming to our unit. He feels that Cassidy should have gotten the position. Of course, she's been filling his head with stuff. He's a hot head, anyway.

It didn't take much to get him on her side. All she had to do was cuddle up to him a little and she had him where she wanted him."

"I can handle him, too," Mark said. "You forget. I was Jim's Second-in-Command and I was Unit Commander of that unit until my accident. I'm not fresh out of the academy."

"I just thought I'd warn you," Don said. "Sometimes it helps to know what you're up against before you get there."

"Thanks, anyway, Don," Mark said. "I'll at least know who to watch out for. Now, let's see your case files. I need to know what you've been working on and how far along you are."

So, Mark spent the rest of the morning going over the case files and familiarizing himself with the different assignments this unit had undertaken. Mark had heard that this was a sloppy unit, but he didn't really know how sloppy until he started reading the case files. He was beginning to wonder if maybe he had made a mistake in taking the position of Unit Commander of this unit. "Well, it's a place to start, anyway," he thought. "I needed a place to start. I guess this is as good a place as any, if I can't have my old unit back."

Mark spent most of Monday going over the case files and on Tuesday, he tried to get acquainted with the members of the unit, but they mostly tried to avoid him. On Wednesday, there was a retirement party for Don, so there wasn't much going on that day, either. They would be off on Thursday and Friday for Thanksgiving, so Mark decided to wait about saying anything to the team, until he would officially take over as Unit Commander on Monday. On Thursday morning, Mark awoke early and drove on out to Cat's cabin. He knew that he would be early for Thanksgiving dinner, but he was anxious to see Cat. He had really missed her the past three days.

When Cat answered his knock, she was surprised to see him so early. "Hi, Mark," she said, as she stepped aside to let him enter. "I didn't expect you this early. Have you had breakfast?"

Mark put his arm around Cat's waist and pulled her to him. "I couldn't wait to see you. I had to come," he said, and gave her a lingering kiss. "No, I didn't take time for breakfast. I just wanted to see you."

"Come on into the kitchen," Cat said, as she tried to calm her racing heart. "I was going to fix breakfast for everyone, so you might as well eat with us. Charlotte and Tyler are here. They stayed with Carol and Skip last night. They'll all be over here shortly. Would you like a cup of coffee?"

"Yes, I would love some coffee. I didn't take time for anything. Thanks," he said, as Cat set a steaming cup of coffee on the table in front of him.

"Well, how did your first few days with Don's Unit go?" Cat asked.

"Not very well," Mark answered. "Cassidy is resentful because she was expecting to get Don's position and everyone else is resentful because they feel that she or someone in their unit should have gotten it. They hardly speak to me at all. If they do, it's something snide or sarcastic. I can't say anything until Monday, when I officially take over as Commander. Then I'll lower the boom on them."

"I wouldn't be too harsh on them if I was you," Cat said. "You may need them to cover you sometime and it's best if they don't have something against you. I would rather have someone who likes me to cover me than someone who hates my guts."

"You're probably right, Cat, but I have to show them who's boss at first. I don't want them to think I'm a pushover, either."

"Just remember what I said. You can catch more flies with honey than with vinegar," Cat replied.

"Yeah, but I don't want to catch any flies," Mark said.

Then their conversation was interrupted, as Sherry, followed by the others, made a noisy appearance.

"Mista Mok," Sherry squealed and ran and hugged Mark.

"Hi, Sherry Rene," he said, as he hugged and kissed her.

"Hi, Mark," Charlotte said, as she came into the kitchen and saw him. "I didn't know you were going to be here."

"Where did you think I'd be?" Mark asked.

Charlotte felt snubbed by Mark's remark and gave him a nasty look and walked over to Cat, who began frying bacon.

"Come read me a story, Mista Mok," Sherry said, as she took Mark's hand and dragged him toward the den.

"Just a minute, Sherry Rene," Mark said. "I want to speak to Tyler and your mom and dad. Hello, Carol, Skip. You, too, Tyler. Did you have a good flight, Tyler?"

"Yes, we did," Tyler answered.

"Mone, Mista Mok," Sherry said, as she pulled at Mark's hand. He gave her a frown, but he followed her on into the den.

"Why is he here?" Charlotte asked Cat. "I thought it was just going to be family."

"He is family, Charlotte," Cat answered. "We're getting married in January."

"I thought maybe you had finally come to your senses and called it off," Charlotte said.

"I love him, Charlotte," Cat said angrily. "You might as well face facts. He's going to be your new brother-in-law."

"Thank goodness I won't have to be around very often to see it," Charlotte said. "I think you're making a big mistake."

Cat ignored Charlotte's remark and continued cooking breakfast. "Carol, will you set the dining room table for me, please?" Cat asked.

"Sure, Cat," Carol said, as she got out plates, napkins and silverware.

When it was ready, Cat called Mark and Sherry and everyone sat down at the table. They had a prayer and then Cat asked who wanted a cup of coffee. She poured coffee and set bacon, eggs and biscuits on the table. Everyone ate hungrily.

After breakfast, Cat shooed the men out of the kitchen and into the den while she and Carol cleaned up the kitchen and started the Thanksgiving dinner. Charlotte sat on a bar stool and watched.

"How is your new job going, Mark?" Skip asked.

"I haven't really started yet," Mark answered. "I start on Monday. I expect some opposition, though. There were others who expected to get it and I'm afraid I'll have trouble with them. Other than that, I guess it's going about as I expected."

"Oh, are you able to go back to work?" Tyler asked. "I didn't know you had started back yet. Charlotte didn't say you were working again."

"I've only been working a few weeks," Mark said. "I'm still not back to full capacity yet, but I'm getting there."

"What are you doing?" Tyler asked. "The same thing you were doing?"

"Yes, I'll be the Unit Commander again. I start on Monday at that position," Mark said, a little uncomfortable by Tyler's questions.

Skip could tell that Mark was getting uncomfortable, so he decided to change the subject. "Tell us about your new movie, Tyler," Skip said. "Are you and Charlotte both in this one?"

Tyler was more than happy to change the subject to himself, so he went into great detail about the movie and the problems that he and Charlotte had already run into.

"Unka Tyla," Sherry couldn't stay quiet any longer. "Did you know Mista Mok sabed me?"

"No, I didn't, Sherry Rene," Tyler said. "Tell me about it."

"You tell him, Mista Mok," Sherry said. "Tell him how you cwimed up and sabed me."

"Maybe Mr. Mark doesn't feel like telling him, Sherry," Skip said, when he saw that Mark was really getting agitated now. "I'll tell Uncle Tyler after while. Why don't you go see what your mother is doing?"

Mark put Sherry on the floor and stood up. "Thanks," he said to Skip. "I think I'll go outside and get a little fresh air," Mark said, as he walked to the front door.

"I wanna go wit you, Mista Mok," Sherry said, as she started to follow Mark.

"Sherry, leave Mr. Mark alone," Skip said, as he picked her up and carried her to the kitchen.

"Carol, your daughter is agitating Mark," Skip said. "Can you do something with her?"

"What did she do?" Carol asked.

"She's just being a pest." Skip didn't want to go into detail, but Carol could tell by the look on Skip's face that something was wrong.

"Where's Mark now?" Carol asked.

"He went outside," Skip said.

"Cat, maybe you better check on Mark," Carol said.

"Why? What's wrong?" Cat asked. She hadn't heard the conversation between Skip and Carol.

"I think he needs you. He's outside," Carol said.

Cat stopped what she was doing and hurried outside. She found Mark walking around kicking leaves.

"You OK, Mark?" she asked.

"I'm OK," Mark said. "What did Skip say?"

"He just said you were outside and maybe I should check on you," Cat said.

"I guess everyone feels like they need to walk on eggs around me, huh?" Mark asked.

"I don't know what you mean, Mark," Cat said. "What happened?"

Mark took a deep breath and put an arm around Cat. "I guess Skip felt that I was about to explode. I was getting a little agitated, so I thought it was best for me to just walk away before I said something I would regret."

"What happened to make you agitated?" Cat asked.

"Now you're doing it, Cat. Can't you just leave me alone for a while. Just let me get myself under control again. I thought I was getting over it, but it seems to have just hidden for a while. I think Tyler was just making conversation, but he touched a sensitive spot. I'm sorry, Cat. It's still hard for me to talk about some things. Maybe I better go."

"No, Mark," Cat begged. "Please don't go. Please stay."

"If I stay, I'll need to be alone for a few minutes. I need to get my head straightened out. Just leave me alone for a while. I'll come back in when I think I can do it."

"Kiss me, Mark," Cat said.

He gave her a light kiss and she said, "Kiss me like you mean it."

Then he took her into his arms and kissed her like he really meant it.

"That's better," Cat said. "I love you, Mark and I'll be with you no matter what you have to go through. Just remember that. I'll go back in, but I expect you to come back in, too. We'll make it through this, Mark. We made it through your recovery. We'll make it through whatever is bothering you now."

She left him wandering around the yard and went back into the kitchen.

"Is Mark all right?" Carol asked when Cat came back without him.

"He's OK. He just needed to be alone," Cat said.

"What did I do?" Tyler asked. "Did I say something to offend him?"

"No, Tyler. He's just really sensitive about certain things right now. He'll get over it," Cat said.

"I was just making conversation," Tyler said, as he went back into the den. "Is there something about his saving Sherry that bothers him?" Tyler asked Skip.

"It's not necessarily that, Tyler," Skip said. "Mark's been through a lot since that accident. I think the doctor said he has PTSD. Do you know what that is?"

"No, not really," Tyler said.

"Well, It messes up your mind," Skip said. "He had a real problem coping a few months ago. He seemed to be getting better, but going back to the job that he was doing when he was injured must have brought it on again, You just have to leave him alone for a while until he can cope again."

"Well, what has that got to do with saving Sherry?" Tyler asked.

"It had a lot to do with that," Skip said. "I think that maybe saving her brought back memories of either saving or failing to save someone else."

Then Skip told Tyler the whole story about how Mark had rescued Sherry from the tower.

"Wow," Tyler said. "I guess he is a hero. I always thought he was just full of hot air, trying to be someone he isn't."

"No, Tyler," Skip said. "He doesn't pretend to be someone he isn't. He's the real deal, but he tries not to let anyone know that he is."

"Wow, I guess I'll have more respect for him now than I did," Tyler said. "I just believed it when Cat said that he let Jim die. I guess that was wrong, huh?"

"Yes, that was wrong," Skip said. "He tried to save Jim, but Jim died anyway. That may be what his trouble is. He may feel guilty because he wasn't able to save Jim."

"Do you think I should go outside and apologize to him and see if he'll come in?" Tyler asked.

"No, Tyler," Skip said. "He'll come in when he's ready. If he wouldn't come in for Cat, he certainly won't come in for you."

After about an hour, Mark came back in and sat down on the sofa. Skip and Tyler were watching a football game and pretended not to notice that Mark had returned. Sherry saw that Mark had come back in and she wiggled out of Carol's lap and ran and jumped into Mark's lap. Carol and Skip held their breaths until they saw what Mark would do.

Mista Mok," Sherry said. "I wondaed whea you wus."

"I had to go outside to think, Sherry Rene," Mark said.

"Whut you tink about, Mista Mok?" Sherry asked.

"Oh, lots of things," Mark said. "I thought about what a pretty little girl you are and I'm so lucky to have you as a friend."

"I lucky to hab you, too, Mista Mok," Sherry said.

Everything was finally ready for dinner, so Carol set the dining room table and Cat put all of the food on the bar. That way they could serve themselves buffet-style.

"Everyone, come to the table. Dinner's ready," Cat called. After everyone was seated, Skip said a prayer of thanks. Then he said, "We are especially thankful this year. God has been very good to us. He sent Mark our way and he gave our precious daughter back to us. If we hadn't had Mark, we might have lost our daughter. Thank you, Mark, for everything you've done for our family." Mark bowed his head and wanted to walk out, but Cat took his hand and squeezed it and he felt better about Skip's praise.

After the meal was over and everyone was still sitting at the table, Charlotte said, "I have an announcement to make. I wanted to make sure that everyone was here when I made it." She paused for a few seconds and then she said. "Tyler and I are going to have a baby."

"You what?" Carol asked. "You're expecting?"

"Yes, Carol," Charlotte said. "That's usually what it means when someone is having a baby."

"When is it due?" Carol asked again.

"Sometime in June," Charlotte said.

"I never thought you'd have a baby," Carol said. "Well, I mean, I didn't think you and Tyler ever had time enough to have a baby."

"Well, we are," Charlotte said.

After everyone got over the initial shock, they all congratulated Charlotte and Tyler.

"While announcements are being made," Cat said. "I want to say that Mark and I have set January 16th for our wedding day."

She really didn't intend to announce it like that, but Charlotte had made her mad and she just let it come out. She looked at Mark and saw the frown on his face and then she wished she could take it back, but it was too late.

"I guess we'll be coming back in January, then," Charlotte said. "I'm glad you finally decided on a date. I was wondering if you were ever going to get married." Mark had been thinking the same thing, but he wasn't about to give Charlotte the satisfaction of knowing it.

Then everyone congratulated Mark and Cat. They wanted to know where the wedding would take place.

"We haven't decided yet," Cat said, as she looked at Mark out of the corner of her eye. She could tell that he was displeased with her, but she had started it now and was unable to stop it. Then she said, "You men can go back into the den and we women will clean up the kitchen."

Skip and Tyler took Sherry and went on into the den. Mark took Cat aside and said, "I need to go, Cat. I need to get on back to the barracks. I wish you hadn't done that, but it's done now. We'll discuss it later. I'm sorry that I've been in such a bad mood today. I guess I've been thinking about Monday too much. Maybe after I get everything at work straightened out, I'll be better. I'll call you sometime next week."

He kissed her then and said, "I love you, Cat. Please just hang in there. I'll get better some day. I might even turn out to be someone you can like. Bye for now."

As he walked to the front door, he said, "Bye, everyone. Sherry Rene, see you later, alligator."

Sherry ran to him and hugged his legs. "Give me kiss Mista Mok."

Mark picked Sherry up and hugged and kissed her. "I gotta go now, Sherry Rene. I'll see you later, alligator."

"See you lata, awagata," Sherry said, as Mark set her down on the floor and opened the door.

"Bye, Mista Mok," she said.

Then Mark was gone.

CHAPTER 16

On Monday morning, Mark was the first one to arrive at Don Gardner's office. He had been given the key to the office by Don before he left. Mark had written a speech and had rehearsed it several times, but he still dreaded giving it. He had thought about what Cat had said, but had rejected it. He had to give a tough speech. He wanted them to know that he intended to be the boss; he didn't plan on backing down any, either.

When they had all arrived, he called a meeting. "In case there are any of you who do not know me," Mark began. "My name is Mark Fuller. I was SIC under Jim Ryan and I became Unit Commander upon his death.

"You may have heard of Jim Ryan. He had the reputation of being the best UC in the country. I was trained by Jim Ryan and I have been following in his footsteps. Jim didn't tolerate any insubordination and I, as well, will tolerate no insubordination.

"Everyone in this unit will go through a two-week training at the training academy in Jonesboro. When I say everyone, I mean everyone. Cassidy and I will take the first two weeks. The rest of the unit will go two at a time until everyone has been through the training. You will be required to stay at the academy during the two-week training.

"Some of you feel that I should not have been given the UC position of this unit. It has been given to me and I have taken it. Therefore, each and every member of this unit is under my command. You may not agree with some of my orders, but I am still the commander. You will obey my orders. If you would like to suggest something, I will listen, if it is presented to me as a suggestion not as a demand.

"If any of you feel that you cannot abide by my rules, you're welcome to transfer to another unit. I'll be more than happy to prepare the paperwork. If you feel that you cannot work with me, I want you to say so right now and I'll be happy to transfer you. Do I make myself clear?"

Everyone was silent.

"Are there any questions?" Mark asked.

"Yeah, I got a question," one of the men said, as he raised his hand.

"What is your name and what is your question?"

"Dave Hightower," he said. "Have you always been such a hard-ass or did you just start when you became Commander of this unit?"

"I guess I've always been a hard ass, but I didn't have to be until I became the Commander of this unit, Mr. Hightower," Mark answered.

"Are there any other questions?" Mark asked.

No one else asked anything, so Mark said, "I assume everyone understands my rules, since there are no other questions. I'll be in my office. If anyone wants a transfer, let's get it over with now. There's no reason to put it off. Mr. Hightower, I would like to see you in my office."

Mark went into his office and sat behind his desk and waited. Dave Hightower knocked on the door and came in.

"Close the door, Mr. Hightower," Mark said. "Sit down. I assume you're unhappy with my rules. Would you like a transfer?"

"No, Sir. I've tried transferring and no one will have me."

"Is that so?" Mark asked.

"Yes, Sir," Dave said.

"So then, you're just unhappy that I'm the new Unit Commander," Mark said. "Is that what you're unhappy about?"

"Yes, Sir," Dave said.

"Who did you want to be the new UC?" Mark asked.

"I don't know," Dave said. "Cassidy was Don's SIC. I guess I thought that she would get it."

"What do you want to do?" Mark asked.

"What do you mean?" Dave asked.

"Do you want to stay in this unit and work under me or do you want out?" Mark asked.

"I guess I'll stay and work under you, since I can't transfer," Dave said.

"How do you feel about working with a hard-ass?" Mark asked.

"I guess it's OK," Dave said.

"Then get out there and go to work," Mark said. "You pick someone else and you two will take the second two-week training."

"Yes, Sir," Dave said and he left Mark's office. Then Mark went to the door and called, "Cassidy, will you come to my office, please?"

"You wanted to talk to me, Sir?" she asked, as she came into Mark's office.

"Shut the door, Cassidy," Mark said. "I know you're pissed because you thought you were getting the Commander position and I got it instead."

"It isn't fair," Cassidy said. "I worked my butt off for that fool Gardner because he told me I would have his job when he retired. Now I have you to look forward to working under."

"Cassidy, if life was fair, there would be no use for wheelchairs," Mark said.

"Now, will you work with me or do you want to transfer?"

"You mean I have a choice?" Cassidy asked.

"If you're willing to obey my orders and work with me, you can stay. Otherwise, you're gone," Mark said.

"Where would I go?" Cassidy asked.

"I have no idea," Mark said. "That would be up to you. I would just sign the transfer papers."

"I guess I have no other choice but to work with you, then. I have no other place to go. I don't want to take that training again, though," Cassidy said.

"If you stay here, you will take the training with me, starting Monday," Mark said. "Do you want to take the training?"

"Yes, Sir," Cassidy said without any feeling.

"Oh, and another thing, while I have you here," Mark said. "Don't try any of your sexual wiles on me. They won't work. I'm marrying Cat Ryan in January and she's the only woman I want. I would not even look at another woman, so forget it."

"What makes you think I would even bother to entice you?" Cassidy asked.

"I know how you work," Mark said. "Remember, I worked with Jim Ryan. Also, I don't want to see or hear of your trying that on any of the men in my unit. Do I make myself clear?"

"What I do on my own time is my business," Cassidy said. "You cannot dictate my personal life."

"I can if it affects the morale of my unit and that would affect my unit. Now, if you want to remain in my unit, you'll do as I say. If not, I want you to pack your gear and leave now," Mark said through clenched teeth.

"All right. You win," Cassidy said. "I don't have anywhere else to go. I'll do as you say, but I don't like it. I never would have expected you to be such a 'hard ass' as Dave said."

"I guess going through what I've gone through the past few months made me this way," Mark said. "Like I said before, if you don't like it, you can leave. I'm not stopping you."

"Who's gonna be your SIC?" Cassidy asked.

"I haven't decided yet," Mark answered. "I expect that person to be loyal to me and to the unit. Who would you suggest?"

"I'm, or was, Don's SIC," Cassidy said.

"I know that," Mark answered. "Can I trust you to have my back or do you shoot me in the back when my back is turned?"

"I don't know, Mark," Cassidy said. "Right now, I'd like to

shoot you in the back or front or anywhere else. If I knew I'd get the Commander position I might try it."

"Well, you're honest, anyway," Mark said. "I guess I know about how you feel.

I should have gotten the Commander position of my unit when I recovered from my wounds. It was taken from me and given to Ted Ames. I felt like ripping Ted's heart out. Is that how you feel about me right now?"

"Just about," Cassidy said.

"Well, I guess I know how you feel, then," Mark said. "I had to work under Ted for two weeks before my transfer came through. He gave me every menial job there was to do. I did everything he asked me to do, not because I liked the guy, because I hated his guts, but because he was the Unit Commander. I respect the title even if I can't respect the man. Do you feel that way about your Unit Commander?"

"I don't know if I could do that or not," Cassidy said.

"Well, you think about it and, after our two-week training session, you can let me know," Mark said. "You may go now. Just remember what I said about your sexual behavior. I won't put up with it."

"I heard you the first time, Sir," Cassidy said, emphasizing the word sir, as she walked out of Mark's office and slammed the door.

Mark was busy looking at the case files the rest of the morning and, at noon, he decided to go to McDonald's. He hoped that Cat might have brought Sherry and he would be able to see them again.

He placed his order and looked around the room while he waited, but there was no sign of Cat. He got his order and found a small table over next to the window. As he ate, he looked out the window to see if he might catch a glimpse of Cat, but he still had no luck.

"Hi, Mark," Jason said and startled Mark.

"Oh. Hi, Jason. I didn't see you come up," Mark said. "Sit down."

"How was your first day?" Jason asked.

"Well, I think I got my point across," Mark said.

"Yeah, I heard you were a hard-ass," Jason said.

"You must have been talking to Dave Hightower," Mark said.

"Yeah, him and others," Jason said. "It sounds like you were pretty rough on them the first day."

"I wanted them to know where I stand," Mark said. "It's better to be honest on the first day and let them know what I expect of them than to let them think I'm a nice pushover and find out later that I'm not."

"I guess you're right there," Jason said. "Did you still want me to transfer to your unit?"

"Whatever you want to do, Jason," Mark said. "I would love to have you, but it's going to be a long time before I get them into shape. I have to be there, but you don't. Not unless you really want to be there with me."

"I want to work with you, Mark, but I'm afraid to take that step right now. Debbie wants to get married soon and I'm just not certain what's gonna happen to you and that unit," Jason said.

"I understand, Jason," Mark said. "As much as I would love to have you in my unit, I can understand your hesitation. You've been too good a friend to me for me to force you into something you're not sure about. Maybe later on, when I've made a real unit out of them, then you can transfer. How about that?"

"Yeah, Mark," Jason said. "That would be great. Well, I better get on back. You know how Ted is. If he caught me talking to you, I'd be on his black list. See you later."

"Yeah, Jason. See you later," Mark said, as he watched Jason walk out of the restaurant. His heart sank a little, though. He had really wanted Jason on his team again.

Maybe he would be later, but right now he had to be satisfied with what he had.

"Well, I guess I have the reputation of being a hard-ass now," Mark chuckled at that. He really hadn't intended to get a reputation like that, but maybe it was best. Now they knew he meant what he had said. He was going to shape that unit into a decent unit or die trying. He shuttered at that. If he wasn't careful, he just might die the next time. So far, God had kept him alive. He might not be so gracious the next time.

"Well, I guess I'd better get on back to the office," Mark thought. "It doesn't look like Cat's coming."

During the rest of the week, Mark spent time getting ready for the two-week training. He rearranged his office to suit himself. He didn't like the way Don had it arranged. He straightened up the files and put them into an easy order so that he could find what he was looking for at a glance. He made a schedule for the remaining team members for their two-week training and left orders for the unit to follow while he was gone. He called Dave Hightower into his office on Friday afternoon.

"Dave, would you mind taking charge while Cassidy and I are in training for two weeks?" Mark asked.

"You want me to be in charge while you're gone?" Dave asked incredulously.

"That's what I said, wasn't it?" Mark asked.

"I thought I didn't hear you right. Yeah, I'd like to be in charge while you're gone," Dave answered.

"OK," Mark said. "Here's what I want you to do while I'm gone. When you're finished, I want you to write a complete report and leave it on my desk. Do you think you can handle it or do I need to get someone else?"

"No, I can handle it," Dave said. "You don't have to get someone else. I just didn't think you liked me. You know because I called you a hard-ass."

"Liking you has nothing to do with why I put you in charge," Mark said. "I put you in charge because I feel that of all the other members, you're the one most likely to be able to handle it. Now will you do as I ask or not?"

"Yeah, I'll do it," Dave said. "I still think you're a hard-ass, too."

Mark chuckled and told Dave he would leave everything on top of his desk. "I'll lock my office door when I leave this afternoon. Here's a key for you to be able to get in on Monday morning. I expect everything to be in order when I get back. If you ever want to be put in charge again, it had better be in order. You can put the key in an envelope and slide it under the door on Friday, since you'll be reporting to the training academy when I come back. I guess I'll see you in four weeks then. Here's my cell phone number. If you have any problems, you can call me on it. Do you have any questions?"

"No," Dave said. "It looks like you made everything pretty clear on these sheets. I hope you and Cassidy have a good training session."

"Thanks," Mark said, then he dismissed Dave and prepared to leave. He hadn't been able to call Cat all week long and he was longing to see her. He decided to stop by the barracks for a few minutes and pick up some clean clothes and go spend the week-end with her. He wanted to go to church with her on Sunday, so he took a suit and a shirt and tie to match. As he was walking from the barracks to his car, he was cornered by Ted Ames.

"Hey, Mark, you old thief you," Ted said. "Why are you trying to steal my SIC, now? Is it because you don't have anyone that would qualify as a decent Second-in-Command?"

"Ted, I don't have any idea what you're talking about," Mark said. "I don't have time to discuss it with you right now, anyway."

"I'm talking about Jason," Ted said. "I know you're trying to get Jason to transfer to your lousy unit. I saw you talking to him the other day."

"For one thing," Mark said. "Jason is a friend of mine. I can talk to him whenever I want to. For another thing Jason doesn't want to transfer to my lousy unit, as you called it. And for another thing, I have team members who are capable of being my SIC. Now get out of my way."

Ted took a swing at Mark and when he did, Mark ducked and

Ted fell to the ground. When Ted got close to him, Mark could smell the awful smell of alcohol.

"Ted, you're drunk," Mark said. "Go on home and try to sober up."

Then Mark continued on to his car. He had just gotten to his car and hung his clothes up inside it when Ted hit him from the back. Mark automatically turned around and swung at Ted. Ted landed on the ground again.

"I'll kill you, Mark Fuller," he said, as he got up and tried to hit Mark again. By this time, a crowd had gathered to watch the fight. A security guard from the barracks came running out and pulled Ted up from the ground.

"What's going on here?" the guard asked.

"I don't know," Mark said. "I was just going to my car and he jumped me."

Some of the bystanders agreed that what Mark had said was what had happened.

"You're drunk and disorderly, Sir," the guard said. "I'm afraid I'm going to have to arrest you." He then put handuffs on Ted and pulled him toward the building.

"I'll get you for this, Mark Fuller," Ted yelled. "Do you hear me. I'll get you for this."

Now Mark's week-end had been ruined. He was in a bad mood and hated to go see Cat like that. The last time he saw her, he was in a bad mood. He wanted to be better this time. Maybe he should just forget about seeing her for now. No, he couldn't do that. He really needed to see her and hold her and kiss her. She could make him feel better. He got into his car and headed toward Cat's cabin.

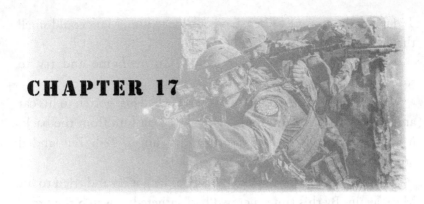

CHAPTER 17

It was almost 6:00 p.m. when Mark arrived at Cat's cabin. He decided to knock on the door first before taking his clothes in. He wanted to make sure that he would be welcome first.

When Cat opened the door and saw him standing there, all doubt as to his welcome was removed. "Oh, Mark," Cat cried. "I'm so glad to see you. I've waited all week for your call, but no call came. I was afraid you were mad at me. I thought maybe you blamed me for what happened at Thanksgiving."

"Come here and kiss me, you little fool," Mark said, as he put his arms around her and passionately kissed her.

"Come on in out of the cold," Cat said, as she pulled Mark into the warmth of the cabin and started to close the door.

"I came to stay for the week-end, if I'm welcome," Mark said. "I left my things in the car until I asked."

"Of course you can stay," Cat said. "Get your things and take them up to your room."

Mark went back out and got his things and carried them to the top of the stairs. He started to walk to his room, but stopped in front of Cat's room. It was just about a month and a half until their wedding. Why wouldn't she let him stay in her room with her? Then he knew why and went on into his room and hung his clothes in the closet.

When he came back downstairs, Cat asked if he was hungry.

"I'm always hungry for you," Mark said, as he grabbed her and pulled her to him.

He gave her another passionate kiss, then Cat pushed him away and said, "I mean do you want something to eat? I have some vegetable beef soup in the refrigerator."

"Yes, I would love some of your vegetable beef soup," he said.

"Come sit down while I warm it up," Cat said, as she led the way to the kitchen.

While they were eating, Cat asked, "How did your first week as Unit Commander go?"

"It went about like I expected," Mark said. "I gave them my talk on Monday. I did what you told me not to do. They resented it. They called me a hard-ass."

Cat laughed at that. "I guess you were a hard-ass," she said.

"Yes, I guess you could call it that," Mark answered. "I wanted them to know right off that I wasn't a pushover. I'm not gonna tolerate insubordination. Several of them wanted to transfer, but no one wanted them, so they had to stay.

"Cassidy, you remember Cassidy don't you?"

"Yes, of course I remember Cassidy," Cat said, becoming a little tearful.

"Yeah, I thought you would," Mark said, not really wanting to dredge up some sad memories.

"What do you mean by that?" Cat asked.

"Nothing, just forget I said anything," Mark said. He decided he had better be careful what he said around Cat from then on. He didn't know if Cat had forgotten about the lawsuit and Cassidy giving Jim so much trouble or what happened when they tried to rescue Cassidy and Don, but he didn't want to bring it back up if she had forgotten it, especially since she was having so much trouble letting go of Jim now.

"Anyway, Cassidy is really pissed," Mark continued.

"What about?" Cat asked.

"She thought she would get the Commander position when Don

retired. She said he had already promised it to her. I told her she was going to have to take the two-week training at the academy and she didn't like that either. She said she had already had it. I told her this is something new and I think that might have appeased her some. She still thinks she should at least be my Second-in-Command."

"Have you decided who that will be yet?" Cat asked.

"No, not really," Mark answered. "I was hoping Jason would transfer, but it looks like that isn't going to happen. Right now, I've made Dave Hightower Acting Commander while I'm gone for the two-week training."

"I'd like to see that training," Cat said. "Would it be possible for me to watch?"

"I don't see why not," Mark said. "I'll check on it and let you know. You're still a unit member. I don't think you have even been taken off the list. You can probably even take the training if you want to."

"No, I don't want to take the training," Cat said. "I just want to watch you."

That night, Cat had a hard time going to sleep. She was keenly aware that Mark was in the bedroom just across the hall. She longed to be with him, but she knew it was best the way it was. She needed the protetion that the hallway between them gave her. She knew if she gave in one time, that would be the end of her resolve to make Mark wait until after their wedding. She tossed and turned and wondered if he was having the same problem sleeping that she was having. Finally, just before dawn, she fell into an exhausted sleep, but awakened as soon as the sun peeped through the crack in her blinds.

When she went downstairs, Mark was already sitting at the kitchen table drinking a cup of coffee.

"Good morning, beautiful," he said. "I already made coffee. I hope that was OK with you."

"Yes, it's fine," Cat said, as she poured a cup and added sugar and creamer. "Did you sleep well?" she asked, hoping that he would say no.

"Yes, thank you," he said instead. "I slept like a log. Thank you for letting me stay here. It's hard to sleep at the barracks. The bed is very uncomfortable."

"You're welcome," she answered, a little disappointed in his answer. "You're welcome to come here anytime you want to.'"

Cat fixed breakfast and, after they were finished eating, she asked, "Did you have something you wanted to do today?"

"Nothing in particular," Mark answered. "I just wanted to be with you. I brought clothes to wear to church tomorrow. I thought, since I was going to church with you, I might as well come and spend the night."

"Yes, that was a good idea," Cat answered. "I'm sure Sherry will want to see you while you're here," Cat said. "Would it bother you to spend some time with her? I know she made you nervous at Thanksgiving."

"She didn't make me nervous, Cat," Mark said with a frown on his face. "It's that egotistical brother-in-law of yours. I'm sorry, but he and I do not get along. He was just baiting me and I took the bait. I'm sorry I ruined your Thanksgiving. To answer your question, yes, I would love to spend some time with Sherry. She always makes me feel better. Even when I'm deep in depression, she lets in the sunshine. Sure, call and see if she wants to come over."

"Carol," Cat said when she answered the phone. "Mark's here. He said he'd like to see Sherry. Can you bring her over for a while?"

"Are you sure he wants to see her?" Carol asked. "I thought she got on his nerves at Thanksgiving."

"It wasn't her. It was Tyler, I guess they've already gone, haven't they?" Cat asked.

"Yes, they left early this morning," Carol answered.

"Anyway, Mark wants to see Sherry. Are you busy? If you are, we can come over there."

"That's OK," Carol said. "I'll bring her over. We won't stay long. I don't want her to make him nervous."

Shortly, there was a knock on the front door and Sherry burst into the room followed by Carol and Skip.

"Mista Mok," Sherry shouted and ran over to the sofa where Mark was sitting and climbed up into his lap and kissed him.

"Hi, Sherry Rene," Mark said. "How have you been? Hi, Carol, Skip."

"I ben lonely," Sherry said. "I miss you Mista Mok. When you comin home?"

"Well, it might be a while before I come home to stay, but I may be able to come on the week-end again. Would you like that?"

"Yes, Mista Mok. I would welly wik dat," Sherry said, as she gave him a big hug.

"I brought you something, Sherry Rene," Mark said. "It's upstairs in my case. Hop down and I'll go get it."

"Oh, goody," Sherry said, as Mark put her on the floor and headed for the stairs. When he came back downstairs, he had a neat children's book. "Look at this, Sherry Rene," he said, showing it to her. "See. It talks."

"Oh, Mista Mok. I wuv it," she said hugging it to her heart.

"Mark, you're going to spoil her," Carol said. "She'll think you're supposed to bring her something every time you come, now."

"That's OK," Mark answered. "Maybe I will."

"You'll make her wish you were her Daddy instead of me," Skip said, as he gave Mark a dirty look.

"I think she knows who her Daddy is," Mark said. "Don't you, Sherry Rene?"

"Yes, I wuv my Daddy," Sherry said, as she went over to Skip and gave him a big hug.

As Carol and Skip left, Carol asked, "Do you want us to pick you up in the morning?"

"No," Mark answered before Cat could say anything. "Cat and I will go in my car. I'll probably have to leave right after we eat. She can ride home with you."

The rest of the day went by quickly and soon it was bedtime

again. Cat dreaded another sleepless night. She kissed Mark and went into her bedroom to get ready for bed. She saw the light in the hallway go out and assumed that Mark had gone into his bedroom.

Soon, there was a soft tap on her door. "Cat, are you asleep?" Mark asked. Cat was silent at first and then Mark asked again, "Cat, may I come in?"

She wanted so badly to say yes, but she knew she should say no. Before she could say anything, though, Mark opened the door a little and squeezed through it.

"Cat, I brought you something, too," he said, as he sat down on the bed next to her. He pulled it out of his pocket and put it into her hand. It was a beautiful, delicate, gold necklace like the one he had bought for Sherry to give to Carol.

"It's beautiful, Mark," Cat said, as she turned on the bedside lamp so she could see it.

"Why?" she asked. "What's the occasion?"

"It's a Just Because gift," he said. "Just because I love you."

"Oh, Mark," she said, as she hugged him. "I love you, too."

Then he bent over and kissed her passionately. He kissed her again and again until she couldn't stand the longing anymore.

"Mark, please," she said. "This isn't right. I'm finding it hard to resist you. Please stop."

"Why, Cat?" Mark asked, as he gasped for breath. "Why don't you just give in? It's only a little over a month."

"Because I can't, Mark," she said. "Not like this. Please stop."

"OK, Cat," Mark said, as he pulled himself away from her. "If I have to, I guess I'll just wait. I don't want to, but if you say so, I guess I'll have to wait."

Then he went over to his bedroom and tried unsuccessfully to go to sleep. "Maybe this was a bad idea after all," he thought. It was pure torture to be so close to her and not be able to make her completely his. "Soon," he told himself. "If I can hold out that long, the wait will be over soon."

The next morning when Cat came downstairs, Mark was again

sitting at the table drinking a cup of coffee. He was wearing a suit with a matching shirt and tie. He had already shaved and he smelled of after shave or cologne, Cat wasn't sure which.

"You're up early," Cat said, as she poured a cup of coffee and doctored it up. "Did you sleep well last night?"

"No, you know I didn't," Mark said angrily. "I think you're doing that on purpose," he said grumpily.

"Doing what?" Cat asked.

"You know what," Mark said. "I shouldn't have come. I would have been better off at the barracks. At least I wouldn't have to have you so close, but so far away."

"Mark, I..." Cat started to say something, but thought better of it.

She sat down at the table next to Mark and started to put her hand on his, but he pulled it away. "No, Cat. Don't touch me right now," he said, as he got up and walked to the den with his cup of coffee.

She felt that he was trying to get back at her for last night, so she just shrugged her shoulders and started breakfast. When she got it ready, she called Mark to the table.

"I'm not hungry, Cat," he said.

"Mark, you're acting like a spoiled little boy," Cat said. "Come eat breakfast."

"I'm sorry, Cat, but I'm not hungry right now," he said. "What time do we leave for church?"

"Do you want to go for Sunday School and church or just church?" she asked.

"Just church," he answered. "I don't think I can handle both this morning."

"We won't have to leave until 10:30 then," she said.

Mark didn't answer her, so she walked into the den. Mark was lying on the sofa shaking. His face was flushed and when she put her hand to his forehead, it almost burned her hand.

"Mark, you have a fever," she said. "Why didn't you tell me you were sick?"

He didn't answer her, so she went to the kitchen and got a glass of water and a couple of aspirin. She took his temperature and it was 103 degrees.

"Here, take these aspirins," she said, as she handed him the tablets and the glass of water. After about an hour, she felt of his forehead again and it felt cool. She took his temperature again and it was normal.

"How do you feel now, Mark?" she asked.

"I feel better, now," he answered. "I don't know what happened," he said. "I was OK one minute and then, boom, I felt awful. Is it time to go, yet?"

"I don't think you need to go to church this morning," Cat said.

"I'm OK now, Cat," he said. "Come on, let's go."

"Are you sure you feel like going to church?" she asked.

"Yes," he said, as he tried to get up. He almost fell back down on the sofa, but he tried again and was successful that time.

"I just had a little bug. It's gone now. Come on, let's go," he said, as he headed toward the door.

Cat grabbed her coat out of the closet and her Bible that was lying on the table and ran after Mark. He was already in the car and had the engine running by the time she locked the front door and got into the car.

"Mark, I really don't...," Cat started, but Mark interrupted her.

"Cat, don't say it," he said. "I'm going to church today. I'm going back to the barracks after we eat and I'm starting my two-week training tomorrow. I'm OK. I have these spells every now and then. They last for about an hour and then they're gone. I picked up something on one of my assignments in Asia. It only lasts for a short period of time. I'm OK."

Then he drove out of the driveway and toward the church. The church was almost full, but they saw that Carol had saved them seats next to them. When Cat and Mark sat down, Carol knew something was wrong by the worried look on Cat's face.

"What's wrong?" she whispered to Cat.

"I'll tell you later," Cat said.

The services had started and she didn't want to get into it during the service. Carol could hardly wait until after the service to find out what was going on. Mark didn't even want Sherry to sit in his lap, which was very unusual.

After the service, Mark didn't wait for Cat. He hurried to the car and leaned his head back on the headrest.

"What's wrong with Mark?" Carol asked.

"I don't know," Cat said. "He was acting really strange and when I took his temperature, it was 103 degrees. I gave him a couple of aspirins and his fever went down and he said he felt better. He insisted that we come to church, though."

"Maybe he has some kind of bug," Carol said.

"That's what he said," Cat answered. "I don't know, though. He was really acting strange. He wouldn't eat and didn't want me to touch him."

"Yeah, and he didn't want Sherry in his lap," Carol said. "That really hurt her feelings."

"By the way, where is Sherry, anyway?" Carol asked.

They looked over at Mark's car and there she was trying to get into Mark's car.

"Mista Mok," she said. "Let me give you kiss. Open da doa so I can gib you kiss."

"No, Sherry. Mr. Mark is sick. You can't kiss him today. Save your kisses for the next time, OK?" he said.

"But Mista Mok," she said. "I mak you feel betta."

"Not this time, Sherry," he said. Then he said again, "Save your kisses for next time. I have to go, now. Cat, will you come on. I need to go."

"I better go, Carol," Cat said, as she hurried to Mark's car. "I'll talk to you later."

"Do you want to go with me or do you want to go ahead and go to the restaurant with them?" Mark asked.

"I want to go with you," she said.

So he drove back to Cat's cabin. "Cat, I need to lie down for a while before I go back to the barracks," Mark said.

She helped him out of the car and he leaned on her, as she helped him into the cabin and over to the sofa. He sat down on the sofa and she helped him remove his tie and put his feet up. He lay back on the pillow that he always lay on and she took his shoes off and covered him with a blanket.

She got another glass of water from the kitchen and a couple of aspirins and walked back to the sofa. Mark was asleep when she came back. She felt of his forehead and it was hot again. She wondered if she should waken him so he could take the aspirins or just let him sleep and give them to him when he was awake. She decided to let him sleep.

Cat sat down in a chair in front of the sofa and watched Mark and worried. His sleep was fitful. Sometimes his legs would jerk and he would toss from side to side. He seemed to be having a nightmare. She thought about waking him from his tortured thoughts, but she didn't know what was best, to let him sleep or awaken him from his terrible nightmare. She finally decided it was best to awaken him.

"Mark," she called softly and touched his arm. He awoke with a start. He looked at Cat with glazed eyes. "Where am I?" he asked.

"You're safe, Mark," Cat said. "You're in my cabin."

Then he looked around, as if he was lost and didn't seem to recognize anything. He looked down at his suit and at Cat with a questioning look.

"How did I get here?" he asked.

"You drove here," she answered.

"No," he said. "I can't drive."

Then he looked at Cat again, as if he didn't even know who she was. He shook his head and tried to stand up.

"Don't try to get up Mark," Cat said, as she gently pushed him back onto the sofa.

He didn't resist, as she pushed him, but his eyes became wide with terror. He looked at Cat again, but didn't say anything. Then he closed his eyes for a few minutes. When he opened them again, the terror was gone and he looked at Cat with a look of recognition. He put his hand to his head and shook his head a few times, as if to clear his eyesight. He closed his eyes and opened them again. Then he asked, "What happened?"

"You started running a fever and you started acting really strange," Cat answered.

Then he was silent for a few minutes. "May I have a drink?" he asked, as he pointed to the glass of water Cat had placed on the coffee table beside the two aspirins.

"Sure," she said, as she handed him the water. "Would you like these aspirins?"

"Yeah," he said and took them out of her hand and swallowed them with a drink of the water.

"Can I stay here tonight?" he asked.

"Of course you can," Cat answered. She wondered about his gear that he would need for his training, but she would wait and ask him about that later. Then Mark lay back down on the pillow and closed his eyes for a few minutes. After a while, he raised up and said, "Will you help me get out of this jacket?"

"Sure," she said, as she helped him take it off.

"Do you feel better now?" she asked.

"A little," he said, as he unbuttoned the top two buttons of his shirt. Then he lay back down and closed his eyes again. Cat didn't know if he was asleep or just had his eyes closed, so she sat there silently and just watched him. Her heart went out to him. He was just getting over a devasting injury and now this. She didn't even know what this was. She knew it had really knocked him for a loop, but what was it? Would this ever happen to him again? Had it ever happened before? He said it happens to him every now and then, but why? There were a lot of questions she wanted to ask him, but she knew she couldn't ask him right now. Then the phone rang. He immediately jerked awake and sat up. "It's just the phone, Mark," Cat said, as she went to answer it.

"Cat, how is Mark?" Carol asked.

"He's a little better, but he's really had a bad time of it," Cat said, as quietly as she could.

"What happened?" Carol asked.

"I don't know, Carol. Let me call you back after awhile, OK?" Cat said, and she hung up the phone. Then she went back and sat down in the chair again.

"Was that Carol?" Mark asked.

"Yes, it was," Cat said.

"I guess she wanted to know what happened to me?" he said matter-of-factly.

"She was worried about you," Cat said.

"I'm glad," he said. Then he closed his eyes again.

After a few more minutes, Mark said, without opening his eyes, "Cat, I'm sorry."   "What are you sorry about?" Cat asked.

"Ruining your day," he said.

"You couldn't help it that you got sick," Cat said.

"I shouldn't have come," he said.

"I'm glad you were here so I could take care of you," she said.

"You don't mind taking care of me, then?" he asked.

"No, I don't mind taking care of you. That's what I've been doing for the last few months," she said. Then he sighed and went back to sleep.

About 6:00 p.m., Cat started getting hungry, so she went into the kitchen to fix something to eat. When she opened the refrigerator, she saw that there was still quiet a bit of the vegetable beef soup left, so she took it out and put it on the stove to warm up.

Soon, Mark woke up and said, "I think I smell soup. Am I right?"

"Yes, you are," Cat answered. Would you like some?"

"Yes, I would. Will you help me to the table?" he asked.

She went into the den and helped Mark stand up and then she put her arm around his waist and helped him to the table.

"Do you feel better now?" she asked.

"Lots better," he said.

She put the soup into bowls and set the bowls on the table. After a short prayer of thanksgiving, they began to eat the soup.

"Have you ever had that before?" Cat asked.

"You mean the soup?" Mark asked.

"No, you know I didn't mean the soup," Cat said. "I mean the bug or whatever it was."

"Yes, I've had it before," Mark said. "I don't want to talk about it, though. It isn't contagious. It's just something I have to live with. I got it when I was in the jungle once. Are you afraid to marry me now?" he asked.

"No, I'm not afraid to marry you," Cat said.

"If you are, just say so and I'll get out of your life forever," he said.

"No, I don't want you to be out of my life," Cat said, as she put her hand on his. He didn't pull it away this time. Instead, he took it and squeezed it.

"Cat, there are a lot of things in my life that you don't know about," he said. "A lot of things I don't want you to know about. If you want to get out of this engagement, I'll understand. I love you more than anything else in this whole world, but I'm willing to give you up if you don't think you can accept me the way I am. I may not be able to change. Not even for you."

"Oh, Mark," she said and began to cry. "I love you and I'll take you any way you are. Maybe I can help you change, if you don't like the way you are. Just don't shut me out. Let me help you." Mark gave a deep sigh and got up and went and lay back down on the sofa. He was finished with that conversation.

CHAPTER 18

"**C**at, I'm going up to my room now," Mark said after he had lain on the sofa for a while. "Will you get me up about 5:00 a.m.? I need to go to the barracks and get my gear. I have to be at the training academy by 8:00 a.m. I just can't make it there and back tonight."

"Sure, I'll get you up," she said.

The next morning, Cat got up at 5:00 a.m. and woke Mark up. She quickly dressed and fixed a quick breakfast and made a pot of coffee while Mark was dressing. When he came down the stairs, she asked, "Mark, would you like for me to drive you?" She expected him to decline her offer, but instead, he said, "That would be nice. Thanks."

After they hurriedly ate breakfast, Cat drove them to the barracks, where Mark assembled his clothes and his gear and loaded it into the trunk of Cat's car.

"Do you know how to get to the academy?" Mark asked.

"I'm not sure," Cat said. So Mark gave her the directions and lay his head back on the headrest and slept while Cat drove to the academy.

At the academy, Cat helped Mark unload his gear and check in. While they were waiting for Mark's room assignment, Cassidy walked up, carrying her gear.

"Well, look who's here," she said when she saw Cat. "Are you taking the training, too?"

"No, I just came to watch," Cat answered.

"I heard that you and Mark were engaged," Cassidy continued. "I guess you came to make sure no other woman carried him off, huh?"

"No, I didn't," Cat said, a little peeved at Cassidy's insinuation. "I trust Mark. I don't think he would be unfaithful to me."

"Unlike someone else, huh?" Cassidy said, and Mark gave her a nasty look and pulled her over to his side. "Did you bring all of your gear?" he asked her, as he headed her out of Cat's hearing range. He gave her another hard look and said, "Don't," under his breath. "I don't want you to even hint at the attraction Jim had for you. She's having a hard time getting over Jim's death this year and I don't want you to make it any harder on her. Do you understand me?"

"Oh, so that's a no-no," Cassidy said in a low voice. "I'm glad you told me. I'll have to watch that," she said, sarcastically. "Yes. I understand you quite well. She doesn't want me to even mention how Jim almost fell for me, does she?"

"Shut up, Cassidy," Mark said through clenched teeth. "If you want to remain where you are, you'll forget that whole incident."

"You don't threaten me," Cassidy said, but she shut up when Mark grabbed her wrist and said, "I said shut up. Cat has tried to forget all about the fixation Jim had on you and how you tried to ruin him. I don't want her to be reminded of it. She's having a hard enough time getting over his death this year as it is. She doesn't want to remember that Jim ever even looked at another woman after he married her, especially a woman like you."

"What's that supposed to mean?" Cassidy asked.

"You know what I mean," Mark said. "Cat thinks Jim was a saint and I intend to let her continue thinking that way. If you even say one bad word to her about Jim, I'll make your life a living hell. Do you understand?"

"My life already is a living hell," Cassidy said.

"I can make it even worse," Mark said.

"Oh, so you are threatening me," Cassidy said.

"Call it what you like, but if you say one bad word to Cat about

Jim, believe me, you'll regret it," Mark said. "I don't want you to tell her that we ever dated, either. That was a long time ago. I was having my own problems then and you were available. It didn't mean anything, so I prefer that you don't even say anything about it. If you do as I say, I might even make you my SIC."

"It's not like Jim and I had an affair," Cassidy said. "You made sure of that. After he didn't transfer me to his unit like he said he would, I felt I had to bring charges against him."

"I can't understand how anyone married to Cat could ever be infatuated with you, anyway," Mark said.

"Maybe he saw something in me that you don't see," Cassidy said.

"Maybe so," Mark said. "I sure can't see it now."

"You're not anything like Jim, either," Cassidy said.

"Cat has pushed out of her memory the incident about the fixation Jim had on you before you brought the charges against him and I don't want her to ever have to think about it again," Mark said angrily.

"You remember that I dropped the charges and apologized to him and Cat after they rescued Don and me, don't you? I'm still grateful to Cat for that, so I wouldn't intentionally want to hurt her by bringing it up," Cassidy said angrily.

"Yes, I remember. I still don't want you to say anything bad about Jim to Cat. I don't think she could handle it right now. I would really appreciate your trying to not hurt her," Mark said.

Cat was standing over to the side where Mark had left her when he had pulled Cassidy over to the other side of the room. She wondered what they were talking about. It looked as if they were arguing about something. Then, when Mark grabbed Cassidy's wrist, it looked like he had intentionally done it to hurt her. "Why did Mark do that?" Cat wondered. She was just about to walk over and find out, when the receptionist said their rooms were ready and they could take their gear to their rooms.

"Come on, Cat," Mark said as he took her arm and led her to his room. "There probably won't be much going on the first day. You can either stay and watch or go back home and watch when you come back to pick me up."

"I'll just stay and watch today," she said. "I want to make sure you're OK now. Since I'm already here, I might as well stay."

"Suit yourself," Mark said, as he opened the door to his room. There were two beds in the room and Cat wondered if the receptionist had thought that she had planned on staying. It really didn't matter, anyway. She was going back home tonight. She just wanted to make sure that Mark was all right before she left.

Mark threw his gear into the closet and headed back out the door. Cat followed him out. He went directly to the registration desk without saying another word to Cat. He just assumed that she was following him. Mark went up to the registration desk and said, "I'm Mark Fuller, Unit Commander."

"Yes, here you are," the attendant said, pointing to Mark's name on his list. "May I see your ID? I see you're the replacement for Don Gardner's Unit. Is this Cassidy Love?"

"No, this is Catherine Ryan," Mark said. "Cassidy will be here in a few minutes."

"Catherine Ryan," the attendant said. "Didn't you train at the academy several years ago when we were in the FSC Building? I remember you because you made such high scores. Aren't you Jim Ryan's widow? I'm sorry about your husband."

Cat murmured a soft thank you and then the attendant continued. "Are you here for training, too?"

Before she could answer, Mark said, "No, she's just here to observe."

"Oh, I see," the attendant said. "You're welcome to observe, Mrs. Ryan. From where would you like to watch?"

"Will you hurry up. There are others waiting," Mark said, getting agitated.

"Sure," the attendant said. "Commander, you go over there

against that wall where the others are. The instructor will be here
shortly. Mrs. Ryan, will you wait here for a few minutes?"

Mark went on over to the spot that the attendant had pointed
out, but he kept looking back to see where Cat was.

"This was a mistake," Cat thought. "I should have just let Mark
out and gone on home. I really don't think he wanted me to stay
here."

"Now, Mrs. Ryan," the attendant said, as he called someone to
take his place at the registration desk. "Come with me, Mrs. Ryan.
I'll take you to a nice spot where you can see everything that's going
on. We have a nice observation tower for visitors who have just come
to observe."

"Thank you," Cat said. "I'm sorry. I didn't catch your name."

"I apologize for not introducing myself. My name's Darin. Darin
Rowe. Is Commander Fuller always so hyper?" he asked.

"Not really," Cat said. "He just had a bad week-end. He caught
some sort of bug. It really did a number on him."

"Oh, I'm sorry to hear that," Darin said. "I hope it doesn't
keep him from being able to do the training. This is really intense
training. It's really even harder than it was when you were here. How
long ago did you say you were here?"

"Five years. It's been five years," Cat said thoughtfully.

"Well, I wish you were taking the training again," Darin said.
"I'd love to see how you do at it now."

"Thanks, Darin, but I'm not in the unit any longer," Cat said.
"Not since Jim died."

"Oh, I'm really sorry about your husband," Darin said again. "I
didn't mean to cause you any grief."

"That's OK, Darin," Cat said. "It was a long time ago."

"You know, I was wondering," Darin said. "Didn't Commander
Fuller belong to your husband's unit?"

"Yes, he did," Cat answered.

"I just wondered why he wasn't Commander of that unit. You

don't have to answer if it's none of my business. I just wondered," Darin asked.

"It's a long story, Darin. I don't want to go into it right now," Cat said.

"OK," Darin said. "Here we are. See, you can see everything from here. There's the field where the shooting range is. There's the simulated area to test reaction time. Over there is the obstacle course. Well, you get the idea."

"Yes, thank you," Cat said.

"If you need anything, you can call me on this phone here. Just push this button and it'll ring me. All you have to do is tell me what you want and I'll get it for you."

"Thank you, again, Darin. I'll be all right," Cat said.

"We'll break for lunch at noon. You can come back to the registration desk and I'll take you to the lunch room. That's where Commander Fuller should be."

"Thanks, again, Darin," Cat said, as she sat down and got comfortable and picked up a pair of binoculars. She finally picked out Mark, and Cassidy was right next to him. Mark still looked like he was mad about something. I wish I could hear what he's saying to Cassidy," Cat thought. "He really seems to be chewing her out about something."

Mark didn't do very well during the morning training. Cat figured it must have been because of his weakened state. She hoped he would do better after lunch. She hurried down to the registration desk, where Darin told her to meet him. He was there waiting for her.

"Well, were you able to see everything?" Darin asked.

"Yes, thank you, Darin," Cat said. "As a matter of fact, I think I saw too much. Mark didn't do too well. I'm sure it's because of the bug he had, though. I hope he does better this afternoon."

"I'm sure he will," Darin said. "Here we are. There's Commander Fuller over there. I think he must be looking for you. I'll leave you two alone now. Come back to the desk after lunch and I'll take you back to the tower."

"OK. Thanks, Darin," Cat said.

"Where have you been?" Mark asked gruffly, when he walked up to Cat.

"I was in the observation tower," Cat said.

"I had no idea where you went," Mark said. "That guy just told me to go over to the wall and then he left with you. Why didn't you tell me where you were going? I was worried about you all morning. I couldn't even concentrate on what I was doing. I made a mess of everything."

"I'm sorry, Mark," Cat apologized. "I didn't think to tell you where I was going. Darin just told me to follow him and I did. Are you OK?"

"No, I'm not OK. I still feel dizzy. I wish I had canceled my training and done it another time," Mark answered.

"Can you cancel it now?" Cat asked.

"No," Mark answered. "Come on. Let's get you something to eat."

Mark led Cat to the line and showed her where to get a plate and silverware. He also got a plate and fork for himself, but hardly put anything on his plate.

Then he led her to a table and set his plate down. "I'll go get us something to drink. What would you like ?" he asked.

"If they have it, I'd like a Diet Coke," Cat said.

When he came back, he set her drink down and sat down across the table from her. Soon, Cassidy came over and joined them. "Do you mind if I eat with you?" she asked.

Cat said, "No, I don't mind," but Mark frowned at her and shook his head.

"Oh, I see someone I want to talk to," Cassidy said and she picked up her plate and left.

"That was rude, Mark,"Cat said.

Mark didn't say anything. He just shrugged his shoulders and took a drink of his Coke.

"Mark, is it bothering you that I'm here?" Cat asked. "If it is, I'll leave and come back on Friday to get you."

"I don't really care right now, Cat," he said. "Do what you want to do. Maybe I'll feel better this afternoon. Why don't you stay?"

So Cat stayed to see how Mark did that afternoon. As he had said, he did a lot better. "I guess he was worried about me," Cat thought. "I guess that's why he did so poorly this morning."

The training ended at 4:00 p.m. and Cat went back to the registration desk. She hoped that Mark would look for her there. Sure enough, she had just arrived there when she saw him heading toward her.

"Come on, Cat," he said. "Let's go to my room." When they got to Mark's room, he turned on the TV. "They said there's a storm coming. I want to see what the weather forecaster has to say."

Sure enough, the forecaster predicted an early snowstorm. There would be from one to three inches of snow in some places. This was unusual for this early, but the weather had been unusual all year, so the forecaster said that everyone needed to heed the warning. It was coming.

"Cat, you can't go home tonight," Mark said. "You might get caught in that storm."

"If I leave right now, maybe I'll beat it," Cat said.

"No. I won't let you go tonight," Mark said. "It's too risky."

"I can make it home before it hits, Mark," she said. "I don't have any clothes and I can't stay here in this room with you."

"Yes, you can," Mark said. "You don't need any clothes, either. Just wear the same clothes you have on. You're not leaving tonight."

So Cat resigned herself to stay and soon it started snowing. Great big, fluffy flakes were falling. It wasn't long before the streets were covered with snow and soon became impassable.

"Well, it looks like you'll be staying tonight," Mark said, as he pulled her to him and began kissing her.

"Mark, stop," Cat said. "If I stay, you'll have to behave."

"I am behaving," he said, as he kissed her again. Then he lay down on the bed and turned on the TV again. There were already numerous wrecks, since everyone was trying to get home at the same time.

"Look at that mess," Mark said. "That's what you would have been in, if you had gone on home."

"OK, Mark," Cat said. "You were right. I needed to stay."

About 6:00 p.m., Mark said. "They serve dinner at 6:00. Come on, let's go get something to eat. I'm hungry."

They got their food and sat down at a nearby table. They had just finished their blessing on the food, when Cassidy walked up with her tray. "May I sit with you two?" she asked.

Cat started to say OK, but she hesitated to see what Mark would say.

"Sure, sit down," Mark said.

"How did you like the new gear?" Cassidy asked Mark.

"It's great isn't it?" Mark answered. "It looks like it would be uncomfortable, but it isn't. I really like it. How about you?"

"Yes, I like it, too," Cassidy said.

"I'll have to get some for our unit when we get back home," Mark said. "Cat, I'd like for you to try it on tomorrow to see how you like it."

"No, Mark," Cat said. "I don't want to try it on. I'm just here to watch, not to participate."

"I just thought you might like to try it on just to see how it feels," Mark said.

"No, Mark. I said I don't want to try it on. Just leave me alone, OK?" Cat said frowning. "If Jim had had gear like that, he might still be alive," she thought.

"OK, Cat, I won't ask you again," Mark said, a little peeved at Cat's refusal to even try the gear on.

"Cat, it looks like you'll be staying tonight," Cassidy said.

"Would you like to borrow some of my clothes for tomorrow. I brought some extra things."

"That would really be nice of you. Yes, I would appreciate it," Cat answered.

After they finished dinner, Mark went to his room and Cat and Cassidy went to her room. Before he left, Mark briefly put a finger to his lips and gave Cassidy a look that she knew meant "Keep your mouth shut."

Cat picked out some of Cassidy's clothes and tried them on. They fit quite well, since she and Cassidy were just about the same size.

"I guess you didn't know it, but I really had a crush on Mark at one time," Cassidy said.

"No, I didn't," Cat said.

"Yeah," Cassidy said. "We had a couple of dates, but I knew I didn't have a chance with him. He was too hung up on someone else."

"Oh, I'm sorry," Cat said. She didn't know what else to say.

"I think the one he was hung up on was already hung up on someone else, because he never got anywhere with her. He was still pining for her the last time I saw him. I hadn't seen him for a while until your unit came to rescue Don and me. He still seemed to be pining for that someone he couldn't have."

"Is there some reason you're telling me this, Cassidy?" Cat asked.

"Yeah, there is," Cassidy said. "I just thought you ought to know."

"Do you know who this person was?" Cat asked.

"Yeah, I think I know," Cassidy answered.

"You're not saying, though?" Cat asked.

"No, I think you'll find out if you don't already know," Cassidy said. "Let me give you a little advice, though. When I knew him years ago, Mark was a very faithful guy. I found out that when he loves someone, he loves that person completely, and would do anything for that person, no matter what it is. He might even die for that person and would do anything to keep that person happy. I really envy that person. Oh, to be loved like that. Mark is a nice guy most of the time, but sometimes he can be cruel. Just don't ever cross him. He can be a hard-ass at times. You'll see what I mean. I learned that the hard way when he became commander of my unit. I don't know if I even still like him at all now. He has really become a hard-ass."

"Thanks for the clothes, Cassidy," Cat said, as she headed for the door. "I'll send them back by Mark when we get home."

At the door, Cat turned and looked at Cassidy. "Thanks for the advice, too. I'll try not to cross him." Then she went back to Mark's room. When she got there, he was lying on the bed watching TV.

"Is it still snowing?" Mark asked.

"Yes, it is," Cat answered, as she brushed snow off her shoulders. "It's also colder than the dickens."

"Aren't you glad I talked you into staying?" Mark asked. "You wouldn't have made it halfway home before it started."

Then Cat turned, pulled the curtain back and looked out the window. Mark could tell by the look on Cat's face that Cassidy must have said something to her. As Cat stood at the window watching it snow, Mark turned in her direction and ordered her to come there. "Come here, Cat," he said.

"What did you say?" Cat asked angrily, testing what Cassidy had just told her.

"I said come here, Cat," Mark said with an authoritative tone.

"Look here, Mark Fuller," Cat said angrily. "I'm not one of your team members that you can order around. If you want me, you can politely ask me to come there. You don't order me to come there." Cat was determined to let Mark know that he wasn't going to treat her like he had done his team members.

"OK," Mark said sheepishly. "Cat, will you please come here?"

"No, I will not," she answered.

"What is your problem?" Mark bristled.

"I told you," Cat said. "I'm not one of your team members. You don't order me around."

"Did Cassidy say something to you to make you act like that? I'll get her if she did. What did she say to you?" Mark asked.

"What do you think she said?" Cat didn't know what Mark was referring to, but she figured that if she acted like she knew what he meant, he would reveal what he didn't want her to know.

"I just wondered what she said to you. It doesn't really matter. I just wondered what she said," Mark answered, assured that Cassidy must not have said anything bad about Jim or Cat would have acted differently.

That didn't work out the way Cat had expected. Mark hadn't revealed anything to Cat. She still didn't know what Mark was afraid Cassidy would tell her. "What do you think she said?" Cat asked again, hoping that Mark would reveal what he meant.

"Forget it. You don't need to know what I thought she said. Just forget I even asked," Mark answered, relieved that Cassidy didn't say anything.

Now Cat was very curious. Didn't Mark know that not telling her would just make her even more curious as to what he was talking about. What was so bad that he had tried to keep it from her? Cassidy had said that Mark had been in love with someone else. Who was this person that he was so much in love with? Is the identity of that person what Mark wants kept a secret? Cat thought that Mark was in love with her. At least he said he was. Of course, Cassidy could be just trying to cause trouble between her and Mark. Maybe that was what Mark was afraid of.

"Come here, Cat, please," Mark said, as he motioned for her to come sit on the bed next to him. "I apologize, Cat," he said. "I said please. Will you please come here, Cat?"

"Since you asked so nicely, I'll come over, but don't get any ideas," Cat said, as she walked slowly over to the bed. When she was within his reach, Mark put his hands on her hips and pulled her down to him and began kissing her passionately.

"Mark, stop," she said. "This is not the time for that."

Mark took a deep breath and sighed. Then he let her go. Cat stood up and walked back across the room. "This isn't going to work, Mark," she said. "It's too much of a temptation for you."

"What are you going to do?" he said. "You can't go home in a snowstorm. You'll just have to stay here tonight. Please come back over here."

She knew that he was right. She couldn't go out after dark in a snowstorm. She didn't even want to drive during daylight when it was snowing. So she gave in and walked slowly back over to the bed.

"Come on, Cat," Mark said. "Lie down here with me and watch TV."

She decided that being in the room here with Mark wasn't a whole lot different from being in her cabin with him, so she propped up a couple of pillows and leaned up on them next to Mark.

He put his arm around her shoulders and pulled her up close to him. It really felt good to be so close to him. She was almost intoxicated by his cologne. Before she knew it, she had fallen asleep on his shoulder. She was awakened about 10:00 p.m. by his kisses on her forehead.

"Wake up, Cat," he said. "We need to pull the covers back and go to bed properly."

"Oh, was I asleep?" Cat asked. "I guess I was making up for last night. I didn't sleep much last night."

She stood up and helped Mark pull the covers back. Then she went to the other bed and pulled the covers back.

"What are you doing?" Mark asked.

"I'm turning the covers back, so I can go to bed," Cat answered.

"Why not just sleep over here with me?" Mark asked. "I promise I'll be good."

"I think I'll just stay over here," Cat said, as she lay down and pulled the covers up over her.

"Dang," Mark said, as he turned out the bedside lamp and pulled the covers up.

During the night, he crept over to Cat's bed and lay down beside her and pulled her up close to him. She was so sound asleep that she didn't even move. Soon, he was asleep with his arms around Cat and his cheek against her back.

As soon as it began getting light, Cat awoke. When she discovered that she couldn't move because Mark was holding her so tight, she said, "Mark Fuller, what are you doing? I thought you said you would be good."

"I'm sorry, Cat," Mark said drowsily. "I guess I lied."

"Let go of me," she demanded. "I should have known better than to trust you."

"You can't blame me for trying," Mark said, as he got out of bed. "I just wanted to be close to you. I didn't do anything."

"I know you didn't," Cat said. "Only because I was asleep."

"No, Cat," Mark said seriously. "I wouldn't have done anything against your will. I guess I just wanted to be close to you. I promise, if you'll stay for the rest of the week, I'll be good. I won't beg you to sleep with me and I won't do anything to irritate you. Just stay here until Friday afternoon and then we'll go home together."

"I can't stay here," Cat said. "I don't have any clothes. I can't keep wearing Cassidy's clothes the rest of the week."

"That's OK," Mark said. "There's a Wal-Mart just down the street. When the streets are clear, you can drive down there and buy what you need. Here, you can use my credit card."

"I don't need your credit card. If I decide to stay, I have some money. I also have a credit card I can use," Cat said.

"Stay then, Cat," Mark said. "They'll probably plow the main streets today and you shouldn't have any trouble getting to Wal-Mart."

"If I can get to Wal-Mart, then maybe I can get home," Cat said.

"It's just a few blocks to Wal-Mart and it's about 100 miles home," Mark said.

"No, I won't let you go home."

"OK, if you're going to insist that I stay, I'll go to Wal-Mart after lunch and get some things. Maybe by then, they'll have plowed the roads," Cat said.

"Now, we need to hurry and get dressed if we're going to have breakfast. They start serving at 6:00 a.m.," Mark said, as he went into the bathroom to shower and shave.

Cat changed into the clothes she borrowed from Cassidy in the bedroom while Mark was in the bathroom. She decided against a shower. She figured she would just wash her face and take a shower after she got some things from Wal-Mart.

When Mark came out of the bathroom, he was surprised that Cat was already dressed. "I hurried with my shower so you could use it," he said.

"I'll just wash my face and take a shower after I go to Wal-Mart," she answered.

"OK. If you're ready, let's go get something to eat," Mark said, as he led the way to the lunchroom. There were some icy patches along the sidewalk, so Mark put his arm around Cat's waist and helped her over the bad spots.

They got their food and sat down at a table to eat. After they said their blessing on the food, Cassidy appeared and asked if she could join them.

"Sure, sit down," Mark said.

"You look good in my clothes, Cat," Cassidy said, as she sat down.

"Thanks," Cat said. "I really do appreciate your lending them to me. I think I'll go to Wal-Mart after lunch and get some things. Do you need anything?"

"As a matter of fact, I do," Cassidy said. "There are a few things I forgot to bring. I'd appreciate it if you'd get them for me. I'll give you a list before you go."

Then, they carried on a light conversation while they ate their meal. Mark kept glowering at Cassidy, as if he was afraid she would say something he didn't want her to say. After they were finished,

Mark said, "Cat, you go find your friend and see where you need to be and Cassidy and I'll go find out what we're supposed to do today."

As Cat headed toward the registration desk, Mark took Cassidy's arm and pulled her over to the side of the room away from everyone else.

"What did you say to Cat yesterday?" he asked.

"What do you mean?" she asked.

"I mean, what did you say to her. I know you said something by the way she acted when she came back. Now what did you tell her?"

"I didn't tell her anything," Cassidy said, "not what you think, anyway."

"What did you tell her, then?" he asked.

"It's not really any of your business what we talked about," Cassidy said, as she started to pull away from Mark. "It was just girl talk."

"I know you well enough to know you didn't just talk girl talk. Now tell me what you said to her," Mark said.

Cassidy just pulled her arm out of Mark's grasp and walked on ahead of him.

Cat didn't find Darin, so she started to go back into the lunchroom to see if he was there. She didn't see Darin, but she did see Cassidy and Mark arguing. Mark had Cassidy's arm in a tight grip and she was trying to pull away. He pulled her back each time she tried to pull away.

Cat wondered what they were arguing about. She wondered if it was the same thing they had argued about when Cassidy had first gotten there. It must have had something to do with what Mark had thought Cassidy had told her. She let her curiosity get the better of her and she slowly inched her way toward them, hoping that she could catch some of their conversation.

"I'm warning you, Cassidy," she heard Mark say. "If you say one word to her about that, I'll make you regret it."

"I told you, Mark," I didn't say anything to her. Oh. Hi, Cat," she said, as she spied Cat when she turned to face Mark.

Mark turned a startled face toward Cat and said, "Oh, Cat. I didn't hear you come up. Couldn't you find your man?"

"No, I couldn't find him," Cat said. "I thought maybe he was in here."

"Well, maybe you better go look for him, then." Mark could hardly breathe. He had no idea how long Cat had been standing there before they saw her.

"We were just going to find out where we are supposed to be," Mark said. "Come on, Cassidy. We need to go."

Cat watched them as they walked away. She could tell that Mark was still angry. He kept giving Cassidy an angry look. When they were out of her earshot, it looked like he was chewing her out some more. What could Mark have been hiding that was so important that he and Cassidy kept it a secret from her. Was it that other woman that Mark was in love with? Who was she, anyway? Why was he marrying her if he was in love with someone else? It just didn't make sense. It hurt Cat's head to try to think about it, so she just tried to forget it.

CHAPTER 19

At lunch, Mark found Cat where Darin had put her to observe his training. They went through the line and got their food. They found a table and said their prayer as usual, but Cassidy never did show up.

"I wonder where Cassidy is," Cat said, as she was eating.

"I guess she's eating with some of her friends," Mark said.

"Yeah, I guess she is," Cat said, as she looked around to see if she could see her. "She was going to give me a list of the things she wanted from Wal-Mart. I wonder if she forgot."

"Maybe she did," Mark said. "I'll find her after we eat and get it from her."

"Thanks," Cat said, but she still wondered where Cassidy was and why she hadn't come to eat with them.

When they had finished eating, Mark said, "Why don't you go on back to the room and I'll see if I can find Cassidy. Here's the key to the room. Just lock the door and keep the key until you come back from Wal-Mart. I won't need to get in until after you get back. I'll get the list and bring it to our room." Then Cat went toward their room and Mark went in the opposite direction.

After about 30 minutes, there was a knock on the door of the room and, when Cat opened it, Mark was standing there with a piece of paper in his hand.

"Here's Cassidy's list. Are you sure you don't want to use my credit card?" he said, as he handed her the list.

"Yes, I'm sure," Cat answered.

"I'll see you after while, then. I have to run now," Mark said, as he gave her a quick kiss.

Cat closed the door to the room and carefully made her way to her car. As she expected, the main street had been plowed and there were piles of snow heaped up along the side of the street. "Boy, this will be rough in the morning after this stuff melts and refreezes," she thought. "I guess Mark is right again. I need to stay here until Friday when he can drive us home."

She made it to Wal-Mart and made her purchases. She bought a couple of outfits to wear for the next two days, as well as the toiletries and other things she needed. Then she carefully made her way back to the academy.

She took her purchases to the room and decided to leave Cassidy's there also until after the training session. It was getting close to 4:00, so she knew they'd be finishing soon, so she decided to go in search of Mark and Cassidy. She found Mark, but Cassidy wasn't with him. "I have Cassidy's stuff I bought for her," Cat said. "Do you know where she is?"

"She probably went to her room," Mark said. "Give it to me and I'll go see."

"It's in our room," Cat said. "I'll go get it."

"That's OK," he said. "I'll just go with you and get it and you can stay in the room until time for dinner."

Cat really didn't like for Mark to order her around, but what he said was logical. She had wanted to give the things to Cassidy herself, but she figured Mark wanted to give them to her, so she let him do it.

Mark found Cassidy's room and knocked on the door. When she opened it, he didn't wait to be invited in, he just pushed her aside and walked into the room. "Here's the stuff Cat bought for you," he said, as he threw it on the bed. "I think it's best if you don't eat with us any more," he said.

"Why? Did I say something that upset your precious Cat?" she asked sarcastically.

"No, not yet and I don't want you to, either," Mark said. "I don't want anything you might accidentally say, to hurt her. I love her, Cassidy, and I'll do anything in my power to make sure she's happy. Anything. I would even kill to make sure she's safe and happy. Do I make myself clear?"

Cassidy started to ask if that was what happened to Jim, but she decided against it. Instead, she answered "Yes, Mark. You made yourself perfectly clear. I'll try to stay out of her way."

"Don't just try. Do it," he said, and then he walked out the door without a backward glance.

Cat couldn't help but wonder about what Cassidy had said. She wondered with whom Mark had been madly in love. The thing that kept going through Cat's mind was how many times Mark had told her he loved her. He really sounded sincere, and when he kissed her. Wow! When he kissed her, there were sparks. Millions of shooting stars. She could feel his need for her in those kisses. No, it had to be real. A person couldn't fake that, but who was this other woman and what had happened to her? Did she die before Mark had met Cat and fallen in love with her? She had to stop thinking about that. It was beginning to give her a headache.

There was a knock on the door and Cat assumed it was Mark. She opened the door and there he was. Her heart skipped a beat when she saw him. He could always make her heart race like that.

"Hurry up and get in here out of the cold," she said. "Did you find Cassidy?"

"Yes, she was in her room," Mark answered. "She said to tell you thanks. Here's the money for the things."

"Oh, I wasn't going to take anything for them," Cat said. "I was just going to get them for her as a return favor for the loan of the clothes."

"Well, there's the money, anyway," he said, as he pitched the money onto the bed. Then he pulled his shoes off and lay down on the bed to watch the news and weather before time to go to dinner.

"I wanted to see if they were expecting more snow," he said. "I heard that the older people believe that if a snow stays on the ground for three days, another one will come on top of it. That's probably an old wives, tale, but this snow has been here several days. Yes, the weather forecaster says another one is predicted. Snow flurries, he said. I hope we make it home before it gets bad."

There was another snowfall, but this one wasn't as heavy as the last one. It did prevent all of the outside training, though. Everything was done inside except for Friday morning, when the snow had melted enough for them to use the shooting range. It was so cold that their fingers almost froze as they tried to pull the trigger on their weapons. Cat wasn't able to go back to the observation tower, but Darin set her up inside with an equally effective observation site. She could see that Mark was doing great, even though she knew that his fingers must have been about frozen. Cassidy was doing well, even though she wasn't doing as well as she had done when they were taking the training before.

Cassidy hadn't come to eat with them again, but Cat wanted to see her before going home. The trainees were going to be dismissed at noon and they could either go home for the week-end and return on Monday morning or stay for the week-end. Some of the trainees decided to go home and finish up their training later when the weather was better. Since Cat and Mark were going home for the week-end, Cat searched for Cassidy to tell her goodbye. She wanted to thank her again for lending her the clothes and tell her that she would send the clothes to the barracks with Mark when he got back home.

She finally found her in her room getting ready to leave. "Are you going home for the week-end?" Cat asked when Cassidy opened the door to her.

"Yes, I thought I would. Then if it's still bad on Monday, I'll tell Mark to cancel the rest of my training until the weather's better. I guess you won't be coming back with Mark when he comes back," Cassidy answered.

"No, I only came with him this time because he was sick and I was afraid he couldn't make it by himself," Cat said.

Cassidy gave a little snide laugh and said, "I can't imagine Mark not being able to do anything by himself."

"I just wanted to tell you bye and thanks for the clothes," Cat said. "I'll launder them and send them back to the barracks by Mark, if that's OK with you."

"Sure, that's fine," Cassidy said. "Did he come with you?"

"No, I came by myself. I think he's still finishing up at the desk," Cat said.

"I can't believe you got away without him," Cassidy said.

"I don't understand," Cat said.

"Never mind," Cassidy said. "I hope you have a safe trip home."

"I hope you do, too," Cat said. "Oh, before I go, I was wondering. You weren't mad at me for some reason were you?"

"Of course not," Cassidy said. "Why do you ask?"

"I just thought I might have said or done something to make you mad and that was why you stopped sitting with us."

"No, of course not, Cat," Cassidy said. She wanted to say that Mark had told her to stop, but decided against that. "I just started eating with some friends of mine."

"I'm glad to hear that," Cat said. "I was afraid I had made you mad. I didn't want to do that. Well, I guess I'd better go find him. He gets upset with me when he can't find me."

"I know what you mean," Cassidy said knowingly. "Good luck on your marriage. You'll need it."

"Thanks, Cassidy," Cat said. "Maybe I'll see you around."

Cassidy watched as Cat carefully picked her way down the sidewalk to Mark's room and said under her breath, "Probably not."

When she got to the room, Cat knocked on the door, just in case Mark was there. He opened the door and pulled her inside. "Where have you been? I've been ready to go for 30 minutes."

"I was saying goodbye to Cassidy," Cat said. "And how did I know you were ready to go?"

"I'm sorry, Cat," he said. "I just wanted to beat this bad weather. Did you see Cassidy?"

"Yes, I saw her," Cat said.

"Is she staying or going home?" Mark asked.

"She's going home," Cat answered. She wondered why Mark was so interested in whether Cassidy was leaving or not, but she didn't ask why.

"Do you have all of your stuff ready to go?" Mark asked.

"It's ready to load into the car," Cat said, as she picked up several bags and headed toward the door. Mark took them out of her hands and loaded them into the trunk of the car.

"Make sure you got everything just in case I decide not to come back next week," he said.

"I've got everything," Cat said, as she went to the car and sat down in the passenger's seat. She figured that Mark would be driving. He got into the driver's seat and started the engine. Mark had driven for an hour before he said anything, then he asked if Cat would like to stop for a few minutes.

"Yes, I would," Cat answered, so at the next service station they came to, Mark pulled into the gas pump and Cat got out and went in search of the restroom.

After Mark finished pumping the gas, he found Cat and asked if she was hungry.

"I am a little hungry," she answered, so they bought some chicken and Cokes and sat down at a table and ate.

Mark didn't stop again until he pulled into the driveway of Cat's cabin.

"We're finally home," Cat said, as she climbed out and stretched her stiff legs.

Mark opened the trunk and took Cat's stuff out. Cat unlocked the door and opened it so Mark could take her things inside.

"Just set them down anywhere," she told Mark when he brought her bags inside. "I'm going to get the heat going."

"I need to get down to the barracks, Cat," Mark said. He gave her a quick kiss and started toward the door. "I don't know if I'll see you this week-end. I have a lot to do at the office. I probably won't go to church on Sunday. If the weather's better, I'm going back to the academy on Monday. I love you."

When he was gone, Cat felt like she had just made it through a whirlwind. Mark had hardly spoken to her all the way home. She knew that he was concentrating on his driving, though. There were still patches of ice here and there and Mark had to be careful to avoid skidding on the ice. Even though he was concentrating on his driving, she still felt that something was wrong. She didn't know what it was, but she felt that Mark was angry with her about something. It was getting to where she had to be careful what she said or did around Mark. It seemed like he was always mad about something.

"Oh, well," Cat thought. "I need to call Carol and tell her I'm home."

"Oh, Cat," Carol said when she answered the phone. "I'm so glad you're finally home. I've been so worried about you and Mark driving on those icy roads. Did you have any trouble getting home?"

"No." Cat said. "Mark drove and he's a really good driver. Most of the roads were in pretty good shape. Mark was really careful and avoided the icy spots."

"Is Mark there now?" Carol asked. "Sherry's been asking when he's coming home."

"No," Cat said. "He said he had a lot of work to do at his office and he left."

"Sherry will be disappointed," Carol said. "When will he be back?"

"I don't really know," Cat answered. "He said he probably wouldn't see me until he gets back next week-end."

"Oh, no," Carol said. "Sherry will bug me to death if she has to wait that long to see him. Well, I'll talk to you later. Bye."

Cat carried her things upstairs and started putting them away. About 6:00 p.m., there was a knock on the door.

"I wonder who that can be," she said, as she ran down the stairs and opened the door. Mark was standing there with a container of KFC and said, "I couldn't stand to be away from you for that long. May I come in?"

"Yes, of course," Cat said, as she opened the door wider for him.

"I brought enough chicken for Carol's family, too," he said, as he set the food on the table. "Will you call her and ask them to come over?"

"Of course," Cat said. "She's going to be really happy to see you. She said Sherry has been bugging her all week about when you were coming home."

Carol said that they would be right over and in a few minutes, there was a knock and then Sherry burst into the room like she always does.

"Mista Mok, Mista Mok," she said, as she ran to Mark and hugged his legs.

Mark leaned over and picked her up and gave her a big hug and a kiss. Sherry began kissing him and didn't stop until she had tried to kiss every inch of Mark's face.

"Save some of those kisses for later," Mark said. "I can't hold that many at one time."

"I have pwenty moa fo lata, Mista Mok," Sherry said. "I missed you,"

"I missed you, too, Sherry Rene," Mark said, as he carried her to the table and sat her in one of the chairs. "We need to eat the chicken before it gets cold."

Cat took the chicken, biscuits and vegetables out and put them on the table while Carol got plates, napkins and silverware. Then Cat fixed drinks for everyone.

"It's ready," Cat said when she had everything on the table. They all sat down and had a word of prayer and began eating.

"I thought you had a lot of work to do at the office," Cat said to Mark.

"I did, but I decided that this was more important," he answered.

"I gwad you came," Sherry said, as she reached over and patted Mark's hand. "I been missin you."

"I missed you, too, Sherry Rene," Mark said. "That's why I decided to forget the office and come see you."

After they had finished eating, they all went into the den and visited. Skip wanted to know all about the new gear that Mark had been using. Mark was excited about it and went into great detail describing it and its uses. Mark had talked more to Skip than Cat had ever seen him talk to Skip before and she was amazed that they were getting along so well.

About 8:00 p.m., Carol said, "I'm sorry to break up such a happy gathering, but I need to get my child home and get her ready for bed."

"No, Mama, us don't go yet," Sherry pouted.

"We have to go, Sherry," Carol said. "I'm sure Mr. Mark is tired and would like to get ready for bed, too. Wouldn't you Mr. Mark?"

"Yes, Sherry Rene," Mark agreed with Carol to her relief. "I've really been working hard all week and had a really long drive home. I'll see you tomorrow. See you later, alligator."

"See you lata, awagata," Sherry said, as Skip picked her up and headed for the door.

Carol gave Cat a hug and said, "I'm glad you're home. I'll talk to you tomorrow. Goodnight."

"Goodnight, Carol, Skip." Then she hugged and kissed Sherry and said, "I'll see you later, alligator. Goodnight, Sweetie,"

"I need to bring my stuff in," Mark said after Carol, Skip and Sherry had gone. "I didn't know whether to bring it in or not, so I left it in the car."

"Why would you think you couldn't bring your things in?" Cat asked.

"I guess I just thought you might be mad at me," Mark said.

"Why would I be mad at you?" Cat asked.

"I don't know," he answered. "I just thought you might have

been. I thought that Cassidy might have said something that made you mad. You hardly said anything all the way home."

"Well, I'm not mad. Cassidy didn't say anything to make me mad," Cat said. "Go get your things."

Mark went out to the car and brought his things into the cabin and on up the stairs to his room. He thought that since they had shared a room at the academy, she might allow him to share her room, but he didn't want to push his luck. He didn't want to get kicked out altogether. He wondered if Cassidy had said something to Cat. Cat said she hadn't, but maybe Cat was keeping it to use on him later. At least she was peaceful tonight. Maybe Cassidy took him seriously and kept her mouth shut.

When it was time for bed, Mark hinted that it would be nice to cuddle up to a nice warm body on such a cold winter night, but Cat didn't take the hint. She gave him a quick goodnight kiss and went into her room and shut the door. Mark stood at her door with his hand paused to knock on it for a few minutes and then gave up and went into his own bedroom.

CHAPTER 20

The next morning, Mark was up early and went down to the kitchen and made the coffee. He didn't get much sleep and awoke with a headache. He hoped, just to be mean, that Cat didn't sleep well either. "It would serve her right if she didn't," he thought.

Cat came into the kitchen just as he was pouring his coffee. "Oh, good. You made coffee," she said. "I need a cup of that."

"Did you sleep well?" he asked, as he poured a cup of coffee for Cat.

"Yes, I did," she answered. "It was nice to get back into my own bed again."

"Well, there went that idea," Mark thought. "Are Carol and Sherry coming over today?" he asked, as he took his coffee over and sat down at the table.

"They may come over for lunch, if I fix it and invite them over," Cat said. "Did you want them to come over?"

"Yes, I did," Mark said. "I have something for Sherry. I'd like to give it to her today."

"I'll fix lunch and invite them over, then," Cat said. After breakfast, Cat called Carol. "Would you all want to come for lunch?" Cat asked when Carol answered the phone.

"I really have a lot to do today, Cat, but if you don't mind if we leave right after lunch, we'll come. I know Mark wants to spend as much time as he can with Sherry and she wants to spend as much time as she can with him."

When Cat got lunch ready, she called and Carol, Skip and Sherry came over. After lunch, Mark said, "Come into the den with me, Sherry Rene. I have something for you."

"A pwesent?" Sherry asked.

"It's not really a present," Mark said. "It's just something I saw and thought you might like."

Mark picked up a package and handed it to Sherry.

"Tank you, Mista Mok," she said, as she opened it. It was a small bear standing on a large ball. There was a small crank on the bottom and when you turned the crank, the bear moved.

"Here, let me show you how it works," Mark said, as he turned the crank and the bear wiggled.

Sherry giggled and said, "Let me do it, Mista Mok."

Mark gave it to her and she cranked and giggled. "I wuv it, Mista Mok," she said.

"We need to go, Cat," Carol said, as Skip carried Sherry and they walked toward the door. "Skip and I have papers to grade and lesson plans to write. I'm sorry we have to eat and run."

"That's OK, Carol," Cat said. "I knew you had to leave early, when you came. I'll see you tomorrow. Bye. Bye Sherry. Bye Skip."

"See you lata, awagata," Sherry said.

"See you later, alligator," Mark said. "I'll see you tomorrow."

As Carol started out the door, she asked, "Are you and Mark coming to church tomorrow?"

"Yes," Cat answered. "We want to talk to Rev. Baxter after services."

"Mark, I have some things I need to do," Cat said, as she walked toward the kitchen. "Can you keep yourself entertained?"

"I have some work I need to do on my laptop," he said. Then he went upstairs and brought his laptop downstairs and set it up on the coffee table in the den. He stayed busy working on his laptop while Cat did what she needed to do.

When it was time for dinner, Cat heated up some vegetable soup, since the air was getting pretty cool. When she called Mark to the table, he was glad to see the hot soup.

It gave him a nice warm feeling, which he needed on a cold night.

After dinner, Cat cleaned up the kitchen while Mark went back into the den to work on his laptop.

About 10:00 p.m., Cat said she was going to bed. "Do you want to go to Sunday School or just church, Mark?" Cat asked.

"Let's just go to church tomorrow," Mark said. "I don't really feel like staying there that long. You wanted to talk to Rev. Baxter afterwards, too, so let's just go for church."

"OK," Cat said. "I'm going to bed. I'll see you in the morning."

Mark turned on the TV to see the weather and worked on his laptop a little longer. The forecast was for more snow, but it wouldn't be arriving until the end of the week. The weather was going to get even colder, though. Mark had to remember to go by the barracks and get some warmer clothes before going back to the academy. After the weather, Mark turned off the TV and went upstairs.

He hadn't really said goodnight to Cat when she went upstairs, so he knocked lightly on her bedroom door and softly called her name. "Cat, may I come in?" he asked. When she didn't say anything, he assumed that she was asleep and he started toward his room.

"Come in, Mark," Cat answered.

He turned around and opened the door. "I just wanted to say goodnight," Mark said, as he just stuck his head inside the door.

Cat sat up and leaned against the headboard. "You were busy when I came up," she said. "I didn't want to disturb you. Come on in."

Mark couldn't believe that Cat had actually invited him into her room. He hurried in and sat down on the bed next to Cat. "I just wanted to say goodnight," he said again.

"Goodnight, Mark," Cat said, as she waited for him to kiss her goodnight.

Mark was disappointed. He thought she was inviting him to

stay. The curt way she said goodnight left him no doubt that it wasn't an invitation. He stood up and leaned over and gave her a short, goodnight kiss and said, "I'll see you in the morning." Then he went to his own room.

The next morning, Cat fixed a quick breakfast, then went upstairs to get ready for church. She was ready to go about 10:30 a.m. "Mark," she called. "Are you ready to go?"

He appeared at the top of the stairs in a navy blue suit with a light blue shirt and tie on. He was so handsome, Cat caught her breath and her heart skipped a beat. "Mark," she thought," if you had come into my room last night looking like that, I probably would have fallen into your arms."

When Cat and Mark walked into the church and sat down next to Carol, all the women in the church gave Mark an admiring look. Sherry came running out of her Sunday School classroom and ran and jumped into Mark's lap.

"Mista Mok, wook wut I drawed," she said.

"That's really pretty, Sherry Rene," Mark said. "Show it to Aunt Kitty, too."

She showed it to Cat, but since the service was beginning, Carol tried to get her to be quiet. She finally made her sit in Skip's lap, where she sat sullenly and pouted. Mark hated that she had gotten into trouble. He made a mental note to make it up to her later.

After services, Cat told Carol and Skip to go on to the restaurant and they'd meet them there after they talked to Rev. Baxter.

"Rev. Baxter," Mark began when he was finally able to ask what they wanted. "Cat and I want to get married on January 16. We'd like for you to perform the ceremony and we'd like to use this church."

"I wondered when you two would be getting married," Rev Baxter said. "Yes, I'd be happy to marry you, but you need the permission of the church members to use the church. If you can come back tonight, I'll ask them."

"I can't come back tonight," Mark said. "I have to go out of town this afternoon. I can be here next Sunday morning, though."

"That'll be OK," Rev. Baxter said. "I'll ask them tonight and have their answer next Sunday."

"There's something I want to discuss with the two of you, though," Rev. Baxter said. "Whenever a couple comes to me to be married, I always like to find out how they stand with God first off. Have the two of you ever accepted Jesus as your Savior?" he asked.

Cat said, "Yes, Sir. I accepted Jesus as my Savior when I was a teenager. I'm a member of Landmark Baptist Church. When my husband died, I couldn't attend that church any longer. It hurt to go there without him."

"I can underatand that," Rev. Baxter said. "And you, Mr. Fuller? How do you stand with God?"

At first, Mark didn't answer Rev Baxter's question. Then slowly he said, "I was raised in a church orphanage, Rev. Baxter. I had to go to church whether I wanted to go or not. I promised myself that when I was an adult, I would go only if I wanted to go. If I didn't want to go, I didn't go. I never made a commitment to God."

"Do you realize that you are a sinner?" Rev. Baxter asked.

"Yes, I do, Rev. Baxter," Mark answered. "I reckon I've broken almost every one of the ten commandents. I haven't committed adultery, though. Only because I figured Cat wouldn't go along with that."

Cat gave Mark a startled look, but didn't say anything.

"Would you like to pray with me, Mr. Fuller?" Rev. Baxter asked.

"No, I wouldn't," Mark said. "I'm not ready to make a commitment yet."

"You know it's dangerous to put it off, don't you?" Rev. Baxter asked.

"Do I have to do that before I can get married here?" Mark asked.

"No, of course not," Rev. Baxter answered. "You can get married here if the church agrees to let you. You need to get right with God because it's dangerous to go on without accepting Jesus as your Savior."

"I'm not ready to take that step yet, Rev. Baxter," Mark said.

"OK, Mr. Fuller," Rev. Baxter said. "Just don't wait too long."

"Are we through here?" Mark asked haughtily.

"Yes, until I find out what the church members want to do," Rev. Baxter said.

"Let's go, Cat," Mark said. "Carol and Skip are waiting. We're through here." Then he took her arm and led her to his car.

When they entered the restaurant, Carol said, "Where have you two been? I was beginning to think you weren't coming."

"Mista Mok, sit hea by me," Sherry said.

"I will in a minute, Sherry Rene," Mark said. "Let me fill my plate first." Mark was still upset with what Rev. Baxter had said, so he really didn't want anything to eat. Since he was planning on leaving for the academy whenever they left the restaurant, though, he figured he had better eat something.

"Well, did you make arrangements to have your wedding at the church?" Carol asked.

"We have to wait until next Sunday to find out," Cat answered.

They sat and visited while they finished eating, then Mark said, "Cat, I need to go. I have to go by the barracks and get some warmer clothes on my way back to the academy. I need to get you back home first."

"I can ride back with Carol and Skip if you want to go on," Cat said.

"I have to get my things at your place, anyway, so you might as well ride with me."

As they were going back to Cat's cabin, she asked, "Mark, I thought you were a Christian. You're really the reason I started going back to church. You really need to think about what Rev. Baxter said."

"I will, Cat. When I'm ready," Mark said angrily. "Now, don't bug me about it." Then he was silent for the rest of the trip.

At Cat's cabin, Mark went upstairs and got his things and walked back downstairs. "Cat, do you want to go back to the academy with me?" he asked.

"No, Mark. I don't want to go back," she answered.

"I'd like for you to go back with me," he said.

"I need to get back to work," she answered.

"I really wish you'd go with me," he almost pleaded.

"Why do you want me to go back, Mark?" Cat asked.

"I want you to try some of the training," he said. "Maybe you'll like it."

"No, Mark," Cat said. "I wouldn't like it. No matter how much you want me back in your unit, I'm not going to do it. I've had all of that that I want. So forget it. I don't even want anything to do with the FSC again. I would not change my mind if I went back to the academy with you."

"OK, Cat," Mark said. "I need to go. I'll see you when I get back."

Then he kissed her and headed for his car. Cat stood in the door and watched him leave. She was worried about him now, but she couldn't go back to the FSC. That was a part of her past life. Her life now had no room for the FSC. The only contact she wanted with it, was that Mark was a Unit Commander. If it wasn't for that, she would have nothing at all to do with them. She said a prayer that God would protect Mark and bring him back safely to her. She also asked God to help Mark make a commitment to Him and accept Jesus as his Savior.

CHAPTER 21

The week went slowly. Cat really missed Mark. She worked at the paper a couple of days and did volunteer work at the children's hospital, but the days dragged by, anyway. Friday finally arrived with gray, snowy skies. Before lunch, big, fluffy flakes were coming down fast and covering the roads and yards.

Cat stood looking out the window watching the snow come down and praying that Mark would make it home safely. She was hoping that he would make it home by 4:00 p.m., but 4:00 came and went and there was no Mark. By 6:00 p.m., Cat was pacing the floor. She had called Mark's cell phone several times and had gotten only his voice mail. She had left him several messages to call her, but he still hadn't called.

Finally, about 6:30 p.m., the phone rang and Cat grabbed it on the first ring.

"Cat, I'm sorry," Mark said. "I know you've been worried, but I didn't have a chance to call you until now. I had an accident and my car is inoperable. Will you come get me?"

"Yes, of course," Cat said breathlessly. "Are you all right?"

"I'm OK," he answered. "Just come as soon as you can."

"Where are you?" Cat asked.

"I'm in the emergency room at the hospital in Wynne." Then he gave her directions to where the hospital was. "Be really careful. The streets are really slick. See if Skip or Jason will come with you."

She called Skip as soon as she hung up the phone. Carol answered and Cat said, "Carol, I need to talk to Skip."

"What's wrong, Cat?" Carol asked. "You tell me before you talk to Skip."

"Mark's had an accident," she said. "I need to go get him and I need Skip to go with me."

"What's wrong, Cat?" Skip asked when he answered the phone.

"Mark's had an accident. He's at the hospital at somewhere called Wynne. He wants me to come get him. Can you take me?"

"Sure, I'll be right over," Skip said.

Shortly, he pulled up in the driveway and Cat ran out and got into his car. As Mark had said, the roads were very icy, but Skip was a good driver and he was very careful. They arrived at the hospital about 9:00 p.m. When they walked into the emergency room, Mark saw them and hurried to them. His left arm was in a sling and there was a large bandage on his forehead above his left eye.

Cat's heart sank when she saw him. "Not another sling," she thought. Mark grabbed her and hugged her. "Am I glad to see you. I thought I was going to have to spend the night here. You, too, Skip."

Then he went to the nurse's station and said, "These are the ones I've been waiting for. I'm ready to go now."

"OK," the nurse said. "I have some papers for you to sign and a prescription for some pain medicine. Who's going to drive you home?"

"My brother-in-law," Mark said.

"He needs to sign this paper stating that he's doing the driving and he will not allow you to drive. You've been given a sedative and are not to drive until the sedative wears off."

"Skip, I told her my brother-in-law is driving me home," Mark said. "You need to sign a paper stating that you're driving and won't let me drive."

"Sure," Skip said. "Where do I sign?"

After the nurse had given Mark instructions and the prescription for some pain pills, they were finally ready to go.

"I'm sorry for the lie, Skip," Mark said. "I didn't know what else to call you."

"Brother-in-law is fine," Skip said. "I'll be that soon, anyway."

"I have a prescription for some pain pills," Mark said. "I guess all of the pharmacies are closed by now. Would you check with Wal-Mart and see if they're still open?"

As luck would have it, the pharmacy in Wal-Mart was just closing, but when Mark told them his problem, they filled the prescription for them before they closed.

Mark took a pill before he got back into the car. Then he leaned back and slept the rest of the way home. When they got to Cat's cabin, Skip woke Mark up and helped him into the den and onto the sofa.

"Thanks, Skip," Mark said. "Let me know if I can ever do anything for you. I'll be happy to return the favor."

The next morning, Mark said he had to go back to Wynne to get his things out of his car. "I have some very expensive gear in my car. I have to go back and get it," Mark said.

"OK," Cat said. "I'll call and see if Skip can go back with us. If he can't, maybe Jason can." So, Cat called Carol again. "Carol, may I speak to Skip," she asked when Carol answered the phone.

"What is it this time, Cat?" Carol asked testily.

"Mark needs to go back to Wynne and get his things out of his car," Cat answered.

"I thought maybe Skip would go with us again."

"Cat, can't it wait until Monday?" Carol asked. "Skip is really busy today."

"No, it can't wait until Monday, Carol," Cat answered. "He has some really expensive equipment in the trunk. He really needs to get it out."

"OK," Carol finally conceded. "I'll get him and see what he says."

"Skip, can you go back to Wynne with us?" Cat asked when Skip answered the phone.

"When did you want to go?" Skip asked.

"As soon as possible," Cat answered.

"OK, I'll be over shortly," he said, but Cat could tell by the tone of his voice that he really didn't want to make that long trip on such bad roads again so soon. Soon, Skip pulled up into the driveway and honked his car horn, anyway. Cat and Mark hurried out and got into the car.

"OK, Mark," Skip asked. "Where do we go?"

"The place is called Joe's Body Shop," Mark answered. "I think it's just on the other side of town. It shouldn't be too far out, from what the police officer said."

As Skip was driving, he looked over at Mark and said, "Cat told me what Rev. Baxter said to you and what you said to him. Mark, I think you need to consider what he said. You know God has given you two warnings. The next time, he may not give you a warning. You're treading on dangerous ground."

"Don't preach to me, Skip," Mark said. "I had enough of that when I was a kid. You don't have to tell me what I am. I know I'm a sinner. I'm just not ready to make a commitment yet."

"If you know you're a sinner and you know what you need to do, why don't you do it?" Skip asked.

"Because I'm not ready to do that, yet," Mark said raising his voice. "Stop preaching to me. Just leave me alone."

"I can't just leave you alone, Mark," Skip said. "I care about you. My daughter is crazy about you and I would hate to see you die and go to Hell."

"I told you, I'm not ready, yet," Mark said. "Now just leave me alone," Mark said and he turned his face toward the window.

Cat sat in the back seat and prayed that maybe something Skip said would sink into Mark's heart and change whatever was keeping him from repenting of his sins and giving his life to Jesus.

The rest of the trip was made in silence. Each one was deep in their own thoughts. When they got to Wynne, Skip drove through the town and on to the outskirts and came to a place that had a high fence around it. "Is this the place?" Skip asked.

"I think so," Mark answered. "Pull up to the office and I'll get out and see."

When Mark came back, he said that this was the place. "Cat, it's really cold," Mark said. "You might as well stay in the car. I think Skip and I can handle it."

Mark led Skip into the office, where the owner was waiting with a clipboard and pen in his hand. "You need to sign this certificate," he said. "It states that you have taken everything of value out of your vehicle. You need to get everything that you want out now, because when your insurance company totals it, it's gone."

"That's what I intend to do," Mark said, as he signed the form that the man handed to him.

When Mark opened the trunk of his car, Skip said, "Dang, Mark, no wonder you were in such a hurry to get your things. Do you use all of these weapons and all this gear?"

"Yes, I do," Mark answered. "I thought you knew what I do."

"I guess I thought you just carried a revolver," Skip said. "I never knew you did all this. Does Cat know you do this?"

"Of course she does," Mark answered. "You forget that she was in my unit when Jim was alive."

"I guess I just didn't know what the two of you really did," Skip said. "I guess I should have more respect for the two of you."

"Don't let my expertise with these weapons influence the respect you have for me," Mark said. "This is my job. Just like teaching is your job. I do it everyday, so it isn't anything unusual to me."

"Your job is nothing like my teaching job," Skip said.

"Yes, it is, Skip," Mark answered. "If you think about it. Come on. Let's get this stuff transferred to your car before someone sees it."

They got Mark's equipment and weapons transferred to the trunk of Skip's car and headed home. On the way home, Skip asked, "What about Jim? I never really knew how he died."

"Sometime when we have time, I'll tell you," Mark said. "Not everything, but what I can, but not now. Not with Cat here."

"Oh, yeah," Skip said. "I forgot she was back there."

"I guess now I have even more to be jealous of you about," Skip said. "My daughter practically worships you and now I find out what a hero you are."

"I'm not a hero," Mark said. "I just do my job. A job I love. That's probably not any more than you do."

"I considered you a hero when you saved Sherry," Skip said.

"That was something I did because I had to do it," Mark said. "Your daughter is wise beyond her years. When she first met me, she saw I needed someone like her. She's helped me through a very rough time in my life. I'll always be grateful to her. When she sees that I no longer need her in that way, she'll come back to you. That time is almost here now."

"I don't think she'll ever stop caring for you like she does," Skip said.

"I hope not, but I know that my need that she filled will soon be met by someone else and I won't need her as much. I think she'll know when it's time."

"Well, I'll be glad to get my daughter's affection back," Skip said. "If you know what you're talking about."

"I think I do," Mark said. Then he leaned back and slept the rest of the way home.

When they arrived at Cat's cabin, Mark and Skip unloaded Mark's equipment and Cat opened Jim's old office and let them put it in there. Then Mark took his clothes up to his bedroom.

"I need to get on home," Skip said. "I'll see you two in the morning. Are you only coming for church?"

"Probably," Cat said. "We'll see you tomorrow. Thanks again for your help."

"Yes, Skip," Mark said. "I really appreciate all you've done for me. I'll talk to you some other time about that other matter."

"I'll see you tomorrow at church, then," Skip said, as he left.

The next morning, the roads were still icy, so church was canceled. Cat fixed a large pot of vegetable beef soup again and asked Carol if they wanted to come down for lunch. She, of course, said yes.

God had laid it on Skip's heart to talk to Mark about his salvation, so when they came in, Skip asked Carol to take Sherry into the kitchen with her. "I need to talk to Mr. Mark alone, Sherry," Skip said. "You go into the kitchen with Mama and Aunt Kitty."

"But I want Mista Mok to read me a story," she pouted.

"He can do that after lunch. Right now, I need to talk to him alone," Skip said.

"Sit down, Mark," Skip said. "I want to talk to you about your soul."

"Skip, I told you I don't want to listen to your preaching," Mark said. "I know I'm a sinner and I need God to forgive me of my sins, but I'm not ready for that yet."

"When do you think you'll be ready?" Skip asked. "When it's too late?"

"There's something in my life that I can't forgive myself for, so I don't expect God to forgive me," Mark said.

"God can and will forgive you of all your sins and help you to forgive yourself of whatever it is that you cannot," Skip said. "Here, I have my King James Version of the Bible. I want you to follow along with me while I read something to you."

"I told you, Skip, I don't want to listen to it," Mark said.

"Just give me a few minutes, Mark," Skip said. "Look, Romans 3:23 says *'For all have sinned and come short of the glory of God.'** "You're not the only one to have sinned and felt guilty about it.

"Look at this verse. Romans 6:23 tells what the outcome of sin is." *'For the wages of sin is death; but the gift of God is eternal life through Jesus Christ our Lord.'**

"The outcome of sin is death, but we don't have to have that outcome. Look, Mark. Look what Romans 10:13 says, *'For whosoever shall call upon the name of the Lord shall be saved.'**

"All you have to do to be forgiven is to call on the name of the Lord and repent of your sins and you'll be forgiven.

"Look, here, Mark. Look at Romans 5:8 *'But God commendeth His love for us, in that while we were yet sinners, Christ died for us.'**

"Christ's death on the cross was a substitutionary sacrifice. Christ's life for yours. When you accept Christ as your Savior, His blood covers all of your sins and God cannot see your sins through Christ's blood. All you have to do is accept the gift of eternal life that God has given you.

"Mark, look. This is the most beautiful verse in the Bible, John 3:16 *'For God so loved the world, that He gave His only begotten Son, that whosoever believeth in Him should not perish, but have everlasting life.'** (**KJV The Holy Bible*)

"All you have to do is accept that gift of everlasting life, so why is it so hard for you to do that?"

Mark started to weep. "Skip, you don't understand. I just can't forgive myself. How can God forgive me?"

"God forgives you because His Son gave His life so that God would forgive you," Skip said. "You don't have to do anything except trust that God does forgive you, and He does. If you ask Him to forgive you, He does. What is it that is so bad that you can't forgive yourself?"

"Skip, I wanted Jim out of my way," Mark said. "I wanted his job and his wife. I didn't want him to die, I just wanted what he had. Then when he died, I felt it was because I somehow willed it to be so."

"Mark, there's no way you could have willed Jim's death. What happened to Jim wasn't your fault. You tried to save Jim. Stop blaming yourself for something that you couldn't have prevented."

"I know that, Skip," Mark said. "I know how hard I tried to save him, but I still feel guilty. I don't feel worthy to accept God's forgiveness."

"Mark, no one is worthy of God's forgiveness. It's just through

His mercy that He forgives us. Will you kneel down and pray with me that God will forgive you. I know that He will if you only ask Him. Are you ready to ask Him now?"

"Yes, I think I'm ready now," Mark said, as he knelt and prayed that God would forgive him and help him to forgive himself.

"Next Sunday, you need to make known your commitment to Christ," Skip said.

"You should present yourself as a candidate for baptism to our church. Do you want to do that?"

"Yes," Mark said. "I'd like that."

Cat slowly walked into the den and saw that Mark looked like he had been crying. "Did I miss something?" she asked.

"I've just accepted Christ as my Savior," Mark said. "Skip helped me see my need for the Lord."

"Oh, Mark, I'm so happy for you," Cat said, as she gave him a big hug. "You'll never regret it."

"I'm going to request that our church, Friendship Baptist Church, baptize me next Sunday," Mark said.

"That's wonderful," Cat replied. "I think I'll move my membership there, too. Lunch is ready if you two are finished."

"Yes, we're finished and ready for lunch," Mark said. "Come on, let's eat."

While they ate their lunch, the sun came out and melted the snow. It became a beautiful warm winter day. It was only a few days until Christmas and everything was beginning to look a lot brighter for Mark. He said a silent prayer of thanks to God for all the blessings He had given to him. Now he was especially grateful for forgiving him of his sins. Now, he would be able to enjoy his marriage to Cat without the terrible feeling of guilt hanging over him.

On Monday, since the roads were pretty clear, Mark asked Cat if she would drive him to his unit headquarters. His shoulder was still pretty painful and, every time he moved, his two cracked ribs felt like a knife stabbing his side.

"You can just drop me off and I'll get Jason or someone to bring me home," Mark said, as he got out of the car.

"I think I'll come in for a while if you don't mind," Cat said. "I want to return Cassidy's clothes to her."

"Suit yourself," Mark said. Then he went directly to his office. Cat followed him into the building, but instead of going into his office with him, she wandered around the room. She finally saw Cassidy sitting at the side of the room by herself. "Hello, Cassidy," Cat said, as she walked over to her. She had brought the clothes that Cassidy had loaned to her at the academy to give back to her.

"Hi, Cat," Cassidy answered. "I never thought I'd see you here."

"Mark had a wreck going home Friday and I drove him in today," Cat answered. "Here are your clothes. Thanks again for the loan. Did you make it home OK on Friday?"

"Yeah, it was rough, but I finally made it home. So Mr. Know-it-all and Can-do-it-all, couldn't, huh?" Cassidy answered.

"Well, he hit a slick spot and his car kissed the guard rail," Cat answered. "His car is totaled."

"I hate to hear that about the poor car," Cassidy said.

"Cassidy," Cat started slowly. "You and Mark don't get along very well, do you?"

"Not really," Cassidy answered. "Why do you ask?"

"I noticed that you two seemed to have an argument the week I was there at the academy," Cat said. "I just wondered what you were arguing about."

"You're trying to get me into trouble, aren't you?" Cassidy asked.

"No, I don't want to get you into trouble," Cat hastily said. "I was just curious. I just wondered if it had anything to do with me."

"Why would you ask that?" Cassidy nervously asked.

"Because it seemed like he didn't want me to talk to you for some reason," Cat answered.

Mark came out of his office looking for Cat and, when he saw her talking to Cassidy, he said, "Oh, no," and hurried over to them.

"Cat, come here a minute," he said when he reached them. "I have something I want you to see."

Then he took Cat's arm and led her away from Cassidy and gave Cassidy a backward dirty look.

"I have something in my office I want to show you," Mark said, as he led her into his office and shut the door.

"This is the Christmas card I got for Sherry," he said, as he showed her a cute card with a kitten in a Christmas stocking on the front. "Do you think she'll like it?"

"Yes, I'm sure she will," Cat answered. "But that's not the reason you wanted me to come in here was it?" she asked.

"No, not really," Mark answered.

"Are you afraid that Cassidy is going to tell me something?" Cat asked. "If it's what I think it is, you don't have to worry. Jim told me about his fascination with Cassidy. We discussed his fascination with her when she filed charges on him. He said that he had wished that he had never even asked her to transfer to our unit. He apologized to me and said that he had no idea why he was so attracted to her, but he would never do anything to jeopardize our marriage. I believed him, too. I don't think he ever did anything to encourage her and, after a while, he lost interest in her, especially after she filed charges on him. So if that's what you were afraid of, that I would fall apart if she mentioned it, you can stop worrying. Jim and I straightened that out a long time ago."

"I didn't know you and Jim had settled things between the two of you," Mark said. "I was just trying to keep you from being hurt. You have had such a hard time coping with Jim's death here lately. I was just trying to keep you from hurting even more."

"It hurt when he told me about how attracted he was to her," Cat said. "But I was glad that he was honest with me. As far as I know, he never strayed, either. Thank you, Mark, for your concern. I found out what I wanted to know. I guess I'll go to the paper office and work until you're ready to go home. Call me when you're ready to go home."

With that, Mark kissed her goodbye and she left. As Mark watched her go, he was relieved that she didn't know the other reason he didn't want her to talk to Cassidy. She wouldn't have understood why he had had to go to someone like Cassidy to try to forget about his love for Cat. It didn't work out anyway. It just made him love Cat even more.

Mark called a meeting of his team and gave them a report on the academy training. "They'll be closed until after the first of the year, so no one else will get their training until after that. I've made a schedule for you to go by. If you see that you can't make the two weeks I have scheduled for you, let me know in time to substitute someone else. Is that agreeable with everyone?" They all agreed that that sounded good to them.

"I'll let Cassidy tell you about her experience first and then I'll add more," Mark said. "To me, it was a very extensive training, even though the snow curtailed some of it. Cassidy, are you ready?"

Cassidy said she was ready and she gave a detailed report of the training she had received. Then Mark gave his report. "I plan to purchase the new gear and weapons for our unit," he said. "I should have it in by the time everyone has completed his or her training."

About 3:00 p.m., Mark's injuries were beginning to hurt, so he called Cat to see if she was ready to go home.

"Sure, I'll be there to get you shortly," she said.

He told Cassidy that she was in charge and then he left with Cat. On the way home, Mark said that his insurance agent had called him. "The insurance agency has totaled my vehicle," he said. "They'll be sending me a check soon. I'll need you to take me to find another vehicle, if you don't mind."

"Of course, I will," Cat said.

"If it's inconvenient for you to bring me into work each day, I'll move back to the barracks and then I can just walk over to the office," Mark said.

"I don't mind bringing you in," Cat said. "I can either work at the paper office or I can go to the hospital and do my volunteer work.

It's not a problem at all." So, for the next two days, Cat drove Mark to his unit headquarters in the morning and home in the afternoon.

Charlotte and Tyler arrived Wednesday afternoon for the holidays. They stayed at Carol's and Skip's cabin and everyone came to Cat's for dinner. As Charlotte walked into the room, she saw Mark's sling and asked, "What happened to Mark?"

"He had an accident," Cat said.

"Another accident?" Charlotte asked. "He certainly is an accident-prone fellow.

Are you sure you want to marry him? You'll be taking care of him all the time."

"Yes, I'm certain I want to marry him," Cat answered. "I'll be happy to take care of him. I love him, Charlotte."

"It seems like every time we come home, he has his arm in a sling," Charlotte said.

Carol could see that Cat was getting angry, so she said, "Well, I for one, will always be grateful that Mark's around here, even if he does have his arm in a sling. I'll be eternally grateful to him for saving my daughter."

"What do you mean by that?" Charlotte wanted to know.

"I'm sorry," Carol said. "I thought we told you about it. Sherry somehow got to the top of a tower over by the restaurant where we eat on Sunday and Mark climbed to the top of it and rescued her. If he hadn't gone up there, I don't know how we would have gotten her down. He almost fell going up, too."

"Well, I guess he's good for something, then," Charlotte said. "I didn't know about that."

"Now that you know, maybe you should be a little nicer to Mark," Carol said.

They made it through dinner without any more snide remarks. Everyone had a congenial visit and, about 10:00 p.m., Carol said, "I need to get Sherry over to our place and get her ready for bed. I'll see you two in the morning. Sherry, say goodnight to Aunt Kitty and Mr. Mark."

"Goodnight, Aunt Kitty," Sherry said. "See you lata, awagata, Mista Mok."

Cat and Mark kissed Sherry and gave her a big hug. "See you later, alligator," Mark said, as he hugged her.

That night, as Mark passed Cat's bedroom door, he heard her crying. He tapped softly on her door and asked, "Cat, are you all right?"

"Yes, Mark. I'm OK," Cat said as she tried to stop crying.

Mark opened the door slightly and said, "You don't sound OK. You sound like you're crying. What's wrong?"

"Nothing, Mark," she said. "Go on to bed. I'm OK."

"It can't be nothing," he said. "If it made you cry, it must be something. What's wrong?"

"It's nothing. I'm just being silly," Cat said.

"Why were you crying, then," Mark asked.

"If you must know," Cat said. "Charlotte is expecting a baby."

"I heard that she was, but you're supposed to be happy for her and not sad," Mark said. "Why are you crying because Charlotte's going to have a baby?"

"I said I was just being silly," Cat said. "I just want a child so much, too."

"Well, if that's your problem," Mark said. "I can take care of that right now. I'll be happy to give you a baby, if you'll let me."

"No, Mark," Cat said. "Not now. I told you I'm just being silly."

"Let me take care of your problem right now, Cat," Mark said, as he sat down on the bed.

"No, Mark," Cat said. "Not like this. It's only a couple of weeks. You'll just have to wait. Now go on back to your room. Thanks for the offer, but I think I'll wait."

"Cat, you're tearing me up," Mark said. "What difference does two weeks make?"

"It makes a difference to me, Mark," Cat said. "Goodnight. I'll see you in the morning."

The next morning, when Cat went downstairs, Mark was already sitting at the table drinking coffee. "Good morning, Mark," she said, as she poured a cup and stirred in sugar and creamer.

"Morning, Cat," Mark said grumpily

"Gee, you sound grumpy this morning," Cat said. "Didn't you sleep well?"

"You know I didn't," Mark answered. "Why do you torture me like that, Cat?"

"I'm not trying to torture you, Mark," Cat said. "I'm trying to be morally correct. Besides, if I'm not worth waiting for, then I must not be worth anything to you."

"No, Cat," Mark said. "Don't say that. You're worth everything to me. I just want you so much." Then he stood up and walked over to her and kissed her. "Merry Christmas."

"Yeah, Merry Christmas to you, too," Cat said. "I almost forgot. It is Christmas, isn't it? I guess I'd better start breakfast. The others will probably be here soon."

Shortly, the front door burst open and Sherry rushed in. "Mewy Cwismas," she said, as she ran over to Mark and gave him a hug and a kiss.

"What about me, Sherry," Cat said. "Don't I get a hug and a kiss?"

"Mewy Cwismas, Aunt Kitty," she said, as she hugged and kissed Cat.

"Wes open pwesents," Sherry said.

"Don't you want to eat first?" Cat asked.

"No, wes open pwesents first," Sherry said.

"OK, let's go into the den where the tree and the presents are," Cat said, as she led Sherry to the den.

Everyone sat down in the den and Skip passed out the gifts. Cat had a gift from Mark, but he said she should wait about opening it.

"I think you need to wait until we're alone before you open the gift I gave you," Mark said.

She figured it must be something that would embarrass her, so she set it aside and opened the other gifts.

After all of the presents were opened, Sherry noticed that Cat still had an unopened gift.

"Open you pwesent, Aunt Kitty," Sherry said, as she picked it up and handed it to Cat.

"I'm not going to open it right now, Sherry," Cat said, as she tried to hide it behind her.

"I wanna see it, Aunt Kitty," Sherry was adamant. "Open it now."

"No, Sherry," Cat said, getting angry. "I want to wait until later."

"Come on, Sherry," Carol said. "Leave Aunt Kitty alone. She wants to wait until later to open her present."

Sherry started to cry and said, "I want her to open it now." Then she grabbed it and started tearing the wrapping paper. Inside was a sexy, sheer, red and black nightie. Cat grabbed it and tried to hide it, but it was too late. Everyone had seen it. Mark sat behind her with an amused look on his face. "I told you to wait until we were alone," he said.

Cat turned red and grabbed the nightie and headed up the stairs with it.

"Why don't you try it on and let us see how it looks," Tyler called after her.

Everyone except Mark laughed. He gave Tyler a dirty look and followed Cat upstairs.

He walked into her bedroom without even knocking. "Cat, I'm sorry. I didn't know that was going to happen. I never would have let you go through that if I could have stopped it."

"That's OK," Cat said. "It was just a little embarrassment. I can handle it. Thanks for the gift, anyway."

Then he went back downstairs. "If anyone makes another crack like that, Tyler, you'll have to answer to me," Mark said. "You could see that she was already embarrassed enough, you didn't have to add to it."

"I was just joking with her," Tyler said. "I thought she could take a joke. Besides, it was your fault. You should have given it to her when no one else was here."

"Yeah, you're right, Tyler, but don't do that again," Mark said.

"OK, Mr. Smart Alec," Tyler said. "I'll never try to joke with her again."

Just then, Cat came down the stairs and went into the kitchen. "I'll have breakfast ready soon," she said and began fixing breakfast as if nothing had happened.

Sherry was confused. She had no idea what she had done. She just knew that everyone had been having a good time and all of a sudden, no one was having a good time any longer.

As they sat down to breakfast, there was a knock on the door. When Cat opened it, Jason and his girlfriend, Debbie, were there. "Hi, Jason, Debbie," Cat said. "Come on in. We were just about to have breakfast. Have you eaten yet?"

"No, we haven't," Jason said.

"Come on in and sit down," Cat said. "I've cooked enough for an army. You're welcome to eat with us."

So Jason and Debbie found a seat at the table. After Skip said a blessing on the meal, they all filled their plates.

After the meal, Cat said, "Mark, while Jason is here, why don't we finish planning our wedding?"

"What's left to plan?" Mark asked.

"Have you asked Jason to be your best man, yet?" Cat asked.

"Jason, will you be my best man?" Mark asked.

"Of course, Mark," Jason said. "I'd be honored to be your best man."

"Our wedding will be January 16 at 7:00 p.m.," Cat said. "We'll probably have it at Friendship Baptist Church if the members agree to let us use their church," Cat said.

"Will I be in your wedding?" Charlotte asked.

"Carol will be my matron of honor," Cat answered. "I didn't know if you'd be here or if you'd want to be a part of our wedding or not."

"Yes, if Carol's in it," Charlotte said. "I want to be in it, too."

"What do you think, Mark" Cat asked. "We'll need another groomsman if Charlotte's in it."

"Whatever you think, Cat," Mark said. "I just want to get the 'I do's over so I can take you to bed."

Cat turned red and gave Mark a dirty look. "I know that's what you've been waiting for, but I want a wedding first," Cat said in an angry voice.

"OK," Mark said. "Ask Skip if he'll be a groomsman. You might as well make Sherry Rene a flower girl, too. Then you'll have the whole family."

"That's a good idea, Mark," Cat said. "I know you were just trying to be sarcastic, but that's a good idea. Sherry can walk down the aisle in front of me and throw out flower petals. She'd like that."

"You're right. I was being sarcastic," Mark said. "What if she doesn't want to do it? You know how she gets when she doesn't want to do something. She'd ruin the whole wedding."

"No, she wouldn't mess it up," Carol said. "I think she'd love it."

"OK, it's settled," Cat said. "We'll draft Skip to be a groomsman and let Sherry be a flower girl."

"What about Tyler?" Charlotte asked.

"We can't use Tyler," Cat said. "He probably wouldn't want to do it, anyway."

"We have enough," Mark said. "I want to get it over as soon as possible. No more groomsmen and no more bridesmaids. You wanted me to help. I'm helping. I'm putting an end to it right now. Carol and Charlotte can be bridesmaids and Jason and Skip can be groomsmen and Sherry, a flower girl, but that's it." Then he walked out of the kitchen into the den.

"Come on Jason. You and Debbie come here. I want to talk to you," Mark said. They sat down in the den and Mark asked Jason if he was happy with Ted's unit.

"I guess I'm about as happy as I can be," Jason said.

"I really need you on my team, Jason," Mark said. "I know you don't want to transfer to a team that's in as bad a shape as my team is, but I think you and I could straighten it out if we worked together."

"Let me think about it, Mark," Jason said. "I don't want to jeopardize my chances of being a Unit Commander. I know you'd give me your SIC position, but I'd like to be Unit Commander some day. I have to see what will help me get that position."

"I'll do all I can to help you, if you'll help me get my team in order," Mark said.

"Just give me a few days to think about it," Jason said. "Well, I guess we better be going. Debbie's parents want us there for dinner. It was good talking to you. I hope you have a wonderful Christmas."

"Merry Christmas to you and Debbie," Mark said. "If I don't see you before then, I'll see you at our wedding."

"OK," Jason said. "Bye everyone."

Everyone said bye to Jason and Debbie and they walked to the door. Mark walked with them and let them out. As he watched Jason walk to his car, he said a prayer that Jason would come over to his team and help him get it straightened out.

CHAPTER 22

New Year's Day arrived with frosty temperatures, but beautiful sunshine. Charlotte and Tyler had stayed to attend Cat's and Mark's wedding. Since everyone had stayed up late for New Year's Eve and because of the cold temperature, everyone was sleeping late.

About 8:00 a.m., Cat decided to get up and go downstairs to fix breakfast. At the top of the stairs, the wonderful aroma of fresh brewed coffee invaded her nostrils. Sure enough, when she entered the kitchen, Mark was sitting at the table drinking a cup of coffee.

"Good morning, Mark. Happy New Year," she said, as she poured a cup of coffee for herself and stirred creamer and sugar into it.

"Happy New Year, yourself," Mark answered. "Well, it's only two more weeks. Did you get everything lined out the way you want it?"

"Do you mean our wedding?" Cat asked.

"Yes, of course," Mark answered. "That's what's been on my mind constantly for the past few months."

"Oh, you poor deprived man," Cat said, as she massaged his neck and back. "Yes, I think so. I asked Tyler if he would walk me down the aisle. That way, Charlotte can be happy that he has a part in our wedding. Is that OK with you?"

"I told you, whatever you decide is fine with me. I just want to get it over and get you into bed," Mark said, as he pulled her down and kissed her. "You know what I want."

"Yes, I know what you want," Cat said, as she blushed.

"How many are coming for breakfast?" Mark asked.

"They're all going to be here," Cat said. "Why do you ask?"

"I just wondered if I was going to have to put up with Tyler's snide remarks this morning," Mark replied.

"You'll have to put up with Tyler for a few more weeks and then they'll go back to Hollywood," Cat answered.

Shortly the door burst open and Sherry ran into the room and straight to Mark.

"Mista Mok, Mista Mok," she shouted. "Happy Nu Yea."

"Happy New Year to you, too, Sherry Rene," Mark said, as he gave her a kiss and a hug.

"How is youa awm, today?" Sherry asked.

"It's better," Mark answered, as he helped Sherry into his lap with one arm. "You did a good job of making it feel better last night."

"I give you big Nu Yea kiss," she said, as she kissed Mark's cheek and gave him a big hug.

"Did you all sleep well last night?" Carol asked.

"I slept like a log," Mark answered. There was no way he was going to say how he tossed and turned all night. Just knowing that Cat was so near and he couldn't be lying next to her had kept him awake all night.

"How did you sleep?" Mark asked.

"Not very well," Carol answered. "Sherry was so excited about the new year that she kept us up all night. She kept wanting to know when the wedding was going to be.

She's excited about being the flower girl. I don't know if I'll last until the wedding."

"I don't know if I will either," Mark answered. "Why don't we call the whole wedding thing off and just elope?"

"I don't think you can do that now," Carol said. "We've already put too much work into it."

After breakfast, the men went into the den to watch football and the women cleaned up the kitchen and visited. When the Tournament of Roses Parade came on the television, the women and Sherry watched the parade.

That's the way New Year's Day went. They watched the Rose Parade and football. Soon, it was time for dinner, so the women returned to the kitchen to prepare a meal. After the meal, there was more football to watch. The day went by fast and soon it was time for Carol and the others to go back to Carol's and Skip's cabin.

When they were all gone, Mark held out his hand to Cat and said, "Come here, my love, I haven't had you to myself all day."

Cat gladly went into his waiting arms. As they sat enjoying each other's company, Mark said, "Cat, I need to go see if I can find a vehicle tomorrow. Can you take me?"

"Yes, of course," Cat replied. "Just let me know when you want to go."

So, the next morning, after breakfast, Cat drove Mark downtown in search of a new vehicle. He looked at a lot of cars and finally settled on a red Ford Fusion. He drove it back to Cat's by being very careful with his sore shoulder. Cat drove her car behind him to make sure he didn't have any trouble.

When they arrived at Cat's cabin, Mark asked Cat to call and have Carol and the others come over and see his new car.

"Mista Mok, I wuv you nu ca," Sherry said when she saw it. "Will you tak me fo a wide?"

"Why don't we let Aunt Kitty take us all for a ride," Mark said. "I have to be careful of my arm until it's well."

So, Cat, Mark, Carol, Skip and Sherry went for a ride in Mark's new car. Then Cat, Mark, Charlotte, Tyler and Sherry went for a ride.

"Mista Mok, I wuv you nu ca," Sherry said. "I wuv to wide in it. Can we go to church in it Sunday?"

"If your mother says it's OK, you can ride with Aunt Kitty and me when we go to church," Mark answered.

On Sunday morning, Cat, Mark and Sherry rode in Mark's

new car and Carol, Skip, Charlotte and Tyler came along behind in Skip's car. When they got to the church, Mark asked Rev. Baxter if he could speak to him. Rev. Baxter took Mark and Cat into his office and shut the door.

"Now, what did you want to talk about, Mark?" Rev. Baxter asked.

"First, I want to tell you that Skip and I had a long talk and I accepted Jesus as my Savior."

"I'm glad of that, Mark," Rev. Baxter said. "I've been praying that you would."

"Now I'd like to be baptized and join Friendship Baptist Church," Mark said.

"I want to transfer my letter from Landmark Baptist Church to Friendship Baptist Church, too," Cat said.

"Good," Rev. Baxter said. "At the end of my sermon, when I give the invitation, you can both come before the church and present yourselves to the congregation. I'm sure there'll be no opposition to your joining Friendship Baptist Church. We'll all be glad to have you. Also, everyone was agreeable to your using the church for your wedding. You just have to abide by our rules. There will be no alcoholic beverages or smoking in any part of the church. There will be no food or drinks in the sanctuary, either. Here's a list of the rules you must abide by. If you agree to these rules, just sign the agreement and that's settled." Mark and Cat, of course, agreed to the rules and were happy to sign the agreement.

After Rev. Baxter's sermon, he gave an invitation and Mark and Cat went up front. Mark presented himself as a candidate for baptism and afterward into full fellowship with Friendship Church. Cat requested that the church request her letter from Landmark Baptist Church to become a member of Friendship Baptist Church. Rev. Baxter took a vote and everyone was in favor of Mark's baptism and Mark's and Cat's membership. Mark's baptism would be scheduled after service the following Sunday morning. Mark and Cat were glad that it would take place before their wedding.

On Monday, Cat took Mark to his doctor's appointment. Before he saw Dr. Nix, Mark was taken to X-ray to have an X-ray made of his shoulder and his cracked ribs.

Mark and Cat waited in the examination room for Dr. Nix to come in with the results.

When Dr. Nix came into the room, he was carrying the X-rays.

"Well, Mr. Fuller," Dr. Nix said, "It looks like your shoulder is healed. I'd still be careful with it if I was you. Your ribs are another thing, though. They may still be painful for a few months. You can still perform your duties, but you may encounter a slight pain in your side that you might have to either learn to live with or try to ignore."

"Doctor, Cat and I are getting married in a week," Mark said. "Will I be able to carry her over the threshold?"

Dr. Nix laughed and said, "I don't see any problem in doing that. Just be careful and don't drop her." They all laughed at that. Then Dr. Nix said, "I guess you're ready to go then, unless you have any more questions for me."

"No, I have no other questions," Mark said. "Do you have any, Cat?"

When Cat said she had no questions, Dr. Nix said, "I guess you can go, then." Then he walked out of the room and Mark and Cat left, too.

Mark decided to drive on the way home. He was very careful at first, but when he was sure that his arm wasn't hurting, he let out the breath he had been holding and started driving the way he usually drove.

"I guess I'll go back to work tomorrow," Mark said. "I need to get back before those guys fall back into the rut they were in when I got there. Do you want to go to the paper office tomorrow?"

"No, I think I'll wait until after our wedding and honeymoon before I go back to work. That way, I can visit with Charlotte and Tyler while they're here," Cat answered.

The next day about noon, Mark was in his office, when Jason came in and asked if he could talk to Mark.

"Sure. Come on in and shut the door," Mark said.

"I think I've made a decision, but first, I want to know if you can guarantee me that I'll get the position of SIC, if I transfer to your unit," Jason said.

"I kinda promised that position to Cassidy, but if you transfer to my unit, the position is yours," Mark said.

"If you promised it to Cassidy, won't she cause trouble if you don't give it to her?" Jason asked.

"Yeah, she'll probably cause trouble, but I can handle her," Mark said.

"Look, Mark, I have that position where I am," Jason said. "I can't risk transferring over here and losing it when Cassidy sues you over it. Even if I do want to work with you, Debbie and I plan to get married soon and I just can't risk it."

"Just a minute," Mark said. "Let me get Cassidy in here and see what she says." Then he called Cassidy to his office.

"Come in Cassidy and close the door," Mark said. "I believe you know Jason Hall. Jason do you know Cassidy Love?"

"I'll get right to the point, Cassidy," Mark said. "I want Jason to be my SIC. How so you feel about that?"

"How do you think I feel?" she asked. "You promised me that position. If you try to give it to someone else, I'll cause you so much trouble, you'll wish you hadn't."

"That's what I thought," Mark said. "If Jason transfers to my unit, then his position in Ted's unit will be vacant. You can transfer there. You don't really want to work with me, anyway, do you?" Mark asked.

"I want the position you told me you'd give me," Cassidy said.

"Come on, Cassidy. Be reasonable," Mark said. "I want Jason on my team. With him as my SIC, my unit can be the best unit in the whole country. Don't you want to be a part of the best unit in the country?"

"How do you know it won't be the best in the country with me as your SIC?" Cassidy asked.

"I don't know for sure, but I know Jason and I know what he's capable of. I know if he's on my team, we're bound to be the best. He was trained by Jim Ryan, who was the best Unit Commander in the country. I want him on my team, Cassidy, and I'll get him whether you like it or not," Mark said.

Cassidy was really mad now. "If you do, Mark Fuller, you'll have your hands full. I'll give you more trouble than you've ever seen," she said, as she walked out the door and slammed it behind her.

"Whee," Mark said. "That went well."

"I'm sorry, Mark, but I can't accept your offer, if it's going to cause that much trouble. I'd really like to work with you, but I think I'd better stay where I am for now," Jason said.

"Just give me a couple of days to bring Cassidy around," Mark said. "I really do need you on my team. I'll talk to Cassidy again and I'll let you know if she changes her mind."

"OK, Mark, but I don't think she'll change her mind," Jason said. "I've got to get back to work. If Ted knew I was over here talking to you, I wouldn't have to think about it. He'd answer for me; he'd fire me. I'll wait a couple of days to hear from you, then. See you later."

"Cassidy," Mark said, as he walked out and found her sulking. "Come on. Let's go to lunch. I'm buying."

"You're not going to change my mind by just buying lunch for me, Mark, so forget that," she said.

"I just need to explain things to you," Mark said. "I'm hoping that you'll be more receptive over a good lunch."

After they had ordered their meal, Mark said, "Look, Cassidy. I really need Jason on our team. I say our team because it is our team. If you stay, you'll be a part of it. I can even make it worth it for you, if you'll cooperate."

"You promised me I would be your SIC," Cassidy said.

"No, Cassidy," Mark said. "I didn't promise you the position. I told you I might give it to you if you didn't say anything to Cat about Jim or that you and I had dated. Well, Cat said that she and

Jim had already settled the problem of you and Jim a long time ago when you filed charges against him and she really doesn't care about you and me dating before she and I got together, so I didn't need to give you the job."

"Why did Cat say that she and Jim had already settled that?" Cassidy asked. "I thought you said she didn't remember anything about it."

"Cat said that Jim apologized to her for even looking at another woman," Mark answered. "When they rescued you and Don and you dropped the charges, they decided to forget the whole incident. Jim said he was sorry that he had ever asked you to join his team and Cat accepted his apology. She remembered all of that and said that if you had mentioned it, she would have just told you to forget it. So, you don't have a trump card after all, Cassidy. So, do you stay with our team and not cause any trouble or do you cause trouble and end up with nothing?"

"I hate you, Mark Fuller," Cassidy said.

"The feeling is mutual," Mark said. "There's a place for you on my team, if you want it, but if you persist in causing me trouble, I will crush you. You need to know that before you start. Now, what is your answer? Are you in or out?"

"If I go along with you, what's in it for me?" Cassidy asked.

"If Jason transfers to our unit, he'll be my SIC," Mark said. "If you behave and obey my orders, you can be an equal to Second-in-Command. If you don't, you're out."

"OK," Cassidy said. "I'll try it and see if you do like you say. If you don't, then I'm giving you all kinds of trouble more trouble than you could ever imagine."

"OK," Mark said. "Do we have a deal?"

"If you live up to your bargain, then I'll live up to mine," Cassidy said.

The next morning, Mark tried to get in touch with Jason, but was unsuccessful. At noon, Mark went to McDonald's hoping that

Jason would be there. He placed his order and found a table and sat down to eat his lunch.

"Hello, Mark," Jason said, as he walked up to his table. "May I join you?"

"Yes, of course," Mark said. "Sit down. I've been trying to get in touch with you."

"Why were you trying to get in touch with me?" Jason asked. "Do you have an answer for me?"

"Yes, I do, Jason," Mark answered. "Cassidy and I have come to an agreement.

If you'll come by my office, I'll explain it to you."

"I have to be careful," Jason said. "Are you sure there'll be no problems?"

"Not on my end," Mark said. "What about Ted?"

"He may be a problem," Jason said. "That's why I want your assurance that there'll be no problem on your end."

"Can you come to my office this afternoon about 5:00 p.m.?" Mark asked. "Then we can discuss it."

"I'll be there," Jason said. "I gotta go now."

So, about 5:00 p.m. that afternoon, Jason showed up at Mark's office. Mark and Cassidy were waiting for him.

"Come on in, Jason," Mark said. "Close the door. Have a seat."

"OK, Jason," Mark started. "If you transfer to my unit, you'll be given the position of SIC. Cassidy will be equal to you. She'll not have the title, but she'll have the same authority you'll have. When I'm unavailable, either of you will be in charge. Does this meet with your approval? Yes or no?"

"I don't understand how that'll work," Jason said. "How can we each have equal authority? What if we disagree on an action? Who'll be right?"

"I'll always have the final say-so on any decision," Mark said.

"What if you're unable to make a final decision?" Jason asked. "What then?"

"You'll just have to work it out," Mark answered.

"I don't know if I like that arrangement," Jason said. "Look, Mark, I'd love to be your SIC, but I don't think I can live with that arrangement."

"I'm trying to be fair, Jason," Mark said. "I want you on my team, but I have to be fair to Cassidy."

"Cassidy," Jason said. "What do you think of this idea?"

"I don't really like it," Cassidy said. "I want the title all by myself. I also want the salary that goes with the position. Mark said that if you come into our unit, I couldn't have it, though. I think the whole idea stinks."

"All right, Cassidy," Mark said. "I thought you agreed to abide by my decision.

Now, are you changing your mind?"

"I guess I am," Cassidy said. "Now that Jason pointed out the flaw in your idea. Who would be in charge, if you're unable to make a final decision?"

"I'm sorry, Cassidy, but it would have to be Jason," Mark said. "He'd be the one with the title."

"Then, I really would have no authority unless both of you were incapacitated. Is that right?" Cassidy asked.

Mark sighed deeply and said, "Yes, that's right, Cassidy. I have no other choice."

"Yes, you do, Mark," Cassidy said, getting angry. "I'm already on your team. You need to give me the position and forget Jason. He doesn't really want it, anyway."

"Yes, I do, Cassidy," Jason said. "I just want to make sure that if I transfer over to Mark's unit, I won't be making a mistake. I already have that position where I am now. I don't want to transfer over here and maybe lose it."

"OK," Mark said, getting agitated. "Let's table this discussion for now. Cat and I are getting married on January 16. We're going to be gone for two weeks after that. You two think about it while I'm gone. You can give me your decision when I come back. If you can't make a decision, I'll just have to give the position to someone else. Jason, you're my best friend. I really want you, but if you feel that you can't abide by my plan, then I'll understand. We'll still be friends no matter what your decision is. I'm through discussing it now. Go on home, now. I'll get your decision when I get back. I'm tired and I'm going home. Goodnight."

Then Mark walked to the door and opened it. Jason and Cassidy realized that the meeting was over, so they walked out.

"If I don't see you beforehand," Jason said. "I'll see you at your rehearsal, Mark."

Mark gave a disgusted sigh, turned out the light, locked the door and headed home.

The next morning, Mark called Cassidy into his office. "Come in, Cassidy, and close the door," Mark said. "Sit down. I need your cooperation, Cassidy. You know I'll be gone for two weeks. I have to leave someone in charge while I'm gone. Do you want that responsibility or do you want me to get someone else?"

"You know I was Don's SIC," Cassidy said. "It's only logical for me to be in charge while you're gone. Yes, I want the responsibility. You'll see that I can do anything that Jason can do."

"OK," Mark said. "I'm putting you in charge while I'm gone. Now, starting Monday, we have an assignment in Florida. Our unit needs to help a unit in Florida in an illegal arms deal. You can show me what you've got then. Be ready to go early Monday morning. You can go back to what you were doing now. I have some things I need to do in the office before I leave for two weeks." Cassidy went back to her desk then and Mark finished his paperwork.

When Mark got home, he hesitated in telling Cat that he was going to be gone the next week. He wasn't sure how she would take it, so he decided to wait until Monday just before he left. He was looking forward to his baptism on Sunday and hoped that that might ease the pain of his leaving for Cat.

After Rev. Baxter's sermon on Sunday, Mark got ready for his baptism. Rev. Baxter was already in the baptistery when Mark carefully entered the water and made his way over to him. Rev.

Baxter took a handkerchief and held it over Mark's nose and mouth and he held his hand up toward Heaven and said, "Upon your profession of faith and by the authority of Friendship Baptist Church, I baptize you, my brother, in the name of the Father, the Son and the Holy Spirit." Rev. Baxter then leaned Mark backwards into the water until he was completely immersed in the water and quickly brought him up again.

Then the members of the church sang some hymns until Mark changed out of his wet clothes and into some dry clothes. Then the members of Friendship Baptist Church gave Mark the right hand of church fellowship. Mark was now a new member of Friendship Baptist Church.

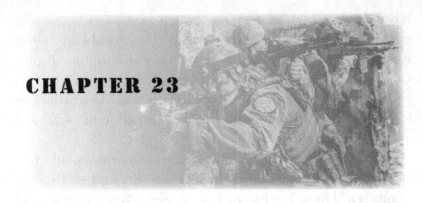

CHAPTER 23

On Monday morning, Mark arose about 5:00 a.m., dressed and went downstairs. He made a pot of coffee and waited nervously for Cat to come downstairs. He thought about waking her up, so he could get on the way, but he felt it would be better to wait until she awoke by herself.

Soon, Cat came downstairs. "Good morning, Mark. You're up early," she said, as she poured a cup of coffee and stirred creamer and sugar into it.

"I have to go out of town, so I need to get an early start," Mark said slowly not knowing what reaction he would get from Cat.

"You're going out of town?" Cat asked. "You didn't say anything about going out of town. How long will you be gone and when did you know you were going to be gone?"

"I'm sorry, Cat, but I have to be gone for several days," Mark said. He ignored her other question.

"Mark," Cat said raising her voice. "Our wedding is Friday and the rehearsal is Thursday."

"I know that, Cat," Mark said. "How could I forget? I'll be back in time for the rehearsal."

"No, Mark," Cat said. "No, you can't go," Cat was getting scared now.

"I have to go, Cat," Mark said. "It's my job."

"No, no, Mark," Cat said. "You cannot go. Please don't go. Please, Mark. Please don't go."

"I promise I'll be back in time for the rehearsal," Mark said.

"Jim promised me, too," Cat said. "He didn't come back in time. No, Mark. I won't let you go. Please don't go," Cat begged and began crying hysterically. "Please, please, Mark," she cried. "Please don't go."

"I have to go, Cat," Mark said again. "It's my job. I promise. I promise I'll be back in time for the rehearsal."

"No, Mark," Cat cried. "Let someone else go. Let Cassidy or Dave go. You can't go. Not now. Please, please don't go."

"Cat, Honey, I have to go," Mark said, as he tried to pull Cat into his arms.

She pushed him away and repeated her plea. "Mark, please don't go. I can't go through that again. If you don't come back, I'll go crazy. I can't do it, Mark. Please don't make me go through that again."

"Cat, nothing can keep me from coming back in time," Mark said, as he tried to embrace her again. "Honey, listen to me. I promise I'll be back in time. Please give me a kiss. I have to go. I can't go away knowing you wouldn't kiss me goodbye."

"No, Mark," Cat said. "I can't kiss you goodbye. If you really love me, you won't go."

"Cat, don't do this to me," Mark said. "I have to go. It's my job. I can't send someone else. I'm being tested. If I fail this test, I may lose my job. I can't let that happen. I've worked too hard for it. I promise, Cat. I'll be back in time for the rehearsal Thursday night. I may be a little late, but I'll be here. Please, kiss me goodbye. I can't leave without a kiss."

"No, Mark," Cat said. "If you go, you go without my blessing. I begged you not to go. I'll not kiss you goodbye and let you think I'm OK with your leaving. I'm not. Please don't go, Mark."

Mark gave a deep sigh and picked up his bag and walked out the door without a backward glance.

Cat sat down at the kitchen table, lay her head on her folded arms and wept uncontrollably. She couldn't believe that he would go when she had begged him not to go. Her memories of Jim overtook her and she could feel that horrible, painful feeling again. She could hardly breathe, as she relived those awful days when she had no idea where Jim was or if he was even still alive. She knew there was no way she could go through that with Mark. She would die first. Then she began to pray for God to take care of Mark and bring him safely back home to her. She suddenly felt a peace come over her and she stopped crying. "Mark will come back," she thought. "He has to come back."

As Mark drove to his unit headquarters, he felt all knotted up inside. "Why can't Cat understand?" he thought. "It's my job. I have to go. I'm just starting as Unit Commander of this unit and I have to succeed. If I don't, I'll never get another Commander's position. Can't she see that I'm not Jim? I'm nothing like Jim. I love her, but sometimes she drives me crazy. I have to go. It's my job." He tried to justify his decision all the way to his unit headquarters.

When he arrived at unit headquarters, Cassidy and the rest of his team were already there ready to go. They loaded their gear and their weapons into their transport vehicle and then everyone boarded the vehicle and headed for the base, where they would board a plane for Florida.

When they arrived in Florida, they were transported to the FSC barracks and there they were met by the Florida Unit Commander with whom they would be working.

"Commander Fuller, I'm Commander Greg Hendrix. I appreciate your coming to assist us. Here's the situation."

Then Commander Hendrix described the situation and outlined the plan of action for Mark. "For the next two days, we'll go by shifts and set up a 24-hour surveillance," Commander Hendrix said. "There are four positions that we need to take, so that will take eight agents at a time. When we're sure of our target and we have all the evidence we need, we'll go in Thursday morning. Does everyone understand what they are to do?"

Everyone said yes, they understood, so Mark paired his team

members and assigned them a time and a position for observation. "Cassidy, you'll be with me. Do you think you can back me up or should I get someone else?"

"I can back you up," Cassidy said. "I happen to be a professional. I don't let personal problems affect my job. I may not like you, but if you're my partner, I'll protect you."

"OK. Come on let's go, then," Mark said. "We need to get this job over, so I can get back to Cat."

"I think you need to forget about Cat until this job is finished," Cassidy said. "Don't forget, you're my back, too. I want you to be thinking about my safety, not your marriage to Cat."

"I'm a professional, too, Cassidy," Mark said. "I don't let personal problems interfere with my performing my job."

Everything went according to the plan on Tuesday and Wednesday, but on Thursday morning, a problem arose. They couldn't catch all of the suspects in the house at the same time. Cammander Hendrix knew that if he didn't get all of them at the same time, he would lose part of the suspects and they would go underground and it would take a long time to discover where they were hiding.

"We have to wait until they're all together," Commander Hendrix said. "If we don't, we'll lose part of them. I don't want that to happen. I've worked too hard and too long on this bust to let anything like that happen."

Mark's heart sank. He had promised Cat that he'd be home in time for the rehearsal. She had begged him not to go, but he went anyway. If he didn't make it, she'd probably never forgive him. He wondered what to do. Then he decided to pray about it.

"Lord, if you see fit to help me out of this mess I've gotten myself into, I'll be forever grateful. I know I haven't done what you wanted me to do. I've mostly ignored You most of my life, but I'd really appreciate it, if You'd help me out this time. I can't let Cat down. Please help me."

As Mark sat watching the house, hoping that all of the suspects would be there at the same time, he began getting more nervous as the hours ticked by. He knew it would take at least four hours to get back to his unit headquarters and then to the church. The rehearsal was set for 7:00 p.m. He would have to leave by 3:00 p.m. and it was already noon. "Why don't those men all get together?" he wondered. He was getting more nervous by the minute. He had begun to sweat until his clothes were wet with perspiration. He wanted to call Cat, but he knew there was no way he could jeopardize the operation by making a phone call. Then finally about 2:30 p.m., the suspects all began arriving. It seemed like something was happening inside the house.

"Come on, let's get 'em," Commander Hendrix said, as he headed toward the house. Everyone followed him. "Federal agents, you're under arrest," Commander Hendrix shouted, as he burst into the building. "Drop your weapons and put your hands in the air. You're surrounded."

It took about an hour to secure all of the suspects and tag the evidence. Mark was getting more nervous all of the time.

"Commander Hendrix," Mark said, when he finally cornered the Commander. "I really need to go. I'm getting married and my fiancee is waiting for me."

"Why didn't you say so, Commander Fuller," Commander Hendrix said. "I never would have made you wait so long."

Then Commander Hendrix called one of his men and told him to get Mark to the base as soon as possible. "I'll call and arrange for a chopper to get you home as soon as possible," Commander Hendrix said. "Thanks for all your help. I hope you make it in time."

"I do, too," Mark said, as he ran to the car. "Please fellow, get me to the base as soon as possible."

As soon as Mark was in the car on his way to the base, he reached into his pocket for his phone. Then he remembered that his phone was in his case. They weren't allowed to carry their phones when they were on a stake-out.

It was 5:30 p.m. when the helicopter took off with Mark sitting nervously in the co-pilot seat. He gave directions to the pilot and asked that he take him directly to the church. Cassidy had said that she would take care of his gear and weapons and make sure that they and his clothes got safely back to the barracks. He hoped that she would do it. Right then, he was more concerned with getting to Cat on time than he was in taking care of his gear.

At 6:00 p.m., when Mark hadn't arrived, Cat started calling his cell phone. Her calls all went directly to voice mail. Carol phoned to see if Cat was ready to go to the church. "Mark isn't here yet," she said, as tears started running down her cheeks.

"Why don't we go on to the church and he can just meet us there," Carol said, hoping that Mark would meet them there.

Cat agreed to go on to the church with Carol, Skip and the others. When 6:30 p.m. came and went, Cat started pacing the floor, crying as she paced. "He'll be here, Cat," Carol said. "He promised you that he would be here and I believe he'll keep his promise."

Cat kept calling Mark's cell phone until it finally wouldn't accept anymore calls. At 7:00 p.m., Rev. Baxter asked Cat if she wantd to go ahead and start the rehearsal without Mark. "I can get someone to stand in for Mark, if you would like for me to," Rev. Baxter said.

"No," Cat said. "If he isn't here by the time he needs to be, we'll just skip his part."

"Where are you, Mark Fuller?" Cat said under her breath. "You promised me you'd be here. Now where are you?"

The organist began to play the wedding march and Charlotte began to walk down the aisle. Then Carol followed her down the aisle followed by Sherry, pretending to throw petals along the aisle, as she slowly walked toward Carol. Tyler had gone to the vestibule with Cat and now he escorted her down the aisle. Just as they arrived in front of Rev. Baxter, they heard a helicopter fly over the church and land in the parking lot.

"Thanks," Mark shouted to the pilot. "I gotta run." Then he

ran into the church and into the spot beside Cat that was waiting for him.

"Who gives this woman to be wed?" Rev. Baxter asked.

"Her family and I," Tyler answered and then he sat down on the front pew.

"Now, do you want the long version or the short version?" Rev. Baxter asked.

"The shorter the better," Mark answered, as he took Cat into his arms and kissed her. "I made it, Cat," he said. "I'm sorry I'm late, but you know you just can't depend on air travel some times. In the winter, there are always delays."

"Oh, Mark," Cat began to cry. "I was afraid you wouldn't make it in time."

"I promised, didn't I, Cat?" Mark said. "I always try to keep my promises."

"Everyone, Barbara has a wonderful meal prepared at my cabin. Let's go eat," Cat said, when the rehearsal was over.

"Jason, do you mind if Cat and I ride with you since Charlotte and Tyler will ride with Skip and Carol?" Mark asked.

"No, that's fine, Mark," Jason answered.

"Cat and I are riding with Jason," Mark announced. "If you don't know the way to Cat's cabin, just follow us."

Jason started up and everyone fell in behind him. Skip came in last.

"Why are you going last, Skip? Charlotte asked.

"That way I can make sure no one gets lost," Skip answered.

"It's only a few miles to Cat's cabin," Charlotte complained. "Who would get lost?"

"You never know, Charlotte," Skip said, as he followed the other cars.

After everyone arrived, Cat had them sit down at the dining room table and Barbara served the meal. After the meal, everyone sat around and visited until about 10:00, then everyone started leaving.

Mark walked Jason and Debbie to the door and thanked him for all he had done for him. "You've really been a good friend, Jason," Mark said. "I couldn't ask for a better friend."

"Did you take Cassidy with you on this assignment?" Jason asked.

"Yes, I did," Mark answered.

"How did she do?" Jason wanted to know.

"She did really well," Mark replied, "better than I thought she would do. Of course, I should have known. Jim was really impressed with her performance at the training academy when she and Cat attended years ago. He tried to get her on his team, but it didn't work out. It took a lot for Jim to be that impressed with an inexperienced agent. She's experienced now, so she should be good."

"Does this mean that you've made your decision about the SIC position?" Jason asked.

"No, Jason," Mark replied. "I told you I'd make my decision when I get back in two weeks, and I still mean that."

"You're leaning toward Cassidy, though, aren't you?" Jason asked.

"I'm not leaning toward Cassidy, Jason," Mark said, beginning to get angry because Jason kept pushing him. "I told you. I'll make my decision when I come back. I want you to decide what you want to do while I'm gone, too. Two weeks should give you time to decide, too."

After everyone was gone, Cat and Mark sat on the sofa in the den. "Cat, I'm sorry that I was so late," Mark said. "I'd have called, but my phone was in my case and I left it for Cassidy to bring home for me. We need to go to the barracks and get my stuff tonight so I don't have to waste time getting it in the morning."

"We might as well go now, then, before it gets any later," Cat said.

"Yeah, we need to go on now," Mark said. "I need to bring my car home, too."

So, they went to the barracks and loaded Mark's clothes and gear into the trunk of his car. What they couldn't get into Mark's trunk, they put into the trunk of Cat's car. "I think I'd better leave a couple of shirts and slacks here in case I have to leave from here some time," Mark said. "I never know when there might be an emergency."

At Cat's cabin, they unloaded Mark's clothes and Mark headed up the stairs with them. At the top of the stairs he stopped. "Do I take these into my bedroom or your's?" he asked.

"Take them into our bedroom," Cat answered.

"Sure," Mark said with a smile and carried them into the bedroom that he and Cat would soon share. Then, Cat opened Jim's old office and Mark stowed his gear and weapons in there. "Here's a key for you," Cat said, as she handed it to Mark. "This is your office now. You can do as you please with it. I won't be going in there for anything."

"Thanks, Cat," Mark said. "I know it must hurt for you to go in there. I'll never ask you to go in there again."

"I'm going up to bed," Cat said, as she walked up the stairs.

"I am, too," Mark said, and he followed her up the stairs. When she started through the bedroom door, Mark continued to follow her.

"Wait just a minute, big boy," Cat said. "You don't sleep in here until tomorrow night."

"Dang, Cat," Mark said. "It's just one day. What does one day matter. Let me sleep with you tonight."

"No, Mark," Cat said, as she pushed him back out the door. "Wait until tomorrow night. I want our wedding night to be special. It won't be if you sleep with me tonight."

So Mark grudgingly walked across the hall to his old bedroom. He lay down on the bed, but couldn't go to sleep. He tossed and turned until about 3:00 a.m. Then he decided to get up and go across the hall.

"I may not be able to sleep with her like I want, but I can at least be close to her," he thought, as he quietly opened the door and lay down beside Cat. Cat was asleep and didn't even stir when Mark lay down. As soon as it started getting light, Mark got up, dressed and went downstairs. He made a pot of coffee and was sitting at the table drinking it when Cat walked into the room.

"Good morning, Cat," Mark said. "Did you sleep well?"

"Yes, I did," Cat replied. "Did you?"

"No, I did not," Mark said grouchily. "I could have slept well, if you had let me, but you wouldn't let me."

"Oh, you poor mistreated baby," Cat said, as she walked up behind him and kissed the top of his head.

Mark grabbed her and pulled her down into his lap. "Cat, I love you so much," he said. "Why do you insist on teasing me like this?"

"Mark, I'm not teasing you on purpose," Cat said, as she tried to pull away from Mark's embrace. "I just want our wedding night to be perfect. I thought you understood. It won't be long now. Surely you can wait a little longer."

"I've already waited what seems like a lifetime," Mark said, as he let her get up. "I guess I can wait a little longer. Just a little longer, though. No longer than I have to wait."

"I won't make you wait any longer than is necessary, Mark," Cat said. "I promise."

The rest of the day seemed to drag by for Mark. Carol, Skip, Sherry, Charlotte and Tyler came over about 4:00 p.m. and ate dinner with Mark and Cat.

"Where are you going on your honeymoon?" Charlotte asked.

"We're going to Hawaii," Cat answered.

"How long will you be gone?" Charlotte asked.

"About two weeks," Cat answered.

Sherry was interestedly listening to this conversation. She hadn't yet understood what a wedding meant. When she heard that Mark and Cat would be gone for two weeks, she knew that meant she wouldn't see either of them for two whole weeks. That was like a lifetime to her.

"Mista Mok, aw you and Aunt Kitty gonna be gone fo two whole weeks?" Sherry asked.

"Yes, we are, Sherry Rene," Mark answered.

"I won't see you fo two whole weeks?" she asked.

"That's right, Sherry Rene," Mark answered.

"I wanna go wit you," she pouted.

"You can't go with us this time," Mark said. "Maybe you can go the next time we go. We're going to see about getting that little girl you wanted us to get. You remember the little girl you wanted?"

"Oh, yeah," Sherry said. "You gonna get a widdle gul fo me to pway wit?"

"Yes, we're gonna try to get a little girl," Mark said, as he winked at Cat, who was turning red. "Come here, Sherry Rene," Mark said, as he picked her up and set her in his lap. "Would you do me a favor?"

"What is a fava?" she asked.

"It's something nice you do for someone," Mark said. "Will you do something nice for me?"

"Yes, Mista Mok," Sherry said. "I wik to do somptin nice fo you."

"Would you call me Uncle Mark instead of Mr. Mark?" he asked.

"You mean wik I call Unka Tyla?" she asked.

"Yes, like you call Tyler, Uncle Tyler," Mark said. "Will you call me Uncle Mark?"

"Yes, but why?" Sherry wanted to know.

"Because, I'll be your uncle after our wedding. Uncle is a lot better than Mr. I would love for you to call me Uncle Mark. Will you?" Mark asked again.

"Of course, Unka Mok," Sherry said. "I wik dat. Unka Mok. It sounds betta dan Mista Mok."

About 5:00 p.m., everyone got ready to go to the church. The females opted to carry their wedding dresses to the church and change after they got to the church. They told Cat that it was bad luck for Mark to see her in her wedding dress before the wedding.

Cat wore a powder blue, street-length dress and a hat with a short veil. She decided that, since she had already worn a white wedding dress with a long train and veil when she married Jim, she would opt for a blue dress. Carol, Charlotte and Sherry wore light pink dresses.

Everything went as rehearsed. When the music began to play, Charlotte started walking down the aisle, followed by Carol. Sherry followed Carol. She gingerly tossed her flower petals all the way down the aisle. She was having a really good time. Carol was afraid that Sherry might be shy about walking down the aisle in front of so many people, but when she saw Mark standing at the front with Rev. Baxter, she was happy to go down the aisle toward him.

Then the music for the bridal march began to play and Rev. Baxter asked everyone to stand while Cat, escorted by Tyler, walked slowly down the aisle.

"Who gives this woman to be wed?" Rev. Baster asked. "Her family and I," Tyler said and he put Cat's hand into Mark's hand and took his seat on the first pew.

Rev. Baxter gave his speech about how marriage was sanctioned by God and that a man forsakes all others for his wife. Then he asked Mark, "Marcus Alan Fuller, do you promise to love, honor and respect Catherine?"

Mark answered, "I certainly do."

Then Rev. Baxter asked Cat, "Catherine Rene Ryan, do you promise to love, honor and respect Mark?"

"Yes, I do" Cat answered.

Then they exchanged rings. "I now pronounce you husband and wife," Rev. Baxter said. "You may kiss your bride."

Mark took Cat into his arms and kissed her passionately. Then Rev. Baxter said, "I now present to you Mr. and Mrs. Mark Fuller."

Then the wedding recessional played and they all marched out. They formed a reception line and greeted all of their friends as they filed out and into the fellowship hall where there was a reception for Cat and Mark.

Mark and Cat had pictures made cutting the cake and feeding each other a bite of cake just like all brides and grooms do. Then they visited with their guests and accepted their congratulations.

After a while, Mark put his arms around Cat's waist and whispered into her ear, "When do we go home, Cat?"

"We can't go yet, Mark," Cat answered.

"When, Cat?" Mark asked.

"Soon," Cat answered. "I have to throw my bouquet and we need to open our gifts."

"Well, hurry and throw your bouquet and we can take the gifts home and open them later," Mark said.

"We can't do that, Mark," Cat said. "Everyone wants to see us open them."

"Well, come on. Let's get it over with," Mark said.

So, Cat gathered the single women and threw her bouquet. Then she talked Mark into helping her open their gifts.

Cat was finally ready to leave, so she and Mark went to his car and everyone threw rice at them. Carol said that she would take the gifts home for them.

When they got to the cabin, Mark carried Cat over the threshold and up the stairs to their bedroom. He lay her gently on the bed and said, "Now, Cat. I don't want to hear, "Stop, Mark," again. It's time. You will be completely mine tonight."

He started kissing her lips. Then he kissed her neck and her shoulders. Cat began to shiver with delight. She was as anxious to become completely his as he was to make her completely his. The lovemaking was wonderful. It was all that each of them had envisioned it to be.

"Oh, Cat," Mark sighed. "You were worth waiting for. You were certainly worth waiting for. I love you with all of my heart."

"I love you, too, Mark," Cat said. Then they went to sleep lying in each other's arms.

Later, Mark awoke and made love to Cat again. When the morning light awakened them, Mark kissed Cat and said, "Good morning, Mrs. Fuller. Did you sleep well?"

"Yes, Mr. Fuller," Cat answered. "I slept wonderfully well, thank you."

Mark again kissed Cat and was beginning to make love again, when the phone rang. "It's Carol," he said. "Should I answer it?"

"Yes, see what she wants," Cat answered.

"Hello, Carol," Mark said grumpily.

"Hello, Mark," Carol said. "It's 8:00 a.m. I just wondered what time you want us to take you to the airport?"

"We don't have to leave until 10:00 a.m.," Mark answered.

"OK, we'll see you then," Carol said. "I hope I didn't interrupt anything."

"You did," Mark answered gruffly.

"I'm sorry," Carol said. "See you at 10:00." Then she hung up.

"That wasn't very nice of you, Mark," Cat said.

"She'll get over it," Mark answered. "Now, where was I?" Oh, yeah. Now I know," he said, as he kissed Cat again.

Later, Cat got up, showered and went downstairs to fix breakfast. Barbara had gone back to the lodge to work again, so Cat went back to fixing their meals.

After breakfast, Cat and Mark finished packing for their trip to Hawaii. Carol and Skip came by about 10:00 a.m. to take them to the airport. Charlotte and Tyler were going to stay with Sherry. They had packed to make the trip home to Hollywood, but they decided to wait until after church on Sunday to leave. They came over with Carol and Skip to say goodbye, then they took Sherry and walked back to Carol's and Skip's cabin.

At the airport, Carol and Skip watched as Cat and Mark boarded the plane. Cat and Mark turned and waved goodbye and then they disappeared inside the plane.

As they watched the plane take off and disappear out of sight, Carol said, "I hope they have a good honeymoon. I know Mark has been looking for it ever since he and Cat became engaged."

"Yeah," Skip said. "I really didn't think Cat could hold him off that long. It looks like she did, though."

"Yeah," Carol said. "Good for her. It didn't hurt for him to have to wait. It just makes it mean more."

"That's right," Skip said. "Like you made me wait. At least I didn't have to wait as long as Mark did."

Cat and Mark spent almost two wonderful weeks in Hawaii. They spent most of it in the hotel room, but they did get out and shop for souvenirs one day and they lay on the beach one day and got a beautiful tan.

"We need to get some sun," Mark said. "We don't want people to think that we spent the whole two weeks in the hotel room, now do we?"

On Thursday morning of the second week, they planned to fly back home, but Cat awoke with an upset stomach. She was so sick at her stomach that even the thought of eating or drinking anything made her run to the bathroom to throw up.

"Mark," Cat said. "You go on and get you some beakfast. I can't eat anything."

"I don't want to eat, if you don't," Mark said. Finally, Cat talked Mark into going to get his breakfast.

"Do you want me to bring you back some coffee?" he asked her.

"No, Mark," Cat said, trying to keep from throwing up again. "Just the thought of anything to eat or drink makes me sicker. You go on and eat."

When Mark came back to the room, Cat was lying on the bed with her feet drawn up to her stomach. "I'm sorry, Mark," she cried. "I can't leave now. I couldn't make it to the airport. Let's stay one more day. Maybe this is just a 24-hour bug and I'll be over it tomorrow."

Finally, in the afternoon, Cat began to feel a little better. Mark found some hot soup and Cat tried to eat a little of it. He got her a Diet Coke and she was able to drink it and it seemed to help the queasiness.

They made plans to leave for home the next morning, but Cat awoke with the same upset stomach as she had the day before. She was determined to go home, though, so she packed her things and took along a sack to throw up in as they went to the airport.

On the flight home, Cat was miserable. She was sick all the way home. Mark had called Carol and asked if they would meet them at the airport and they were waiting when Cat and Mark arrived.

"What's wrong, Cat?" Carol asked when she saw how pale Cat was. She could tell that she wasn't feeling well.

"I got sick yesterday," Cat answered. "I thought I had a 24-hour bug, but it's lasted longer than 24 hours."

"Well, we'll get you home and into your own bed and then you'll feel better," Carol said, as she helped her into the car and fastened her seat belt. She sat in back with Cat and Mark sat in front with Skip

"Where's Sherry?" Mark asked Skip.

"She's with Charlotte and Tyler," Skip answered. "They decided to wait until you two returned before going home. Charlotte said she didn't know when they would be able to see you again, so they would wait until you got home."

"Well, she won't be able to visit with Cat very much," Mark said. "She's been really sick since yesterday morning."

When they arrived home, Cat went directly upstairs to her bedroom. Mark followed her to make sure that she was all right.

"Is there anything you need, my love," Mark asked, as he helped her get undressed and into bed.

"No, Mark," Cat said. "I just want to lie here and try to get over this terrible sick feeling."

When Mark came back downstairs, Carol asked if Cat was OK. "She's still sick," Mark answered. "If she isn't better by Monday, I'm taking her to the doctor."

"What did she eat before she started getting sick?" Carol asked.

"She didn't eat anything," Mark replied. "She just woke up sick at her stomach. She wouldn't eat or drink anything."

"I'm going to go up and check on her before we go home," Carol said. "Skip, I'll be back down in a few minutes."

"Skip, would you like to go sit in the den?" Mark asked. "I know how long a woman's minutes are."

"Sure," Skip said, as he followed Mark into the den. "How did things go otherwise?"

"Everything was great until Thursday morning," Mark answered. "Oh, that reminds me. We brought some souvenirs home. Cat will want to give them to you, when she feels better."

"I wish you would stop getting something for Sherry every time you go somewhere," Skip said. "You're spoiling her rotten. She's beginning to think you're supposed to bring her something all of the time. I think she likes you better than she does me."

"I don't think so, Skip," Mark said. "I know she loves you very much. I'm sorry if you feel that I'm taking her away from you. She showed me love when I really needed it, though. She helped me out of a really dark pit that I had gotten myself into. For that, I will be eternally grateful to her. I hope you understand, Skip. I'm not trying to take her away from you. I'm just so grateful to her, I can't help but get a little trinket for her now and then. If you want me to stop, though, I'll stop, but I really would like to continue getting her something every now and then."

"OK," Skip said. "Since you put it that way, go ahead and spoil her. I think you've already done that, anyway."

Then Carol came down the stairs. "I guess I'm ready to go, Skip. There's nothing I can do for Cat. She's taken some antacid medicine and I got her a cool washcloth to put on her forehead, so I guess that's all I can do for her. Call me, Mark, if you need me."

"Thanks, Carol, I will," Mark replied.

"I'll call tomorrow to see how she's doing," Carol said, as she and Skip walked out the door. "Bye for now."

"Bye, I'll talk to you later," Mark said.

The next morning, Cat was still sick. She stayed in bed and hardly ate or drank anything.

"Cat, if you're not better by Monday, I'm taking you to the doctor," Mark said.

"You need to go to work, Mark," Cat said. "I'll get someone else to take me."

"I'll take you," Mark said with his most authoritative voice. "You're my wife. I'll just have to miss a few hours of work."

Cat began to feel a little better late that afternoon, so she got out of bed and went downstairs. She ate a little soup and drank a little Diet Coke. "Maybe whatever I had is gone now," she told Mark. "I sure hope so."

The next morning, though, she awoke with the same sick feeling. Carol called to see if Cat and Mark were going to church.

"No, Carol," Mark said. "Cat is still really sick. I'm going to take her to the doctor tomorrow. She can't go on like this."

"Charlotte and Tyler are leaving after church," Carol said. "I was hoping that we could all go to church together and then to the restaurant before Charlotte and Tyler left. I guess that's out of the question, now."

"Yes, it is, Carol," Mark said. "You'll have to count Cat and me out. She doesn't feel like going to church and she certainly wouldn't feel like going to the restaurant afterwards."

"Can we come by for a few minutes on our way to church, so they can tell her goodbye, then?"

"Sure, if she feels like seeing them," Mark answered.

So about 10:00 a.m., Carol, Skip, Sherry, Charlotte and Tyler arrived to tell Cat that Charlotte and Tyler were leaving.

"Let me go up and see her alone first, Tyler," Charlotte said.

"Sure, go on," Tyler agreed.

Charlotte knocked lightly on the door and said, "Cat, may I come in?"

"OK, Charlotte," Cat said. "Come on in."

"Cat, we're leaving after church, so I wanted to tell you goodbye," Charlotte said, as she gave Cat a hug. "I don't know when we'll be able to get back down here to see you again."

"I'm sorry that we haven't been able to visit, Charlotte," Cat said. "I've just been so sick."

"Cat, are you taking the pill?" Charlotte asked.

"What pill?" Cat asked.

"You know what pill," Charlotte said.

"No, I'm not, Charlotte," Cat replied. "Mark and I want to have a baby soon. Why do you ask?"

"Well, when I first got pregnant, I was sick every morning just like you are. Do you think you might be pregnant?"

"I don't know," Cat answered. "Do you think that could be it?"

"If you're not on the pill," Charlotte replied. "It could very well be your problem."

"I never thought about that," Cat said. "It's so soon."

"I'm just saying that that could be your problem," Charlotte said. "If it is, you'll be sick for a couple of months, then it'll get better. The doctor can give you something for it if that's it. Just be sure to ask him for something. I'm feeling much better now."

"Thanks, Charlotte," Cat said. "I appreciate that. I'll be sure to ask him."

"Charlotte, are you about ready to go?" Tyler called from the foot of the stairs.

"Yes, you can come up and tell Cat goodbye now," Charlotte said.

Tyler came up and stuck his head into the bedroom and said, "Goodbye, Cat. I hope you get to feeling better. We'll see you the next time we come."

"Come here and let me give you both a hug," Cat said. "I don't have anything that's contagious. I think I don't, anyway."

"I don't think you do either," Charlotte said, as she hugged and kissed Cat goodbye.

Tyler gave Cat a quick hug and said, "Bye, Cat."

"Bye to you both," Cat said, and they went out and closed the door. After Mark let them out, he went up to the bedroom to see how Cat was doing. "How do you feel now, my love?" he asked.

"A little better," Cat answered. "I think I know what's wrong with me now. Charlotte told me what she thought was wrong."

"What is it, then?" Mark asked. "Is it serious?"

"Yes," Cat answered. "It's very serious. Charlotte thinks I'm pregnant."

"No, not really," Mark said in a surprised voice. "You really think you're having our baby?"

"Charlotte thinks so," Cat answered. "And it makes sense. I'll find out Monday when I go to the doctor."

Cat was feeling better that afternoon, but sure enough, on Monday morning, she was sick again.

"Why don't you go on to work, Mark?" Cat asked. "I can go to the doctor by myself. You really need to go to your office after being gone for two weeks."

Cat finally talked Mark into going on to his office. "I'll call you as soon as I find out something," she promised.

"You better," Mark said. "Your appointment is at 2:00 p.m. If I don't hear something from you by 3:00, I'm coming to the doctor's office."

"I might not know anything by then," Cat answered.

"Well, call me anyway," he said. Then he kissed her and walked out and slammed the door.

At the office, Mark called Cassidy into his office. "Come on in and shut the door, Cassidy," he said. "Sit down and tell me how things went while I was gone."

"We got called out on a couple of local assignments," Cassidy said. "I left you a report on your desk. Overall, everything went well. Dave and Greg were back from their training at the academy. I had them give a report and reminded the two that you had scheduled to go these next two weeks that it was their turn to go. You'll find their reports on your desk, also. Is there anything else you need to know?"

"Yes," Mark said. "First, I want to thank you for taking care of my stuff for me. Then, I want to know how you liked being in command and how the other team members took to your being Unit Commander."

"I loved it, Mark," Cassidy said. "I felt like I was meant to be Commander. The team, on the other hand, didn't like it at first. After they found out that I knew what I was doing, they became more receptive, though. I had some trouble with Dave Hightower, but everyone has trouble with him. You even had trouble with him, didn't you?"

"Yes, I did," Mark replied. "I'm glad everything went well. I'll read your reports and let you know what I think."

"Have you made a decision about Jason and me yet?" Cassidy asked.

"Not yet," Mark said. "I'll read your reports and they might have a bearing on my decision. By the way, Cassidy, I still don't want you having relations with any of the other team members in my unit. Please do as I ask. It's bad for morale if you break up. I don't want any bad morale in my unit. I thought I made myself clear when we talked the last time."

"What makes you think I'm having relations with anyone here?" Cassidy asked.

"Because I saw you with Jeff when I drove up this morning. That kiss didn't look like just a friendly greeting to me," Mark answered.

"You know, Mark," Cassidy said sarcastically. "I could get you into a lot of trouble for that remark. It's really none of your business what I do on my own time. I think I could sue you for sexual harassment and I would win."

"You try it, Cassidy, and see how far it gets you," Mark said angrily. "If you want the job of SIC, you'll do as I say. Don't forget, I can get rid of you, too. You're dismissed. Go back to your desk and stay there until I call you again."

"Yes, Sir, Mr. Unit Commander," Cassidy said, as she gave a sloppy salute and turned and walked out the door, slamming it behind her.

"That woman," Mark said under his breath. "If I didn't need her, I would get rid of her so fast….That's the problem, though, I need her and she knows it."

Mark devoted the rest of the morning to reading the reports that Cassidy left on his desk. He was impressed with them in spite of his feeling for Cassidy. "It's too bad she's so good," Mark thought. "I can't find anything wrong to count against her."

At noon, Mark went to McDonald's, hoping to see Jason there. He ordered his food and found an empty table when his order was ready. He had just started eating when Jason walked over.

"Hi, Mark," Jason said. "May I sit down?"

"Sure," Mark said. "I was looking for you. Have you decided what you want to do yet?"

"I'm still not sure yet, Mark," Jason started. "Ted said he intends to retire in a couple of years. It would be easier to get the Commander position if I'm already on that team than if I transferred to your team."

"I understand, Jason," Mark said. "I probably understand more than you realize. I put Cassidy in charge while I was gone. She did one hell of a job. I didn't think she could do it, but she did. She even had opposition from some of the other teammates and she overcame that. She and I clash on some things, but I have to admit, I'm proud of her."

"Yeah, I heard from some of the guys how she was doing," Jason said. "I guess that's another reason I've been hesitating about making a decision. If she's as good as you say she is, she might have an advantage over me if you ever decide to retire. I guess I'd better just stay where I am. I would really like to work with you again, but I think I'd better just stay where I am."

"Maybe you're right, Jason," Mark said. "Maybe you had better just stay where you are. We can still be friends and I guess you can help me out sometime if I need you, can't you? Ted wouldn't keep you from helping another unit in need, would he?"

"I guess not," Jason answered. "I guess we'll find out when the time comes. Oh, by the way, Debbie and I are getting married on February 14, Valentine's Day. Will you be my Best Man?"

"Of course I will, Jason," Mark said happily. "You know I will. Congratulations."

"Thanks, Mark," Jason said, as he stood up. "I guess I'd better be going. Ted holds a tight rein on us. I'll see you around. I'll talk to you later about the wedding."

"I guess I'd better get back, too," Mark thought. He looked at his watch and saw that it was only 1:00 p.m. It was too early to call Cat. He was tempted to go home and get her and take her to the doctor, but he knew she wouldn't like it, so he settled for just calling her at 3:00.

Back at his office, he called Cassidy into his office. "Close the door and sit down, Cassidy," he said. "Do you think you can work with me as my Second-in-Command? I mean really work close to me. You would have to put your prejudice aside. I want someone who likes me to be my SIC. The two of us will have to work really closely together at times. Do you think you can do that?"

"I don't know, Mark," Cassidy said. "Are you offering me the job?"

"I need to know what your answer is first," Mark said. "I know you hate me, but I need to know if you can get over your hatred for me and work closely with me without questioning my authority. I don't want my SIC to be always questioning my authority."

"You know something, Mark," Cassidy said. "At one time, I had a crush on you. Don't get the big head, though, because I got over it. I don't really hate you. I dislike you, though. You're an egotist. This job has just made you even more of an egotist than you were. As a matter of fact, you're just like Jim Ryan was."

"I'm nothing like Jim Ryan," Mark said. "Besides being Unit Commander and being in love with Cat, I'm nothing at all like Jim Ryan was."

"Yes, you are, Mark," she said. "You're just like him. I wouldn't be surprised if that's not why Cat married you. Maybe she thinks by marrying you, she got Jim back. He was like that. Just like you, his word was law."

"That hurt, Cassidy," Mark said. "You didn't have to be so blunt."

"You didn't have to be so tactless, either," Cassidy said. "If I was your SIC, I'd expect to have input into any decision that involved me and the rest of the unit. I respect the fact that you'd have the final say, but I'd expect you to listen, without interruption, to my ideas, too. I'd want you to respect me, also. I know you don't like my lifestyle, but it's my lifestyle. Anything I do on my time that doesn't affect this unit, is none of your business. You said you want your SIC to like you. Well, I say you need to be likable, which you are not, at the present time. That would go both ways also. I'd want you to like me, also. So before I answer your question, what do you really feel about me?"

"OK, Cassidy," Mark answered. "Since you were so bold as to ask. No, I don't like you. I don't like you at all. I don't like anyone who bucks my authority, and you have really done that. I am proud of you, though. I think you're a darn good agent and I would be lucky to have you as my SIC, but we need to do something about our other problem. What are we going to do about that?"

"Can we compromise?" Cassidy asked. "You give a little and I'll give a little. How would that work?"

"I don't care for that idea," Mark answered. "After all, I'm your boss."

"That's your problem, Mark," Cassidy said. "You're always thinking 'I'm the boss. What I say goes.' I'm told that's just like Jim was. Maybe someone else has a better idea. Was Jim ever receptive to someone else's ideas or was he close-minded like you are?"

"What difference does it make what Jim did?" Mark asked. "This is my unit and I'll do what I please."

"There you go again, Mark," Cassidy said.

"If you continue with that attitude, you won't be Commander for long, because your unit will all leave you and go to other units. I'm telling you, Mark, you're going to have to let up a little. You have to compromise."

Mark looked at his watch and saw that it was 3:30 p.m. "This disussion is over for now. I have to call my wife. We'll talk later. You're dismissed."

Cassidy stood up and said, "Think about what I said, Mark." Then she walked out and slammed the door again.

Mark gave her retreating back a mean look, then he called Cat's cell phone.

"Hello, Mark," Cat said as soon as she answered. "I was just going to call you. Dr. Williams said that he can't be sure because it's too early to tell, but he thinks I'm pregnant."

"Oh, Cat," Mark said excitedly. "I hope so. When will we know for sure?"

"He said we might be able to tell in a couple of weeks," Cat said.

"How much longer are you going to be so sick?" Mark asked.

"Maybe about three more months for that," Cat said. He gave me a prescription for something for the nausea. He said it should keep me from being so sick all of the time. I'm going to go by the pharmacy on my way home and have it filled. How did your day go?"

"I'll tell you about it when I get home," Mark said. "Can you make it home OK or do you want me to come get you?"

"I can make it home," Cat said. "You just stay and take care of your business."

"OK, Cat. I'll do that," Mark said. "I love you, Cat. I hope we are having a baby and that's what your problem is."

"I do, too, Mark," Cat answered. "I love you, too."

When Mark hung up, he called Cassidy back into his office. "All right, Cassidy," he said. "Maybe you're right. Maybe I do need to lighten up a little. If I try to be easier on the teammates, will you do some of the things I asked you to do or not do?"

"It depends on what you tell me to do or not do," Cassidy said.

"You know what I want you to not do, Cassidy," Mark said, getting angry again. "I think I've made myself clear on that subject."

"All right, Mark," Cassidy said. "I won't date any of the guys in this unit. Is it OK if I date the guys in some of the other units?"

"I don't care who else you date, as long as you don't date any of the guys on my team," Mark said.

"Do you think you can work with me under those circumstances?" Mark asked.

"If I get the position and the salary, I can manage a little cooperation," Cassidy said.

"OK," Mark said. "I'll start the paperwork, but if you double-cross me, I'll sack you. I mean it, Cassidy. I want to make this unit the best unit in all the country and, if I have to cull the garbage, I'll do it."

"Are you calling me garbage?" Cassidy asked.

"If the shoe fits, wear it," Mark said.

"I don't think I like being called garbage," Cassidy said.

"Well, don't be garbage, then," Mark said. "It's all up to you, Cassidy. You can do whatever you set your mind to do. Now get back to work. I need to leave early. You can take over while I'm gone. I'll see you in the morning."

On the way home, Mark drove by Simmons Drug Store, just in case Cat was still there. He didn't see her car, so he assumed she was already at home or on her way home.

On the way home, Mark started thinking about what Cassidy had said about his being just like Jim. He knew he wasn't anything like Jim, but he couldn't get the idea that Cat might think he was like Jim out of his mind. It hurt to think about what Cassidy had said. Surely, Cat didn't marry him because she thought he was just an imitation of Jim, a weak imitation at that. He tried to force it out of his mind, but it was almost impossible. Now, every time he kissed her, he would wonder if she was thinking of Jim.

When he arrived at home, her car was in the driveway, so he gave a sigh of relief that she had made it home OK. As he came into the cabin, he called her name. "Cat, where are you, Honey?" he asked.

"I'm in the den," she answered. "I took over your old bed," she said. "I hope you don't mind."

"Not at all," he said, as he leaned over and kissed her. "How are you feeling?" he asked.

"A lot better," she answered. "I took one of the pills as soon as I got them. I think they're going to work."

Then the phone rang. "It's Carol," Mark said when he answered it. Then he gave the phone to Cat.

"Hello, Carol," Cat said.

"Hi, Cat," Carol said. "How are you feeling?"

"A little bit better," Cat answered.

"I stopped at KFC on the way home," Carol said. "Do you feel like eating? If you do, we can come over and have dinner with you and Mark?"

"Sure," Cat answered. "Come on over."

"We'll be over in a few minutes," Carol said.

In a few minutes, Sherry burst through the door as usual and ran to Cat and hugged her.

"Aunt Kitty me sorry you sick," Sherry said. "Me kiss you. Make you feel betta." Then she began kissing Cat's face.

"Hey, Sherry Rene," Mark said. "Save some of those kisses for me."

"I got lotsa kisses," Sherry said. "Here, Unka Mok, I give you some, too," she said, as she kissed Mark.

"After we eat, Sherry Rene, I have something for you," Mark said. "I brought you something back from Hawaii."

They ate their meal and visited for a while, then Mark went upstairs to get Sherry's gift. He left the other things upstairs in case Cat wanted to give them to Carol and Skip later.

"Wook, Mommie," Sherry squealed with delight. "It's a widdle hula gul," she said, when she saw the small Hawaian girl dressed in a grass skirt. Whenever Sherry moved her, she did the hula dance. "Wook, Daddy," Sherry said excitedly, as she showed the doll to Skip. "She does da hula when I wiggle hewa."

"Yes, Sherry, I see," Skip said and he gave Mark a dirty look. "Yes, Uncle Mark was very nice to bring you something from Hawaii. Tell Uncle Mark thank you."

"Tank you, Unka Mok," Sherry said, as she hugged the doll to her chest. "I wuv it."

Then Mark took Skip aside and whispered, "I'm sorry, Skip, but I saw the doll and I just had to get it for Sherry."

"OK, Mark," Skip said. "This was a special occasion. I'll let it pass this time, but please don't make a habit of bringing her something every time you go somewhere."

"I hear you, Skip," Mark said. "I thought we had already agreed that I could bring her something every now and then, though."

"Yes, I guess we did," Skip said. "I just didn't realize she would like it so much. Next time try not to make it so appealing." Then Skip walked over to Carol and asked if she was ready to go.

"Sure, Skip," Carol answered. "Will you carry Sherry to the car? Bye, Cat. I'll see you tomorrow. Bye, Mark."

"Bye, Carol. Bye, Skip. See you later, alligator, Sherry Rene," Mark said, as he waved goodbye to Sherry.

"See you lata, awagata," Sherry said. "Bye Aunt Kitty."

"Bye, Sherry and you two," Cat said. "Maybe I'll feel better tomorrow and we can have a longer visit. I'll get your souvenirs then."

"That's fine," Carol said, as she followed Skip and Sherry out the door.

"Now," Cat said. "Now that they're gone, tell me about your day. Was it bad?"

"Well, I guess you might say it was bad," Mark said, as he sat down on the sofa and put Cat's head into his lap. "Jason decided to stay where he was, so I was left with Cassidy for my SIC. We had a, I don't know if you would call it a fight or just a disagreement. Anyway, I got angry and she got angry and I think we both said some things that we wish now we hadn't said. What's done is done, though, and it can't be undone. Anyway, I told her I would give her the position if she agreed to my terms. She halfway agreed. I hope I haven't made a mistake."

"Maybe it'll all work out after things get settled down and everyone has the two-week training," Cat said.

Mark thought for a few minutes. He wanted to ask Cat about

Jim, but he didn't know how to ask without seeming obvious. "Cassidy made a statement today that I was wondering about," he started slowly at first, to see Cat's reaction. "She said I was just like Jim. I never thought of myself as anything like Jim. What do you think?"

"Well, yes, I guess you are a lot like Jim," Cat said. "You're both very handsome and strong. You're both kind and good leaders. You are both controlling, though. I bet that was one of the things that Cassidy said you were alike. Yes, I think you are a lot like Jim. Do you think that's a bad thing?"

"No, I guess not," Mark said. "When you list all those good points. The only bad thing you said was that I'm controlling. Am I as controlling as Jim was?"

"Mark, why are you asking me this?" Cat said. "I really don't feel like talking about Jim right now. Please change the subject."

"I'm sorry, Cat," Mark said, as he leaned over and kissed Cat's forehead. "I just needed to know if you thought I was a lot like Jim. I really never thought I was anything like him until Cassidy pointed it out."

"Yes, Mark, if you must know, I do think you're a lot like Jim, but you're mostly like Marcus Alan Fuller. You're one of a kind. I never even thought of you're being anything like Jim until you asked me. Now, please, let's change the subject."

"Sure, Cat," Mark said. "Tell me about your doctor visit. What did Dr. Williams say?"

"He said that he was pretty sure that I was pregnant, but it's too soon to know," Cat said. "I bought a pregnancy test at the pharmacy. I thought I'd try it in a couple of weeks and see what it shows.

"Dr. Williams said I would probably have this sickness for about three months, but to take these pills and they would help. They're already helping. Maybe I'll be able to sleep tonight and wake up in the morning without feeling like throwing up."

"I hope so, too," Mark said. "Would you like to go upstairs to our bedroom now or do you want to stay down here?"

"I'm ready to go upstairs, if you're ready for bed," Cat said.

"Come on, then," Mark said. "I'll help you get up the stairs."

When they were in bed, Mark pulled Cat to him and kissed her neck. "I love you, Cat," he said. "I can't stand to see you hurt. Tell me what I can do to make you feel better."

"Just being close to you makes me feel better, Mark," Cat said. "Please, don't ever leave me. I need you so much, Mark."

"I'll never leave you, Cat," Mark said. "It would be against my will if I ever did."

"Jim said he would never leave me, but he did," Cat whispered. "Please don't promise me something you can't keep."

"I'm not Jim, Cat," Mark said. "I'm not Jim."

CHAPTER 24

February 14 arrived with lots of sun, but the air was crisp and cold. Mark shivered in his tuxedo, as he stood outside the church waiting for Jason to arrive. The wedding was scheduled for 2:00 p.m., but Mark had misjudged how long it would take for him to get to the church and had arrived at noon.

He had wanted Cat to attend the wedding with him, but she wasn't feeling well when she got up that morning. He was still worried about her. The sickness pills usually helped, but they hadn't helped her at all that morning.

He was scheduled to undertake a new assignment starting on Monday morning and he was expecting to be gone for about two weeks. He was dreading being away from Cat for that long, but there was nothing he could do about it. The unit in Florida needed help with surveillance again. This time it was a ring of illegal gun smugglers. The Florida unit had already done the preliminary work. They just needed Mark and his unit to help round up the suspects and the evidence.

Jason finally arrived and Debbie and her bridesmaids followed him.

"It's about time you showed up, Jason." Mark complained. "I'm freezing. Why are you so late?"

"There was a wreck on the freeway," Jason said. "There was no way to get around it until they had cleared it. I'm sorry you had to wait out here in the cold. The minister was caught in the traffic, also."

Jason unlocked the door to the church and Mark and the girls rushed into the warm sanctuary. "At least the heat's on," Mark said. "Jason, I can't hang around after the wedding. Cat's sick again. I need to get home and see about her."

"Sure, Mark," Jason said. "I appreciate your being my Best Man. You can leave whenever the wedding's over. What's she going to do when you're gone for two weeks, though? Have you thought about that?"

"Yes, Jason," Mark said. "I think about it all the time. Everytime I have to leave for a few days, I think about it. Now that you're getting married, you'll be in the same boat I'm in. I guess we just have to trust God to take care of our wives while we're gone. He can probably do a better job than we do, anyway."

After Jason's wedding, Mark shook hands with Jason and congratulated him again and said, "I'm sorry, Jason, but I really need to get home and check on Cat. I'll talk to you when you get back from your honeymoon. See you later."

When Mark arrived home, Cat was in the kitchen cooking dinner. "Hi, Honey," Mark said, as he gave her a kiss. "Are you feeling better?"

"Yes, I'm feeling much better," she answered. "How was the wedding?"

"About like all the other weddings," he said. "I just wanted it to be over, so I could get back home to you."

"I'm glad you're home," she said. "I missed you."

Then the phone rang. "It's Carol," Mark said when he answered it.

"Hi, Carol," Cat said, as she took the phone from Mark.

"Hi, Cat. How are you feeling?" Carol asked.

"I'm feeling much better," Cat answered. "I'm fixing dinner, if you guys want to come over."

"Not tonight, thanks, anyway," Carol answered. "I've already fixed dinner over here and I was going to ask if you wanted me to bring something over for you. I guess we'll just eat what I fixed and you can eat what you fixed. Oh, while I think of it, do you think you'll feel like attending church tomorrow?"

"I may make it to church, but I don't think I'll make it for Sunday School," Cat answered. "We'll probably see you there."

"OK," Carol answered. "I'll see you two tomorrow."

"Are they coming over for dinner?" Mark asked.

"No, Carol fixed dinner over there," Cat answered.

"I didn't think Carol knew how to cook," Mark said sarcastically.

"Of course she does," Cat said angrily. "I just fix for us and them, too, because I know how busy she is."

"Well, since they're not coming, I'm going upstairs and get out of these clothes," Mark said. "They're very uncomfortable."

"They may be uncomfortable, but you sure are handsome in them," Cat said, as she hugged and kissed him.

"Thanks for the compliment," Mark said, as he ran up the stairs and into their bedroom.

On Sunday morning, Cat was a little nauseated, but after she took one of her pills, she began to feel better. Since she was feling better, Cat got ready to go to church.

At church, they sat in their usual pew next to Carol and Skip. When Sherry came out of her Sunday School room, as usual, she ran and jumped into Mark's lap. "Unka Mok," she said, as she held up a picture for him to see. "See what I drawed. It's a pitcha of Jesus wit widdle wambs. How you wik my pitcha?"

"I love it, Sherry Rene," Mark said. "Why don't you go show it to Daddy. I think he'd like to see it, too."

"Suwa," Sherry said, as she jumped down and climbed into Skip's lap. Skip gave Mark a smile and mouthed the word, "Thanks."

After church, Carol asked if Cat felt like going to the restaurant. "I guess I do," Cat answered. "Mark, do you want to go to the restaurant?"

"Why don't we go back home and eat leftovers?" Mark asked. "I need to get ready to go out-of-state in the morning."

In the car on the way home, Cat said, "I didn't know you were going out-of-state in the morning. Did you tell me?"

"I don't know if I told you or not, Cat, but I have to go back to Florida. I'll probably be gone for two weeks."

"Oh," Cat said.

"What is it, Cat?" Mark asked.

"It's nothing," Cat said. "I just didn't expect you to go out-of-state so soon."

"I'm sorry, Cat, but you know I have to go a lot. You were in the FSC. You know there are times when we have to go out-of-state, even out of the country sometimes."

"I know, Mark," Cat said. "I just didn't know you would go out again so soon."

"Honey, it's been a month since I was in Florida," Mark said. "You just forget how long it's been."

When they arrived at home, Cat went into the kitchen to prepare something for lunch and Mark went upstairs to change clothes and begin packing for his trip to Florida.

When Cat had their meal ready, she called Mark, who came downstairs and sat down at the kitchen table.

They had their prayer and they each filled their plate and began to eat in silence. Mark could tell that Cat was unhappy that he was leaving, but he knew there was nothing he could do. It was his job and he had to do what his job dictated.

The next morning, Mark was up at 5:00 a.m. preparing to leave. Cat was feeling sick again, but she was determined to keep Mark from knowing. She went into the bathroom and took one of her pills and hoped that it would calm her upset stomach. When she was feeling better, she went downstairs to find Mark sitting at the table drinking a cup of coffee.

"Good morning, Honey," Mark said. "Sit down and I'll get you some coffee."

"No thank you, Mark," she said. "I don't want any coffee this morning. What would you like for breakfast?"

"Don't worry about fixing breakfast for me," he said. "I'll get something at headquarters. I need to get on the road. I was the last to arrive the last time. I don't want that to happen this time."

He then took her into his arms and kissed her hard. "I love you, Cat," he said. "If there was any way I could get out of this, I would, but I can't. I have to go, now. Pray that I have a safe trip."

"I always pray for you, when you're gone," Cat said, as she kissed him back and gave him a big hug.

"I'll call you when we get there, but you know I can't call after that, don't you?"

"Yes, I know, Mark," Cat said. "Bye. I love you."

"I love you very much, Cat," Mark said and then he was gone.

Cat watched as his car drove out of sight and then she sat down and cried. "I know he has to leave, but I just can't stand to see him go," she said to herself.

When everyone arrived at the unit headquarters, they stowed all of their gear and weapons in the transport vehicle and everyone boarded it. Then they were driven to the base, where they boarded the plane that would take them to Florida. The trip took a couple of hours and Mark spent the whole time thinking about Cat. He felt bad that she was unhappy that he was leaving, but he knew there would be many more times when he would have to leave her. Some of the times he would be going out of the country. He knew these trips would be the hardest, but he would have to steel himself for them. It was his job. A job that he had wanted for a long time. A job that he had coveted when Jim was alive. Now that he had it, he had to take the good with the bad. It came with the job. He was determined to do a good job. He couldn't let anything, not even Cat, keep him from doing the best job he could do. That included doing some things that he really didn't enjoy doing, but they had to be done.

Sooner than he expected, the plane was landing at the base in Florida. Everyone unloaded, carrying their gear to the transport vehicle that took them to the barracks.

There, they were assigned rooms where they would stay for the duration of their stay.

After dinner, they met with Commander Hendrix, who briefed them on the assignment and gave them their positions. About 8:00 p.m., they were driven to the site and each team took their position.

It was a boring assignment and the days and nights seemed to drag by, but finally the first week was over. By Wednesday of the next week, most of the work had been accomplished. That night, Commander Hendrix said, "It's time. Everything's ready. Let's go."

With their new gear and weapons, Mark's team took their position, while Commander Hendrix's unit stormed the stronghold. The suspects weren't taken easily. There, of course, was a gun battle. Some of Mark's teammates were wounded and were taken to the hospital to be patched up.

As Mark and Cassidy sat in the waiting room of the hospital waiting to see how everyone was doing, Darin Coleman, the SIC of the Florida team, walked into the room. "Hey, you guys," he said. "How's everyone doing?"

"We don't know yet," Mark answered. "How are your guys?"

"Most of them just have superficial wounds," Darin said. Then he sat down next to Cassidy. "How you doing, beautiful?" he asked.

"Better since you came in," Cassidy answered.

"How would you like to go get a drink and celebrate or do you have to stay with your Commander?" Darin asked.

"I'd love to go get a drink with you, handsome," Cassidy answered. "No, I don't have to stay with my Commander, although he might get jealous. He thinks he owns me."

Mark frowned at Cassidy and said, "Sit down, Cassidy. You're not going anywhere, yet."

"You see what I mean, Darin," Cassidy said, but she didn't sit back down. "He's crazy about me. Won't leave me alone and he's married, too."

Mark grabbed Cassidy's wrist and said, "That's enough, Cassidy.

Sit back down. You're not going anywhere until we find out about our teammates."

Cassidy shook Mark's hand from her wrist and said," You can't stop me, Mark. I'm on my own time, now. Come on, Darin. Let's go get that drink."

"That's OK, Cassidy," Darin said. "We can get that drink later. You need to stay here until your Commander says you can go."

"I'm on my own time now, Darin," Cassidy said again. "I don't have to listen to my Commander. Come on, let's go."

"Cassidy, if you walk out that door, you're through," Mark said.

"I'll be back at the barracks in time to get to the transport," Cassidy said. "I'll see you then." Then she and Darin left.

Mark was full of anger, but he stayed at the hospital until all of his teammates were ready to leave. Then they were taken back to the barracks by the transport vehicle.

About 2:00 a.m., Mark heard Cassidy come into the barracks. He got up and confronted her. "Cassidy, I want to talk to you."

"Not now, Mark," she said with a slurred voice. "I'm tired. I just want to go to bed."

"I need to talk to you, now," Mark said, as he grabbed her arm and pulled her to a secluded spot in the barracks. "I don't appreciate what you did tonight. You know I could fire you for insubordination. That crack about my being crazy about you and jealous if you date someone could give me a bad reputation. If that ever gets back to Cat, you'll be very sorry you did that."

"I'm sorry about Cat," Cassidy said. "I didn't think about her."

"That's just it," Mark said. "You weren't thinking. Why did you do that?"

"I just wanted to hurt you," Cassidy said.

"Why?" Mark asked.

"Because you hurt me," Cassidy answered, as tears welled up in her eyes.

"How did I hurt you?" Mark wanted to know.

"I was in love with you," she said. "You didn't even care. You were too hung up on Cat."

"You were married," Mark said. "That's why I broke it off with you."

"Not at first," she answered. "The only reason I married Buck was because I decided to give up on you. I didn't love him. That's why our marriage didn't last. I still loved you."

"It hurts when you love someone who doesn't love you back," Mark said. "I know from experience. You have to just get over it and get on with your life."

"That's not what you did," Cassidy said. "You just kept hanging around hoping you'd get her some day, didn't you?"

"That's none of your business, Cassidy," Mark said. "That still doesn't give you cause for insubordination. When we get back to the office, you will be censured. You get another demerit for showing up at the barracks drunk. Now get to bed. We'll be leaving early in the morning."

That morning at breakfast, Commander Hendrix issued an official commendation to Mark and his unit.

"Thank you, Commander Fuller, again for your help. We appreciate everything you've done for us. Let me know if we can ever do anything for you and your unit," he said.

Then they loaded the transport vehicle and headed to the base and back home. When they arrived back at their own barracks, Mark was almost exhausted. He was glad that he would be getting home early. He thought about calling to tell Cat that he would be home early, but he decided to surprise her.

It was already dark when Mark arrived at home. He unlocked the door and went into the cabin without turning on the light. He didn't want to awaken Cat, if she was sleeping on the sofa in the den.

All at once, he heard the click of a safety being taken off of a pistol and a light in his eyes. "Cat, it's me," he shouted. "Don't shoot."

"Oh, Mark," Cat cried. Then she ran to him and threw her arms around him and sobbed.

"You almost shot me," Mark shouted. "Why were you sitting down here holding a gun?"

Cat stopped crying and didn't say anything for a few minutes. Then she walked into the den and sat down on the sofa.

Mark followed her and noticed the pillow and blanket on the sofa. "Were you waiting for me?" he asked.

"No, I wasn't expecting you until tomorrow," Cat answered.

"Then why were you here instead of in the bedroom? Are you sick again?" Mark asked. "Why the gun?"

Then the telephone rang. Mark grabbed it before Cat could get to it. "Cat are you all right?" Carol asked breathlessly.

"Carol, it's Mark," he said.

"Oh, Mark," Carol sounded relieved. "I'm glad you're home. I guess that was you I heard."

"Yes, I just got home," he answered. "What's going on, Carol?"

"What do you mean, Mark?" Carol asked.

"When I got home, Cat almost shot me," he said. "Now, tell me what's going on."

"I'll let Cat tell you that," Carol said. "I've gotta go now. I just wanted to make sure Cat was all right." Then she hung up before Mark could ask her anything else.

"What's going on, Cat?" he asked sternly.

Cat took a deep breath and said, "I was frightened. I heard a noise."

"What kind of noise?" Mark asked.

"Just a noise," Cat answered.

"Why were you afraid of just a noise?" Mark asked.

"I don't know," Cat said. "Forget it. Let's go to bed." Then she started toward the stairs.

Mark caught her arm and pulled her back down on the sofa beside him. "You're not leaving until you tell me what's going on," he said.

"I just heard a noise. I thought someone was breaking in," Cat said. "Then, when you came in, I thought he had come in."

"He who, Cat?" Mark asked.

"Just he," Cat said. "I don't know who. I just said he."

"Cat, you're keeping something from me," Mark said. "I'm not letting you go until you tell me what it is. Has someone been trying to break in on you while I've been gone?"

Cat started to cry again. "I think so," she said.

"Well, go on," Mark coaxed her. "Tell me all of it."

"That's it," she said. "I thought someone was trying to break in. That's it."

"Cat, I know you," he said. "I know you inside and outside. I know you upside and downside. I know when you're lying to me. Tell me the truth. I mean the whole truth. Why are you trying to hide it from me?"

"I don't want you to do something that you'll be sorry for later on," Cat said.

"What, Cat," he asked. "What would I do that I would regret?"

"You might," she started. Then she hesitated.

"I might what, Cat?" Mark asked again. "Tell me what happened while I was gone."

"It's really nothing," Cat said, trying to make light of it. "I may have made more of it than it really was."

"Anything that makes you so scared, that you would almost shoot me, is serious," Mark said. "Now, start at the beginning and tell me the whole story."

"It all started innocently enough, even before you left for Florida," Cat started between sniffles. "There was this man. Everywhere I went, he was there. I just thought that we shopped at the same stores at the same time, just a coicidence. On day, he bumped into me and I laughed and made some comment about our shopping at the same stores and was he following me. We both laughed and I went on with my shopping.

"I didn't see him in the stores anymore after that. Then one day, while you were gone, I started seeing this car behind me a lot. It was the same car I had seen this man get into one time. I know it was the same car because I noticed the license plate on the front of the car. It said, 'Daddy's Toy.'

"Anyway, after that, I began to see that car everywhere I went. I know it was just a coincidence, but it scared me. I stopped going out. I asked Carol to bring me things that I needed, so I wouldn't have to go out. She wanted to know why, so I told her.

"Then I started feeling like someone was watching me when I was in the cabin. I kept hearing noises outside at night. Skip came over and looked, but he never saw anyone. He even slept over here a couple of nights, but he never saw anyone.

"I really felt uncomfortable when I was upstairs in our bedroom, so I sarted sleeping down here in the den with my gun."

"Why didn't you call the police?" Mark asked.

"I did," she answered. "They came out and looked. They found a couple of footprints under the window after it rained one night, but they said that wasn't enough to make an arrest. They told me to start carrying a gun and shoot if anyone tried to break in on me and then call them and they would handle it from there."

"They what?" Mark asked.

"Anyway, that's why I almost shot you," Cat said. "I know I'm being silly, but I was scared."

"You weren't being silly, Cat," Mark said. "What did this guy look like?"

She didn't answer him at first, but when she hesitated, Mark asked again. "What did this guy look like, Cat? Would you recognize him, if you saw him again?"

"Yes, I would, Mark, but I don't want you to do anything that would get you into trouble," she said.

"Do you know who he is?" Mark asked. "Answer me, Cat. Do you know who he is?"

"I think so," Cat said. "Please, Mark, don't do anything that will get you into trouble."

"Just tell me who he is, Cat," Mark said sternly.

"No, Mark," Cat said. "I won't tell you."

"Tell me who he is, Cat," Mark said again. "Just give me his name. That's all I want. Tell me who he is."

"Promise me you won't do anything to him, Mark," Cat said.

"I can't promise you that, Cat," Mark said, getting angry. "Tell me the dirt-bag's name."

"His name is Grady," Cat finally said. "Grady Polk."

"Grady Polk?" Mark asked. "Grady Polk from Ted Ames' unit?"

"Yes, that Grady Polk," Cat said. "Please, Mark. Don't do something that will get you into trouble."

"I won't, Cat, but the first thing in the morning, I'm going to have a little talk with Grady Polk. Come on, let's go to bed. I really missed you. Why don't you put on the Christmas present I bought you?"

Then all thoughts of Grady Polk were forgotten while Mark made up for the two weeks he was gone.

The next morning, Mark was up early. He made coffee and drank a cup and kissed Cat and said, "I'll see you tonight, Honey. I'll get breakfast at the office."

"Mark, don't do something foolish," Cat said, as she kissed him goodbye.

"I won't, Cat," Mark said. "I'm just going to have a little talk with Grady Polk."

When Mark arrived at FSC headquarters, he went directly to Ted Ames' unit.

"Hello, Mark," Ted said. "What brings you here? Did you come to steal my SIC again?"

"No," Mark said sharply. "I came to see Grady Polk. Is he here?"

"I don't know if he's here, yet," Ted said. "What do you want to see him for? Do you want to try to steal him, too?"

"It's personal," Mark answered. "Will you check for me?"

"I'll page him for you," Ted said. Then he took the intercom and said, "Grady, will you come to my office, please?"

Grady was on his way up to Ted's office when he saw Mark. "Mark, I didn't do anything," he said, as he started backing up. "If she says I did, she lied."

Mark grabbed Grady by the shirt and hit him hard on the jaw. "Don't you ever even come within 100 feet of my wife again. Do you hear me?" Then Mark hit him again.

"I didn't do anything, Mark," Grady said again.

Each time Grady denied doing something to Cat, Mark hit him again until his face was bruised and bloody.

"Mark, stop," Ted said. "I don't know what this is all about, but you can't come into my unit and attack one of my men."

"Leave me alone or you'll be next," Mark said. Then he hit Grady one more time and Grady fell on the floor and didn't attempt to stand back up.

"You stay away from my wife," Mark said. "Do you hear me, Grady Polk. You stay the hell away from my wife."

Then he stormed out the door. Ted ran after him and caught him by the shoulder.   "What was that all about, Mark?" he asked.

"He's been harassing my wife and I want it to stop," Mark said. "She's so scared, she almost shot me last night when I came home early. I don't want him to come near my wife or my house again. If you don't want him shot, you'd better encourage him to stay away from my wife."

Then Mark went to his own office. "Now, to deal with Cassidy," he said, as he sat down at his desk. "Cassidy, will you come to my office, please," he called over the intercom.

"Come in and shut the door," he said, when she came into his office.

"What happened to you?" she asked. "You're a mess. Your hand is bleeding."

"Never mind me," Mark said. "I called you in here to talk about you. If you ever disobey my order in front of another unit member again, you're gone right then. When we're on an assignment, you are to respect me and any order I may give you. Whenever I give you an order, I do have a logical reason for giving it. I don't just give you orders to hear myself talk. I never want to hear you refer to me as being crazy about you again, either. You have really embarrassed me. I'll put a memo in your file, and a copy will be sent to your personnel file in Human Resources. That way, I should have no problem firing you if you ever do it again. From now on, you will address me as Commander, also. Do not call me Mark in front of any member of any of the units of FSC. Do you understand me?"

"Yes, Sir, Commander, Sir," Cassidy said, sarcastically emphasizing the word Sir.

"You may go back to your desk now and wipe that smirk off your face. I can still change my mind and go ahead and sack you now," Mark said.

Mark then called Bill and Greg, who had just completed their two-week training at the academy, to come into his office. "Come in and sit down gentlemen. Shut the door, please. I know you'll enter your report, soon, but I'm anxious to learn what you thought about the training."

"It was great," Bill said. "It was well worth what you had to pay for it and our time spent."

"Yes, I agree," Greg said. "I would have loved to have spent even another week there."

"Did you see anything negative that you would like to report?" Mark wanted to know.

"No, I saw nothing negative about it," Bill said, and Greg agreed with him.

"OK, that's all I needed to know," Mark said. "You can go ahead and turn your reports in as usual. I wanted to make sure you guys are getting something out of it before I send anyone else there."

Then Mark went over to the barracks and cleaned up and put on the clean clothes that he always kept on hand in case of an emergency.

When he came back to his office, he worked on his report until noon. Then he went to McDonald's for lunch. As he waited in line to order his meal, Jason walked up to him.

"Hi, Mark," he said. "Mind if I join you for lunch?"

"Not at all," Mark said. "I'd be glad for the company."

After they got their food and sat down, Jason said, "I heard about your altercation with Grady Polk this morning. What was that all about?"

"He's been stalking Cat," Mark said. "When I got home early last night, Cat wasn't expecting me and she almost shot me. She thought it was Polk trying to break in on her."

"You sure she wasn't trying to kill you and just used Polk as an excuse," Jason joked.

"Jason, that's nothing to joke about," Mark said. "Polk had her scared to death.

If he even looks at her again, I'll beat him to within an inch of his life."

"I guess I'd be the same way if he was doing something like that to Debbie, but you need to be careful, Mark," Jason said. "There are people who do not like you that witnessed your attack on Polk this morning. You could be in deep trouble."

"I couldn't let him get away with doing that to Cat," Mark said. "Maybe I picked the wrong place to do it, but it had to be done."

"Well, I guess I better get on back to work," Jason said. "Good luck. I hope you don't get any bad repercussions from it."

Mark went back to the office and finished his report and sent it to headquarters. He was finished by 4:00 p.m. and so he decided to take off early and go on home and check on Cat.

"Cassidy, I'm leaving early," he said. "You're in charge for the rest of the day."

"Yes, Sir. Thank you, Sir," Cassidy said sarcastically.

Mark stopped at KFC and got chicken and sides on his way home. When he arrived home, he started calling Cat, as soon as he walked into the cabin. He didn't want a repeat of last night.

"I'm in the den, Mark," Cat said, as she came out and kissed him.

"I brought KFC," Mark said. "You wanna call Carol and see if they want to come over?"

"Sure," Cat said. When she called Carol, she said they would be over shortly. When they arrived, as usual, Sherry ran to Mark, who was sitting on the sofa in the den, and she jumped up into his lap. "Unka Mok, wats wong wit you hand?" Sherry asked.

"I had an accident," Mark said.

"Does it hut?" Sherry asked.

"A little," Mark answered.

"Wet me kiss it. Make it well," Sherry said, as she held his hand and kissed it several times.

"Sherry what are you doing to Uncle Mark's hand?" Carol asked.

"I kiss it. Make it well," she said, as she kissed it again.

"What's wrong with your hand, Mark?" Cat asked, as she came from the kitchen to see Mark's hand.

"It's nothing," Mark said, as he pulled his hand out of Sherry's clasp. "I just hurt it at work. It's OK. I just got a few cuts on it. It's fine."

Cat held his hand and said. "Let me get some medicine and put on it. You don't want it to get infected." Then she ran upstairs and brought some antiseptic down and started daubing it on Mark's hand.

"Ouch, Cat, that hurts," Mark said, as Cat daubed a little too hard.

"What did you do, Mark?" Cat whispered, as she daubed again. "Did you do something you shouldn't have done?"

"Ouch, Cat, that's enough," Mark said, ignoring Cat's questions. "It felt better when Sherry Rene was kissing it."

"I kiss it again," Sherry said.

"No, not with the antiseptic on it, Sherry," Cat said. "Come on into the kitchen. Everything's ready to eat, now," Cat said, as she tried to herd everyone toward the kitchen.

After Carol, Skip and Sherry went home, Cat asked Mark again, "Mark, what did you do?"

"I took care of your problem," was all that Mark would say. Cat never did know for sure what Mark had done, but she wasn't bothered by Grady Polk again.

A few days later, Jason joined Mark for lunch at McDonald's. After they were seated, Jason said, "Mark, you don't have to worry about Polk bothering Cat anymore."

"Why?" Mark asked.

"He did the same thing with the Director's wife that he was doing to Cat. He made the mistake of breaking in on her when the Director was home. The Director took care of him."

"Thanks for telling me, Jason," Mark said. "I'll tell Cat. She'll be relieved."

After Mark told her about Grady Polk, Cat began to get out again a little at a time. She went back to working at the paper a few days a week and volunteering at the hospital. She felt she was finally getting her life back. She was even able to arise each morning and feel good with no nausea.

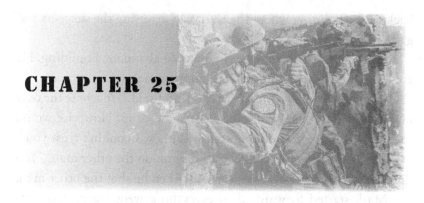

CHAPTER 25

February faded into the past and March arrived as the saying goes, in like a lion. Cat used her pregnancy test and, as she already knew it would be, it was positive. She knew it was too early, but she started looking at baby products. Since she didn't know its sex yet, she was careful to buy only unisex clothes.

Mark hadn't gone on any long assignments lately. He mostly had local assignments. Cat thanked God every day that Mark hadn't gone on any more two-week assignments.

Mark and Cassidy were working out their problems. When Mark needed Cassidy to cover his back, she was there. He was beginning to trust her. They were working on a surveillance of a local illegal weapons group for two weeks and were now ready for an arrest.

Mark assigned a position for each two-agent group. He and Cassidy were to go in together. As they stormed the building, they announced that they were Federal Agents, so there should have been no question that they were being surrounded by Federal Agents.

"Drop your weapons and raise your hands in the air," Mark said, as they came into the building, after first making sure there was no trap.

As they were rounding up the suspects, one of them started to run and Mark started after him. Cassidy followed Mark, but lost sight of him. She looked everywhere, but didn't find him, so she went back to the building where the team was arresting the suspects and gathering the evidence.

Mark followed the suspect into an old abandoned building. He could see his suspect arguing with another man.

"You had to be the one," Mark's suspect said. "You were the only one who wasn't there when the Feds showed up. How else would they have known. You double crosser. I knew I couldn't trust you."

Then Mark saw his suspect pull his gun on the other man. "You don't deserve to live," the suspect said. Then he shot the other man.

Mark started forward, then everything went black. That was the last thing he knew until he came to and heard his suspect and another man arguing.

"He's a Federal Agent, Frank. You can't kill him," the other man said.

"I gotta kill him. He saw me kill that dirt-bag, Wiley," Frank argued.

"You can't kill a Federal Agent, Frank. They go hard on someone who kills a Fed. You can't kill him."

"I told you, Earl, I gotta kill him. He saw me shoot Wiley. He can testify against me. I could spend the rest of my life in prison."

"If you're gonna kill a Federal Agent, I'm outta here," Earl said. "I'm not being a part of killing a Fed."

"What are we gonna do with him, then," Frank said. "We can't let him go."

"I vote to not kill the Federal Agent," Mark said, coming out of his unconsciousness.

"What?" Frank asked. "That guy's awake." Then he walked over to where Mark was sitting on the floor. "What did you say?" he asked.

"I said I vote to not kill the Federal Agent," Mark answered.

"You don't get a vote," Frank said.

"You don't wanna kill me, Frank," Mark said. "The court frowns on someone who kills a Federal Agent. They'll go real hard on you."

"You hear that, Frank," Earl said. "We can't kill this guy."

"That's right, Frank," Mark said. "I have a wife and she's pregnant with our baby. You don't want to make my wife a widow with a baby, now do you? My baby will grow up without a father. You don't want that to happen, do you? Besides that, my wife has already lost one husband. Do you want to put her through that again?"

"If we don't kill him, what can we do with him?" Frank asked.

"You can surrender to me and let me take you to jail," Mark said. "I can put a good word in for you and tell the court that you voluntarily surrendered to me. They may go easy on you, if I put a good word in for you."

"You hear that, Frank?" Earl said. "He'll put in a good word for us. We can't kill a Fed. We'd go to Federal prison. We'd never get out."

"Yeah, Frank," Mark said. "You can't kill a Fed. They would be really hard on you. Come on let me go. Give me your weapons and let me take you in."

"Look, Earl, he saw me kill that dirt-bag," Frank said. "If he takes us in, I'm looking at a murder charge, anyway. What difference would another murder be?"

"No, Frank," Mark said. "You don't wanna kill me. Think about my poor wife and baby. Come on. Untie me and surrender to me and let me take you in. I'll put in a good word for you. I promise. I'll put in a good word for you."

"Come on, Frank," Earl said. "He makes sense. Let him go."

"OK, Earl, but if he double-crosses us, it's your fault." Frank said. "Cut him loose."

After Earl cut the ropes on Mark's wrists and feet, Mark rubbed his wrists to get the circulation going again. "OK, Frank," Mark said. "Give me your guns."

"I didn't say I'd give you my gun," Frank said.

"I thought we agreed that you'd let me take you to jail," Mark said. "I need your weapons," Mark held his breath hoping that Frank would surrender his weapon to him.

"OK," Frank finally said. "Here. You just remember that you promised to put in a good word for us."

"OK, Frank," Mark said. "I told you I would, and I will. Turn around. I need to put these handcuffs on you."

"Why do you need the cuffs?" Frank asked. "I told you I'd go with you."

"It's police procedure," Mark said. "I'm sorry, but I have to put them on you. You, too, Earl."

When he had the cuffs on the two suspects, Mark went outside and called Cassidy.

"Where are you, Mark?" she asked. He gave her his location and said, "I have two suspects. I need to transport them to jail."

When Mark had Frank and Earl secured in the back seat of the police vehicle, he and Cassidy got into the front seat and Cassidy drove them to jail.

"What happened to you, Mark?" Cassidy asked. "I looked all around for you and you were nowhere to be found."

Mark was deep in thought and didn't even notice that Cassidy had called him Mark. He remained silent all the way to headquarters. He took the two suspects to the desk to be booked and the agent on duty asked the charges.

"This one, Frank, was involved in the illegal weapons bust and also is a suspect in a murder," Mark said. "The other one, Earl, was also in on the weapons bust. Oh, and would you put in the record that they voluntarily surrendered to me."

"Sure," the agent said. "I don't know that that will make any difference, but I'll put it in the record, anyway."

When Mark and Cassidy got back to the office, Mark said, "Cassidy, I don't feel well. I'm going home. You have it the rest of the day."

"What's wrong, Mark?" she asked. "You've been so quiet all the way back to headquarters. What happened back there? Where were you when I was looking for you? I looked everywhere and couldn't find you."

"I said I don't feel well and I'm going home," Mark said, as he started out the door. "I'll see you tomorrow." Then he left. He drove all the way home in a daze. He always knew that, in his job, there was a chance that he would be killed. But he never thought that he would be killed in cold blood without even a chance to defend himself. Frank could have just pulled the trigger and killed him without another thought. How could someone be so cold?

When he arrived home, Cat was in the kitchen.

"Cat, I'm home," he called, as he headed to the sofa in the den and sat down. He was still in a daze.

"Hi, Mark. You're home early," Cat observed, as she kissed him.

"I didn't feel well, so I came on home," Mark said, as he lay down on the sofa.

Cat felt of his forehaed and said, "Your head isn't hot. I don't think you have a fever. Where do you feel bad?"

"I just feel bad, Cat," Mark said. "It's nothing I can describe. I just feel bad."

"Did you have a bad day?" Cat asked.

"Yes, Cat I did," Mark answered. "Cat, I...," he started and then he hesitated. How could he tell Cat he was almost killed?

"You what, Mark?" Cat asked.

"Cat, I...," he started again, but couldn't tell her. She would go to pieces.

"Mark, what's wrong?" Cat said, as she sat down in a chair next to the sofa. "I know there's something wrong. What happened today? Tell me, Mark."

"It's nothing, Cat," Mark said. "I just don't feel well. You go finish what you were doing. Is Carol coming over today?"

"Yes, they're coming for dinner. They should be here soon. Why?"

"I just wondered. That's all," Mark said.

Shortly, Sherry burst into the room, as usual.

"Unka Mok," she said, as she ran over to the sofa and jumped into his lap.

"Hi, Sherry Rene," Mark said, as he sat up and set Sherry back onto the floor. "I don't feel well, Sherry," he said. "Why don't you go into the kitchen and see Aunt Kitty."

"What's wong, Unka Mok?" Sherry asked. "Did you hab a bad day?"

"Yes, Sherry Rene," Mark said. "Yes, I had a very bad day. Skip, come upstairs with me, would you? I need to talk to you."

"Sure, Mark," Skip said, as he followed Mark to the stairs.

"Me come, too," Sherry said, as she ran after them.

"No, Sherry," Mark said. "I need to talk to your daddy alone."

Upstairs, Mark took Skip into his old bedroom and motioned for him to sit down.

"What's wrong, Mark," Skip asked.

"I was almost killed today," Mark started without any hesitation.

"That's not unusual is it?" Skip asked. "I thought you were faced with that all the time in your job."

"Yes, but this was different," Mark said. "I was tied up. My hands and feet were both tied. There was no way I could get away. The guy was just going to shoot me. He was going to kill me in cold blood. He would have, too, without even a backward thought, but I talked him out of it. I told him I had a wife and a baby on the way. That my wife had already lost one husband. It would be hard on her to lose another one and her with a baby to have to raise alone. Then I told him it would be really hard on someone who killed a Federal Agent. He finally gave in and let me arrest him, but I think he still wanted to kill me."

"Oh, Mark. That's really bad," Skip said. "I can only imagine how you felt pleading for your life like that. Did you tell Cat?"

"No, I don't want her to know. She'll go to pieces," Mark said. "You're the only one I've told. You're the only one I will probably tell. Skip, I wanted to ask you. You seem like you're so close to God. Do you think God's trying to tell me something? Cat almost shot me the other night and now this today. That's two close calls I've had recently. I just wondered if God's trying to get my attention."

"Well, Mark," Skip said. "It looks like something's going on, but only you can say whether God's talking to you or not. I know when God talks to me, but you're the only one who can determine if God's talking to you."

"Mark, Skip, dinner's ready," Cat called up the stairs. "Come on down to the table."

After they ate, Carol, Skip and Sherry prepared to leave.

"Goodbye, Sherry. See you later, alligator," Mark said, as he kissed and hugged her.

"See you lata, awagata," Sherry said. She then hugged Mark's neck and said. "I wuv you Unka Mok. Don't wet dat mean man make you feel so bad. Jesus wuvs you, too. He won't wet anyting happen to you."

"Hang in there, Mark," Skip said. "See you later."

After they were gone, Cat took Mark's arm and led him to the sofa in the den.

"What's going on, Mark?" she asked. "What happened at work today? Don't lie to me. I know you well enough to know when something's bothering you. Now tell me what it is."

"Cat, I really don't want you to know," Mark said.

"Tell me, Mark," Cat said. "I can just about guess, anyway. It has to be bad or you wouldn't be keeping it from me. You had to tell someone and when you chose Skip, I knew it was really bad. Now tell me before I imagine something even worse than what it really was."

"OK, Honey," Mark said. "I came this close to being killed." He held up his hand and indicated less than an inch. "If it hadn't been for you and our baby, I probably would be dead by now."

"What do you mean, Mark?" Cat asked, getting frightened.

"This guy was about to kill me and I told him that I was married and you were expecting our baby. I told him our baby would have to grow up without a father if he killed me. I guess it must have struck a nerve, because he didn't shoot me."

"Oh, Mark," Cat cried. "I don't know what I'd have done without you. I can't lose you. It was hard enough to get over Jim's death. I could never get over yours. I would have to raise our child alone. She would have no father. You've got to quit that job. You're young. You can go to college and train to do something else. I can't lose you, Mark. I just can't." Then she sobbed uncontrollably.

"Cat. I can't quit my job and you know that," Mark said, as he held her to his chest. "I love my job. I wouldn't be happy at anything else. You knew what kind of job I had when you married me. You certainly should have known, anyway. Maybe I shouldn't have married you and put you through this all over again. I'm sorry, Honey. I didn't want to tell you, but you insisted that I tell you. You'll just have to pray that God will protect me and have faith that He will."

"I love you so much, Mark," Cat said, as she held him tight and kissed him. "I'd want to die, too, if I lost you. Please be careful from now on. Remember, you have a child to consider now. Neither of us can do without you."

Mark kissed her and said that he would be extra careful from now on. In his mind, he was replaying what Cat had said. She really loved him. Maybe she loved him even more than she had loved Jim, if that was possible. It was worth almost dying to find out how much Cat really cared for him. His heart began to sing, "She loves me. She really loves me." Now, he knew for sure that she really did love him. She didn't just feel sorry for him.

CHAPTER 26

After a long, cold March, April finally made an appearance with an abundance of showers and flowers. Cat's world was beginning to be beautiful. Mark's assignments were mostly local now. If he had to go out-of-state, he was only gone for a few days. After Mark's near-death incident, Cat became very clingy, though. Sometimes, Mark felt like he was being smothered, but he understood why she was like that and decided that he could live with it. After all, she was the reason he was still living.

Mark was determined to find out if God had truly been trying to get his attention for some reason. He decided that he and Cat needed to start attending Sunday School as well as church services. He was learning more about God and His Holy Word every Sunday. One thing that he had figured out, was that God intended for every Christian to be a witness for Him, so he began to witness everywhere he went.

The trial for Frank and Earl was getting close and he was preparing himself to face them. He wondered how he would feel toward the man who had almost killed him. He talked to Skip about what he should do as a Christian. Mark had never revealed the fact that he had seen Frank kill Wiley. Frank had voluntarily confessed to the murder and claimed it was self-defense and no one had asked Mark if he had been there when it happened. It still bothered him that he hadn't volunteered the information and become a witness for the prosecution. He told himself that he was just paying Frank back for not killing him, but in his subconscious mind, he knew he was doing wrong. He talked to Skip about it one night when he and Carol and Sherry were there for dinner.

"Am I doing wrong, Skip?" Mark asked. "I don't mean looking at it from a human standpoint. I mean looking at it from God's position. What would God want me to do? After all, no one asked me if I had seen the murder. I guess they assumed that it happened before I arrived."

"Well, Mark," Skip said. "I can't presume to know what God would have you do. All I know is, if it keeps bothering you, then God must be telling you something. The guy has already confessed to killing the guy. It's not like you were telling something that hadn't already been told."

"I know, Skip, but he's trying to get by with self-defense," Mark said. He killed that guy in cold blood, just like he was going to do to me. That's what I can't get over. Would he have claimed self-defense, if he had killed me? That's what keeps bothering me, I think."

"I don't know, Mark," Skip said. "I think you just need to go with your conscience. If it tells you to turn the guy in, then turn the guy in. If it says you can live with yourself and not turn the guy in, then don't turn the guy in. It's as simple as that."

"That's not simple, Skip," Mark said. "It may seem simple for you because you're not involved, but it isn't for me. I'm grateful to the guy for not killing me and I promised him I'd help make it easy for him, but I don't feel right letting him off with a self-defense plea."

"Then do what your conscience tells you to do," Skip said. "Would you like for me to pray with you?"

"Yes, Skip, I would," Mark answered.

So they both knelt and prayed that God would help Mark make the right decision.

When they were through, Mark felt a peace come over him and he finally knew what he had to do.

The next day, instead of going to lunch at noon, Mark made a trip to the jail where Frank and Earl were incarcerated. Before his trip to the jail, Mark found that Frank's last name was Duncan and Earl's name was Betts. He had also cleared it with the authorities before making his trip.

When he got to the jail, he showed his ID and his authorization for visiting Frank. "I need to see Mr. Duncan," he told the officer in charge. "You can have 20 minutes," the officer said. "Let me know when you're ready to leave."

"Hello, Frank," Mark said. "Do you remember me?"

"Yeah, I remember you," Frank said. "How could I forget the guy responsible for putting me here. What do you want?"

"I need to talk to you about Wiley," Mark said.

"What about that dirt-bag?" Frank asked.

"I heard you said you killed him in self-defense," Mark said.

"Yeah. What about it?" Frank asked.

"Wiley didn't have a weapon," Mark said.

"What are you getting at Mr. Federal Agent?" Frank asked angrily. There was menace in his voice as he accented Mr. Federal Agent.

"Remember, Frank, I was there," Mark said.

"Are you trying to blackmail me?" Frank asked.

"No, I'm not trying to blackmail you," Mark said. "I'm just reminding you that I was there."

"And what's that supposed to mean?" Frank asked.

"I think you need to change your plea," Mark said.

"Or what? You'll tell on me?" Frank asked. "I thought you were going to help me out if I didn't kill you."

"I did what I said I'd do," Mark said. "I put in a good word for you. I told the charge officer that you voluntarily surrendered to me. That should make it go better on you. I did my part. Now it's up to you to come clean. I have to admit that I witnessed the murder and when I do, I will not say it was self-defense."

"Don't forget, Mr. Federal Agent," Frank said. "I can still get out on bail. It wouldn't be hard to find where you live. I just might pay that pretty wife of yours a visit. I wouldn't be too hasty in volunteering information if I was you. You really didn't have a good view. You might not have seen what you thought you saw. Do you understand?"

"I understand that you're threatening me and my family," Mark said. "That won't look too good on your record, Frank. If I was you, I'd do what I suggested. It still might work in your favor."

Then Mark told the guard that he was finished and left. He almost held his breath until he was out of the building. His heart was racing. He prayed that he had done the right thing. Now, he'd have to contact the Prosecuting Attorney and tell him what he knew. He only hoped that he wasn't doing the wrong thing. He didn't want to put Cat in danger, but now maybe he'd be able to sleep at night and look himself in the eye in the mirror in the morning.

The next morning, Mark went to the Prosecuting Attorney's office and told him why he was there. The Prosecuting Attorney questioned Mark to see if he would be able to help him get a conviction for Frank Duncan.

"Now, I'm going to record your answers. Will that be OK with you, Mr. Fuller?" the Prosecuting Attorney asked.

Mark said it was OK with him.

"So tell me what you saw, Mr. Fuller," the Prosecuting Attorney said after he turned on the recorder.

"I would appreciate it if you would address me as Commander Fuller, if you don't mind," Mark said.

"I apologize, Commander Fuller," the PA said. "I wasn't aware you were a Commander. Let's start again, then, from the beginning. How is it that you happened to be in the building at the same time as Mr. Duncan and Mr. Betts?"

"I was pursuing a suspect in another case," Mark started. "The suspect entered the building in question and I followed him inside. As I entered the building, I could hear voices. I took cover until I could determine to whom the voices belonged.

"The voices got louder and, as I looked out of my cover, I saw that one of the voices was coming from the suspect I was pursuing,

Frank Duncan. I heard Duncan accuse the other man of double-crossing him. Then he told the man he didn't deserve to live. Then I heard a gunshot. That was the last thing I remember until I awoke to find my hands and feet bound and two men arguing about whether to shoot me or not."

"You say you heard one gunshot?" the PA asked.

"Yes, one gunshot," Mark answered.

"Could you tell who did the shooting?" the PA asked.

"No, not from where I was sitting," Mark said.

"So, conceivably, Wiley could have shot first. That could have been the shot you heard. Then after you were unconscious, Duncan could have shot Wiley. Do you think that could have been the way it happened?"

"I don't know, Sir," Mark said. "Someone hit me on the head after I heard the gunshot and I have no idea how long I was out."

"Then you can't definitely say that you witnessed the defendant kill Wiley in cold blood, can you?" the PA asked.

"No, Sir, I can't," Mark had to admit. "I know he did, though. That's why he said he had to kill me, because I saw him kill Wiley."

"That's just hear-say evidence," the PA said. "That's no guarantee that I could get a conviction from that. I'd like to put you on the stand, though, and have you testify that they were arguing before you heard the gunshot and maybe that he was going to kill you because you witnessed the confrontation."

On the day of the trial, Mark was nervous. He hardly slept the night before and so he got up early, dressed and went downstairs. He was too nervous to eat, so he only had a cup of coffee and prepared to leave for the courthouse. Cat wanted to go with him to give him moral support, but he was afraid for her to go. He didn't want Duncan to see her. Mark felt that if Duncan had seen Cat, he could somehow put her in danger.

The trial started about 9:00 a.m. and there were several witnesses called and questioned before it was Mark's turn to testify. When he was called to the witness stand, he was asked to state his name and if he swore that what he was about to testify was the truth. Mark, of course, said yes.

"Commander Fuller, will you tell the court where you were on March 12 and what you observed?" the Prosecuting Attorney asked.

"Yes, Sir," Mark began. "I pursued a suspect into an abandoned building. While there, I witnessed an altercation between the suspect and another person."

"Can you give us some details about this altercation?" the PA asked. "In other words, could you hear what they were arguing about?"

"The suspect accused the other person of telling the Feds, he called them, about something," Mark answered.

"How close were you to the two men?" the PA asked.

"About as far as from here to the door of the courtroom," Mark answered.

"So, you were close enough to hear most of what was being said. Is that correct?" the PA asked.

"Yes, Sir," Mark answered.

"Then what happened?" the PA asked.

"I heard a gunshot and saw the person with my suspect fall to the floor," Mark answered.

"What happened then," the PA asked.

"I got up and started to go over to arrest my suspect, but I was hit on the head with something and I passed out," Mark said.

"What happened then?" the PA asked.

"When I came to, my suspect and another person were arguing," Mark said, as his heart started racing and he began to have trouble breathing.

"What were they arguing about?" the PA asked.

"Whether to kill me or not," Mark almost couldn't get that out because it was so hard for him to breathe.

"So, who wanted to kill you?" the PA asked.

Mark hesitated and the Prosecuting Attorney said, "Answer the question Commander Fuller."

"My suspect, Frank Duncan, was the one who wanted to kill me."

"Why did Mr. Duncan want to kill you?" the PA asked.

"He said I had witnessed him killing the other person he was arguing with."

The whole audience gasped when Mark said that. The judge hit his gavel on his desk and said, "Order. If there isn't order here, I will be forced to clear the courtroom."

"So, Mr. Duncan wanted to kill you because you witnessed the murder of the other person. Is that correct, Commander Fuller?" the PA asked.

"Yes, Sir, that's what he said," Mark answered.

"Now, Commander Fuller, is the suspect you followed into the building and you witnessed having the altercation with the other person in the courtroom today?"

"Yes, Sir," Mark answered.

"Will you point him out for the court?" the PA asked.

"Yes, Sir. It was the defendant, Frank Duncan."

Everyone gasped again and again the judge threatened to clear the courtroom.

"Thank you, Commander Fuller, that's all I have," the Prosecuting Attorney said and walked over to his table. Then Frank's lawyer got up and walked to the front of the witness stand.

"Commander Fuller," the lawyer started. "You stated that you were as far from the two men as you are from here to the front door. Is that correct?"

"Yes, Sir," Mark said. "Approximately that far."

"Do you see the gentleman standing at the front of the door?" the lawyer asked.

"Yes, Sir," Mark answered.

"Can you tell if he's holding a weapon?" the lawyer asked.

Mark hesitated. He couldn't figure out what the lawyer was getting at, but he didn't think he liked what he was insinuating.

"I don't understand the question, Sir," Mark said.

"I asked you if you could see a weapon in the gentleman's hand.

The one standing at the front door. Do you see a weapon in his hand?"

"No, Sir. I don't see a weapon in his hand," Mark said.

"That's my assistant, Larrry Holmes," the lawyer said. "Larry, are you holding a weapon? If you are, will you please hold it up?"

Then Larry held up a small pistol.

"Now, Commander Fuller, do you see a weapon?" the lawyer asked.

"Yes, Sir," Mark said angrily.

"So, I can assume from that demonstration that Mr. Wiley could have been holding a weapon and you could not see it because your view was blocked by the defendant. Is that correct, Commander Fuller?"

"It's possible," Mark answered.

"You also testified that after you heard the gunshot, you passed out. Is this correct?" the lawyer asked.

"Yes, Sir," Mark answered.

"So, while you were unconscious, do you think it could have been possible for another gunshot to have occurred. A gunshot from another weapon, perhaps?" the lawyer asked.

"I have no way of knowing what occurred while I was unconscious," Mark answered.

"Do you think it was possible that that could have occurred during the time you were out, though?"

"I've already told you, I have no idea what occurred while I was unconscious," Mark said, getting angry again.

"That's all I need to know, anyway," the lawyer said. "I'm finished with this witness."

Then the judge said, "You may step down, Commander Fuller."

Mark stepped down from the witness stand and started to leave, but he decided to stay and see what the outcome would be. There was one other witness and then the judge adjourned for lunch. "Court will reconvene at 2:00 p.m.," the judge said, and everyone began filing out.

As Mark started toward the door, Frank called out, "Hey, Commander Fuller."

Mark turned around and looked at Frank. "Thanks for your help," Frank said sarcastically. Then the bailiff took Frank out the other door.

Despite himself, Mark shivered as if a cold wind had just blown down the back of his neck. "I'm glad I didn't let Cat come with me," he thought. Then he went to McDonald's to eat lunch.

As Mark was waiting in line to place his order, Jason walked up and slapped him on the back. "Hey, Mark," Jason said. "How's it going?"

"If you mean the trial, I guess it's going about like I expected. At least I lived through it," Mark said.

"Did you think you wouldn't?" Jason asked.

"I was hoping it would be easier than it was," Mark answered. "It was brutal."

"I've never had to testify before," Jason said. "I hope I never do. I've heard that those slick lawyers can turn everything you say against you. Is that right?"

"They really know how to rattle you," Mark said. "I don't think I breathed a full breath the whole time I was on the stand."

They got their food and found a table and sat down. "How's Cat doing?" Jason asked.

"She's feeling better," Mark answered. "She doesn't seem to be getting as sick any longer. She has an appointment with an OB-GYN next week. I plan to take off work and take her."

"What did she say when you told her about your brush with death?" Jason asked.

"Just what you'd expect her to say," Mark answered. "She wants me to quit.

She's afraid of becoming a widow again. I told her I can't quit. I think she still thinks she can talk me into it."

"If you quit, I want your job," Jason said, and he grinned. He knew that Mark would never quit. He was like Jim. The only way he would quit, would be if he was dead.

"If I ever get tired of it, you and Cassidy can fight over it," Mark said.

"Speaking of Cassidy," Jason said. "Are the two of you still fighting?"

"No, I think we finally got it settled that I'm the boss and she's the employee," Mark said. "It took a while, but I think I finally got it through to her."

"Well, I guess I better get back to work," Jason said. "Are you going back to the trial or back to the office?"

"I think I'll go on to the office. I've got a lot of work to do," Mark answered.

"Well, I'll see you around," Jason said, as he walked out the door.

Mark threw his trash away and did the same.

Back at the office, everyone wanted to know how the trial was going. "I don't know," Mark said. "I finished my testimony and decided to come back to the office. I'm just glad my part's over."

"Was it that bad?" Dave asked.

"It was pretty bad," Mark answered. "I just hope I didn't say something wrong."

Cat's doctor had made her an appointment with Dr. Lucy Monroe, an OB-GYN, for 2:00 p.m. the following Wednesday. Mark had taken off work at noon, so he could take her to her appointment. Cat was nervous about seeing Doctor Monroe. She had no idea what to expect. When she was called to go back to the examination room, she squeezed Mark's hand and asked if he could go with her.

"Sure," the nurse said. "Many men like to be with their wives when they have a sonogram."

"What's a sonogram?" Cat asked.

"It's an ultrasound," the nurse said. "You'll be able to see your baby."

Then the nurse weighed Cat and took her temperature and blood pressure. "The doctor will see you in a few minutes," she said, and then she left Cat and Mark in the examination room to wait.

"Mrs. Fuller, I'm Doctor Lucy Monroe," the doctor said when she entered the examination room a little later.

"Hi, Doctor Monroe," Cat said. "This is my husband, Mark."

"Hello, Mr. Fuller," Dr. Monroe said. "I'm going to let you wait here while I take Mrs. Fuller to prepare for the ultrasound. When she's ready, I'll come get you so you may see your baby, also."

Mark waited for what seemed to him to be an eternity. Soon, the nurse knocked on the door and said, "You may come with me now."

The room was dark and the nurse had to guide Mark to a seat at the end of the examination table where Cat was lying. There was a screen at the side of the table and when the technician moved an instrument across Cat's stomach, you could see a shadowy figure.

"Is that my baby?' Mark asked.

"Yes, that's your son," the technician said.

"My son?" Mark asked. "It's a boy?"

"Yes, Mr. Fuller, it's a boy," the technician said.

Mark was so thrilled, he was walking on air, as he and Cat were taken to Dr. Monroe's office. "Dr. Monroe would like to speak to you in her office," the nurse said, as she took them to a room and showed them a seat. "Dr. Monroe will be here shortly," she said.

When Dr. Monroe came into her office, she had a copy of the sonogram and pointed out features of their baby. Mark was bursting with pride. He could hardly wait to get home to tell his friends that he and Cat were going to have a boy. The only one who would be disappointed would be Sherry. She really had her heart set on a "widdle gul to pway wit."

Dr. Monroe gave Cat some vitamins and instructions to follow to ensure a healthy baby. Then she told her to make an appointment to come back for a check up, which she did on the way out.

As soon as they arrived at home, Cat called Carol to tell her the news. "Carol, we're having a boy," Cat said excitedly.

"A boy?" Carol asked. "I thought you were going to have a girl."

"We just came from Dr. Monroe's and she said it looks like a boy," Cat answered. "Mark's walking on air. He's so excited. I'm sorry about Sherry. I know she'll be disappointed, but Mark is so happy. Dr. Monroe gave me a copy of the sonogram. I'll show it to you when you come over."

Soon, Carol, Skip and Sherry burst into the door. Cat and Carol headed to the kitchen and Skip and Sherry went to the den with Mark. "A boy?" Sherry asked. "You said you wud git a widdle gul fo me to pway wit."

"I guess God wanted us to have a little boy instead," Mark said. "We'll just have to try for a little girl next time."

"When will you git a widdle gul?" Sherry asked.

"I don't know, Sherry Rene," Mark answered, "but we'll try again for a little girl."

CHAPTER 27

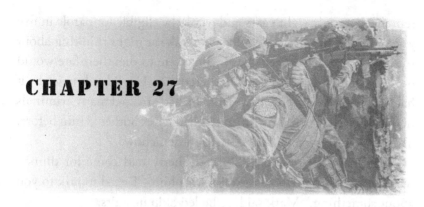

By May, Cat had finally gotten over being sick every morning and she was beginning to have a slight baby bump. The weather had gone from dreary winter weather to warm, beautiful Spring days. On days when it wasn't raining, she would arise early with Mark and, after sending him off to work, she would take a short walk into the woods and back home again.

Mark had to go out-of-state on assignments quite often now and, every time he left, Cat's heart sank. She now worried that some day he might not return to her. She prayed all the time for his safe return and eventually he did return. Sometimes he would have an injury, but nothing like he had already faced before. The new protective gear and weapons that they were using now prevented a lot of injuries. Mark had commented several times that he was glad that he had gone to the training at the academy and had purchased the new gear for his unit.

Mark had been thinking about Frank Duncan a lot lately. It was hard for him to imagine that Frank could just shoot him in cold blood while he was bound hand and foot. It wouldn't have even bothered Frank at all to do it. The man must not have even had a conscience. He wanted to go to the prison and talk to him, but he didn't really know what to say.

Mark had heard that Frank had been sentenced to 20 years for manslaughter for killing Wiley. That would mean that he could be eligible for parole in 15 years with good behavior. Earle was sentenced to only eight years and would be eligible for parole in five years. Sometimes, Mark would stay awake at night thinking about the two men. He realized that if they were to die, their fate would be eternity in Hell. That really bothered him. He didn't know why it had bothered him so much, because he had arrested many criminals in his years as a Federal Agent, and it had never bothered him before. These two men were different, though, somehow.

One day when Carol, Skip and Sherry had come for dinner, Mark asked Skip to come upstairs with him. "I need to talk to you about something," Mark said, as he led Skip upstairs.

"Me come, too," Sherry said running after them.

"No, Sherry, not this time," Mark said. "I need to talk to your daddy alone."

Sherry began to cry, but Mark went on upstairs, anyway.

"Skip, I need your help," Mark said when he got to his old bedroom. "Sit down. I need to talk to you."

"Sure, Mark," Skip said. "What is it?"

"You know that guy who almost killed me, Frank Duncan?" Mark asked.

"Yeah," Skip answered. "What about him?"

"I've been thinking a lot about him lately," Mark said. "It has really bothered me that he could just kill me in cold blood while my hands and feet were tied and not even think a thing about it."

"You mean you want to get back at him or something like that?" Skip asked.

"No, that's just the point," Mark said. "It bothers me that the guy has no conscience. I lie awake at night and think about where he's headed, you know? When he dies."

"You mean you're worried about his soul, is that it?" Skip asked.

"Yes, that's it, Skip," Mark said.

"Mark, God's put a burden on your heart for this man," Skip said. "I understand that, because God does that to me all the time. That's why I talked to you when I did. God gave me a burden for you."

"I want to talk to Frank like you talked to me," Mark said. "I don't know the scriptures you used, though. I know I should have known it since I was raised in a church orphanage, but I don't. Would you come with me and talk to him?"

"Sure, Mark. I'll go with you, but I think you need to learn these verses yourself. You may need them again," Skip said. "You make the arrangements and I'll make arrangements to go with you. Just give me time enough to get a substitute for my class."

"OK," Mark said. "I'll do that and let you know. Now, let's go back downstairs before your daughter has a fit."

The next day, Mark made an appointment with FSC Director Halbert. He was given an appointment for 11:00 a.m. that morning. When he knocked on the Director's door, he was told to come in and sit down.

"What can I do for you Commander Fuller?" Director Halbert asked.

"Director Halbert, I'd like to visit Frank Duncan in prison. I wonder if you could make arrangements for me to do so?"

"Would you tell me the reason you want to visit him?" the Director asked.

"It's personal, Sir," Mark answered.

"I need to know why you want to see him," Director Halbert said. "Does this have something to do with the fact that he tried to kill you?"

"Yes, Sir, indirectly," Mark answered.

"Then, I'm afraid I can't let you do that," Director Halbert said. "I can't let you cause trouble in the prison."

"No, Sir," Mark said. "I don't want to cause trouble. I just want to talk to Duncan. You don't understand, Director Halbert. I need to talk to Duncan. God's laid it on my heart to talk to him about his soul."

"Well, I can't guarantee that you'll get a chance to talk to him, but the warden at that prison is a friend of mine," Director Halbert said. "I'll talk to him and see if he can arrange it."

So Director Halbert contacted Warden Bradley Madison, who was the warden at the prison where Frank Duncan was serving his time.

"Bradley," Director Halbert said. "I have a Unit Commander who would like to visit with one of your prisoners."

"Paul, you know we're always happy to cooperate with the FSC," Warden Madison said. "Who is the Commander and who is the prisoner?"

"The Commander is Mark Fuller and the prisoner is Frank Duncan," Director Halbert said. "This isn't official business, though."

"Isn't Fuller the one who arrested Duncan?" Warden Madison asked. "What's this about?"

"Commander Fuller said it was personal," Director Halbert said. "So if you feel that you can't do it, then I understand."

"It would help if I knew why he wanted to see him," Warden Madison said.

"He said it was something he had to do," Director Halbert said. "Something God wanted him to do."

"Well, all I can do is ask Duncan, then, and see what he says," Warden Madison said. "If he wants to see Fuller, then I'll initiate the paperwork. If he doesn't, tell Fuller to forget it."

"Will do, Bradley," Director Halbert said. "Thanks for whatever you can do."

So Warden Madison asked Duncan if he would like to see Commander Fuller.

"Why does he want to see me?" Duncan asked.

"He says it's personal, is all I know," Warden Madison said, "Do you want to see him or not?"

At first he was angry, then his curiosity kicked in and he said, "Yeah, I'll see him once and see what he wants," Duncan said. He was really curious as to what Mark wanted to see him about. "Send the paperwork through."

So the process of getting Commander Mark Fuller and Skip Taylor approved to visit prisoner Frank Duncan was begun.

It took a few weeks for Mark to get the form from the prison, fill it out and return it. Then the process of running a background check on Mark and Skip took another week. Finally everything was arranged and Mark set up an appointment to meet with Frank at the prison.

On the day that Mark had arranged, he picked Skip up at his cabin and drove to the prison. The guard checked both of their identification cards, checked them for weapons, and, after taking Mark's weapon, let them enter the gate. At the door to the prison, their ID cards were checked again. After they had passed all of the checkpoints, they were taken into a room where they were told to wait and Frank Duncan would be brought in to see them.

"Hello, Frank," Mark said, as Frank was brought into the room where he and Skip were waiting.

"What do you want?" Frank asked gruffly.

"We want to talk to you, Frank," Mark said. "This is my brother-in-law, Skip Taylor."

"What do you wanna talk about?" Frank said angrily. "Didn't you do enough to me already? If it wasn't for you, I wouldn't be in here. If you hadn't been sneaking around and seen me kill that dirt-bag, Wiley, no one would even know I killed him."

"That's what I want to talk to you about," Mark said. "It's bothered me that you could have killed me in cold blood, while you had my feet and hands bound, and it wouldn't have bothered you at all."

"So, why does that bother you?" Frank asked. "I killed that dirt-bag, Wiley, and it didn't bother me, either. Does that bother you, too?"

"Yes, Frank," Mark said. "It bothers me that you can so easily kill someone and not even think about it. It bothers me that you have no conscience."

"Why would that bother you, anyway?" Frank asked.

"It bothers me that you have probably never even considered

where you would spend eternity if you died today," Mark said, getting serious.

"If you're going to try to preach to me, you can forget it," Frank said. "I don't care for your religious mumbo jumbo."

"What Skip and I have to say to you isn't religious mumbo jumbo," Mark said.

"It's a fact that if you die without Christ as your Savior, you'll face eternal judgment alone. That's a very dangerous situation to be in. Will you at least listen while Skip presents the plan of salvation to you?"

"No, I will not listen," Frank said, and then he got up and walked over to the door and told the guard that he was ready to go back to his cell.

As Mark and Skip walked back to his car, Mark was very disappointed. "He didn't even give us a chance," Mark said.

"You really didn't think he would, did you, Mark?" Skip asked. "Don't get discouraged. Remember how many times I had to talk to you before you were ready to listen to me."

"Yes, I guess you're right," Mark said. "It was really hard for me to forgive myself of my sins, so, I didn't think God could either."

"Maybe Frank's the same way," Skip said. "Anyway, we'll keep trying. Maybe we'll get to him someday. We just have to pray that God will convict him and soften his heart enough to let us talk to him."

Mark and Skip made arrangements to visit Frank whenever they got a chance. Sometimes he would come visit them and sometimes he would refuse to see them. Some of the other inmates discovered that Mark and Skip were sharing the Word of God with Frank and they requested a chance to visit with them at times, also.

So, Mark talked with the chaplain at the prison and set up a time to have a regular Bible study. Frank and several of the other prisoners became regular attendees. Mark was overjoyed when Frank finally accepted Jesus as his Savior. After Frank made the first move, several others followed. Mark felt that when God had saved his life that day, He had a plan for his life. God gave Mark something to do in return for saving his life and now Mark was doing it.

CHAPTER 28

May faded into the past and June appeared with bright, warm sunshiny days. Cat was really showing her pregnancy now. Every now and then, she could feel the baby kick. When she did, she would tell Mark so he could put his hand on her stomach and feel the baby, too. Mark was getting so excited; he could hardly wait until his son arrived.

Becoming a father, had made a change in Mark's attitude, also. He was beginning to take things in stride more. He and Cassidy had finally come to terms and had a better working relationship. He knew he could trust her to cover for him and she knew she could count on him to have her back. She still called him Mark instead of Commander and he seemed not to even notice that he had demanded she call him Commander.

All of Mark's teammates had gone to the academy for their two-week training and they were becoming more familiar with their new gear and weapons. Mark was finally shaping his unit into the well-oiled team that he had envisioned them to be. Now, whenever they went out on an assignment, there were fewer injuries. Finally, on the last few missions, there were no injuries. Mark was so proud of his team, he was about to burst. They were fast becoming the best unit in the whole country.

It was getting closer to Charlotte's delivery date and she and Cat were keeping in close contact. Since Charlotte had been showing her pregnancy the last couple of months, her director had begun filming around her, so she had been spending most of her time at home. Since Cat was at home most of the time, they were spending a lot of time together on Facebook or Skype. They were fast becoming good friends. Cat felt that the time they were spending together now was making up for the 12 years that they were apart. When Carol was at home, she would join them and it was wonderful for all three of them to reconnect.

Mark had become very interested in Bible study since the inception of his and Skip's Bible study at the prison. He and Cat had become faithful Sunday School participants. They attended every time Mark was at home.

Skip had been spending some sleepless nights thinking about the Bible study that he and Mark were teaching at the prison. He felt that God was calling him to do more than he was currently doing. One Sunday morning, when Rev. Baxter extended the invitation, Skip announced his call to the ministry. He would later enter the Missionary Baptist Seminary for his training.

On June 18, Christen Lynn Weldon came into Charlotte's and Tyler's life with a good set of lungs. She was screaming at the top of her lungs when the doctor held her up for Charlotte and Tyler to see their new daughter. "Well, she knows how to get your attention," Tyler said, as he swelled with pride.

"Let me hold my baby," Charlotte said. As she held the small bundle of joy, it was love at first sight. "I feel like I've been waiting for you all of my life," she said, as she cradled her daughter and kissed the top of her head. "I can hardly wait to introduce you to my family," she told her. "We'll probably go see your Aunt Cat and Aunt Carol when your Aunt Cat delivers your new cousin."

Cat had wanted to go to Hollywood to be with Charlotte when her daughter was born, but she was now five months along and as big as a barrel, or so she thought. She was hoping that Charlotte, Tyler and daughter would be able to come back home when her baby was born.

On October 4, Cat awoke with a cramping in her stomach.

Mark started to stay home with her, but she said there was no need for him to stay home. It was still too early for the baby to come. She expected the pain to subside, but instead of subsiding, it only got worse all day long.

Mark could hardly concentrate on anything at work. He kept calling Cat to see if she was all right. Finally, when her pains were coming three minutes apart, he rushed home and loaded her into the car and headed to the hospital.

It was 4:00 p.m. when Cat and Mark arrived at the hospital. She was taken to a room and she and Mark waited for the arrival of their son.

Sometimes the labor pains would be so severe that she would squeeze Marks hand and leave indentations where her fingernails dug into the soft flesh of his hand.

Finally, when her pains were two minutes apart, Dr. Monroe arrived to see how she was doing.

"How's my beautiful Mama doing?" Dr. Monroe asked Cat.

"She isn't doing so well," Cat answered between breaths. "Can I have something for the pain?"

"Soon," Dr. Monroe said. "First we have to get that boy into the world."

Then Dr Monroe prepared Cat for delivery. After a lot of pushing and pain, a little head and then arms and shoulders appeared. Soon, at 1:05 a.m., his whole body appeared. Dr. Monroe took the small body, cleaned him up and handed him to his mother. Cat was filled with love. Mark swelled up with pride; he was walking on air.

They had already decided on his name. When Dr. Monroe asked, Cat and Mark said in unison, "His name is James Ryan Fuller. We'll call him Jimmy."

When they brought Jimmy home from the hospital, his Aunt Carol, Uncle Skip and cousin, Sherry Rene, were all there to welcome him home.

Charlotte and Tyler planned on bringing Christen to visit when

Cat came home from the hospital, so they expected them in a few days.

As Cat sat in the den holding her precious son, Sherry stood beside her looking at him. "You gots a boy," she said. "I tawt you wus gettin a widdle gul."

"Well, God wanted us to have a little boy, so he sent Jimmy to us," Mark said. "We'll just have to try for a little girl next time."

"Don't you think you can love Jimmy?" Cat asked.

"Yes. I wuv Jimmy alwedy," Sherry said. "I still want a widdle gul, though."

"Well, we'll try to get one next time," Mark said again.

After Carol, Skip and Sherry went home, Mark took his son in his arms and held him close to his heart. His heart was so full of love, it was about to burst. He knew how much he loved Cat, but he never dreamed he could ever love another person as much as he loved his son. He looked at his son's beautiful face and said, "Little man, if you live up to be half the man your name sake was, you'll be a great man some day, James Ryan Fuller." Then he thought, "Well, Jim Ryan, I was finally able to compete with you, and it looks like I won."

Printed in the United States
By Bookmasters